THE GUNKS (SHAWANGUNK MOUNTAINS) RIDGE AND VALLEY TOWNS

THROUGH TIME

RONALD G. KNAPP AND
MICHAEL NEIL O'DONNELL

Now photography by
Fred Gerty, Maxine Kamin, Glenn Koehler, Susan Koehler,
Susan Lehrer, Michael Neil O'Donnell, Carol Rietsma

FONTHILL

Dedicated to

DENNIS O'KEEFE (1951–2006)

Friend, early collaborator,

Collector of postcards,

Enthusiast about the history of New Paltz,

Engaged citizen of the Gunks community

All proceeds from this project will benefit The Mohonk Preserve

AMERICA THROUGH TIME is an imprint of Fonthill Media LLC

Fonthill Media LLC
www.fonthillmedia.com
office@fonthillmedia.com

First published 2015
Reprinted 2024

ISBN 978-1-63500-014-6

Typeset in Mrs Eaves XL Serif Narrow
Printed and bound in England

Connect with us:
www.twitter.com/usathroughtime
www.facebook.com/AmericaThroughTime

Introduction

Located within a half-day's drive of some 20 million people in New York, New Jersey, and Connecticut, the Shawangunk Mountains—the Gunks—are renowned for stunning landscapes on and off the ridge. With names that vary as one travels northward from Georgia, the northern reaches of the Appalachian Mountain system embrace the well-defined Shawangunk Mountain range. To the south in New Jersey, the range is called the Kittatinny Mountains on the east side of the Delaware River, and in Pennsylvania they are referred to as the Blue Mountains, which lie on the eastern edge of the broader Appalachian chain.

In New York State, the Shawangunks traverse three counties—Orange, Sullivan, and Ulster. In this book, the ridge land focus is on Ulster County, specifically the areas enclosed within the Shawangunk Mountains Scenic Byway that has at its core the Mohonk Preserve and Minnewaska State Park Preserve, as well as the towns in the adjacent river valleys. Thus, the subtitle "Ridge and Valley Towns" defines the geographic scope of the book. The Mohonk Preserve is New York State's largest private member and visitor supported land trust and nature center. The Minnewaska State Park Preserve, which is managed by the Palisades Interstate Park Commission, has long been considered the jewel of the New York State park system.

In 1887, Arnold Guyot, the first Professor of Geology and Geography at Princeton University, remarked "Few spots on our continent unite so much beauty of scenery, both grand and lovely, within so small a compass, to be enjoyed with so much ease."

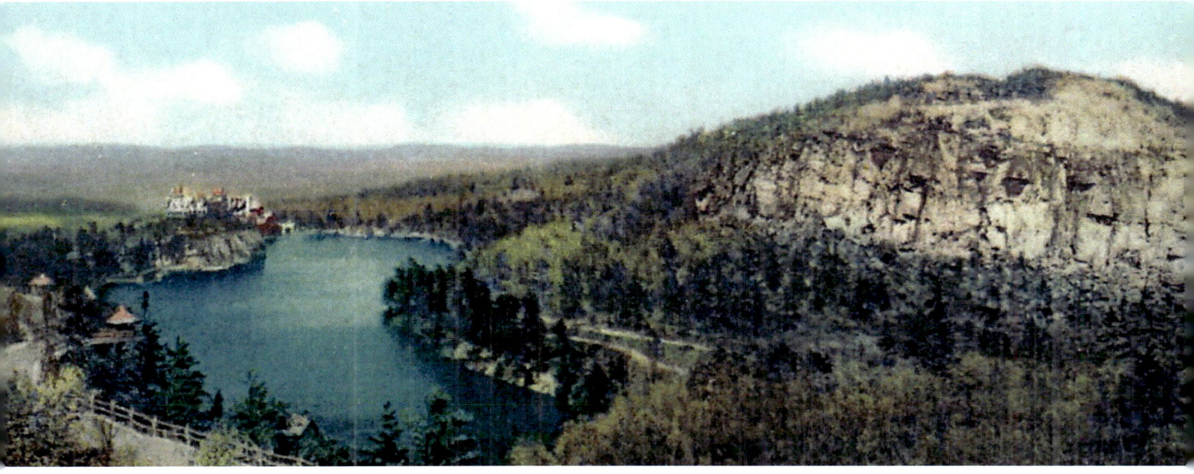

View from Eagle Cliff across Lake Mohonk. Sky Top without a tower is on the right and the Mohonk Mountain House on the left, 1910s.

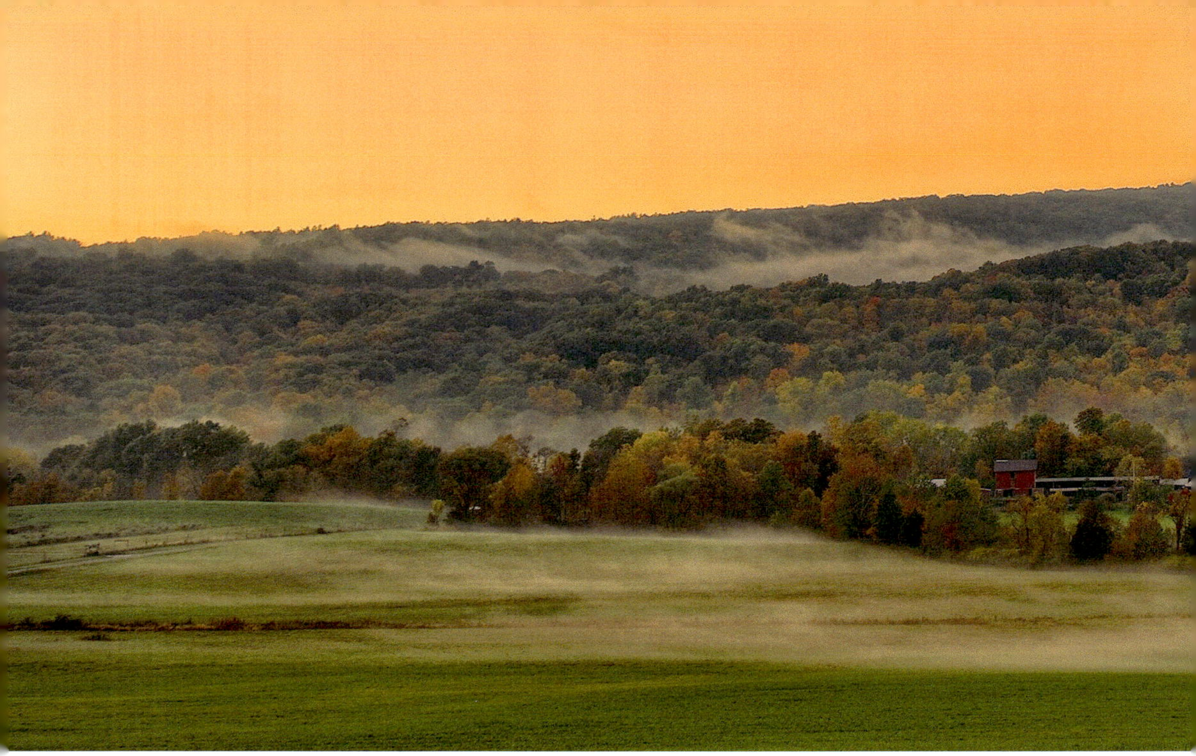

This is a sentiment that resonates with visitors today. While the mountain elevations are not high—nowhere exceeding 2240 feet—they present a rugged topography with glistening grey-white escarpments, jumbled boulders called talus at the base of cliffs, deep crevices, extensive slabs, as well as precipitation-fed "sky lakes." Ancient pitch and dwarf pine barrens, gnarled by the action of the wind and secured by roots that tap into small rifts in the rocks, are clustered erratically at higher elevations amongst rare and endangered species of flora and fauna. Renowned for its biodiversity as well as scenic character, the Shawangunk Ridge has been designated by The Nature Conservancy as one of "Earth's Last Great Places."

The grey-white rock of the cliff faces is called conglomerate, which is comprised of somewhat milky quartzite, a mixture of pebbles and sand of different dimensions cemented together with calcite or silica. An incredibly hard rock resistant to abrasion and erosion, Shawangunk Conglomerate—sometimes called Shawangunk Grit—became the material for making millstones during the late eighteenth and early nineteenth century. Quarried only along the western slopes for about ten miles, the millstone industry died out in the late 1930s as new forms of grinding machinery came to the fore.

Beginning in 1935, a new use for Shawangunk conglomerate began to unfold as the vertical surfaces beckoned several European immigrant rock climbers, notably Fritz Wiessner and later Hans Kraus, who saw the cliffs as remarkable and intimidating challenges. Both of these accomplished free climbers established nearly a hundred first ascents along the cliff faces of the Gunks that continue to be popular today. Within decades, the long easterly-facing ridgeline of the Gunks with approximately 2000 routes with pitches for every level of climber had become the premier climbing area in the eastern United States.

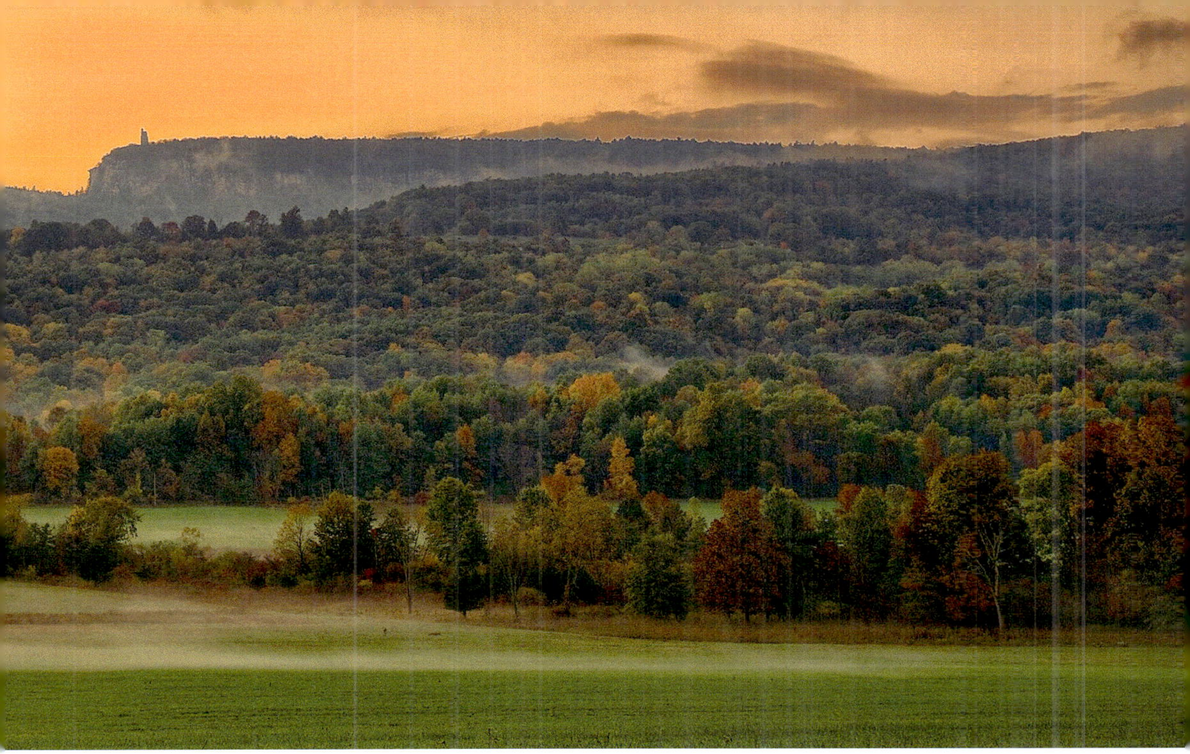

Above: View westward towards the Mohonk Preserve Foothills and Sky Top with the Albert K. Smiley Memorial tower above Lake Mohonk

Below: From Millbrook looking north towards the Trapps and Sky Top.

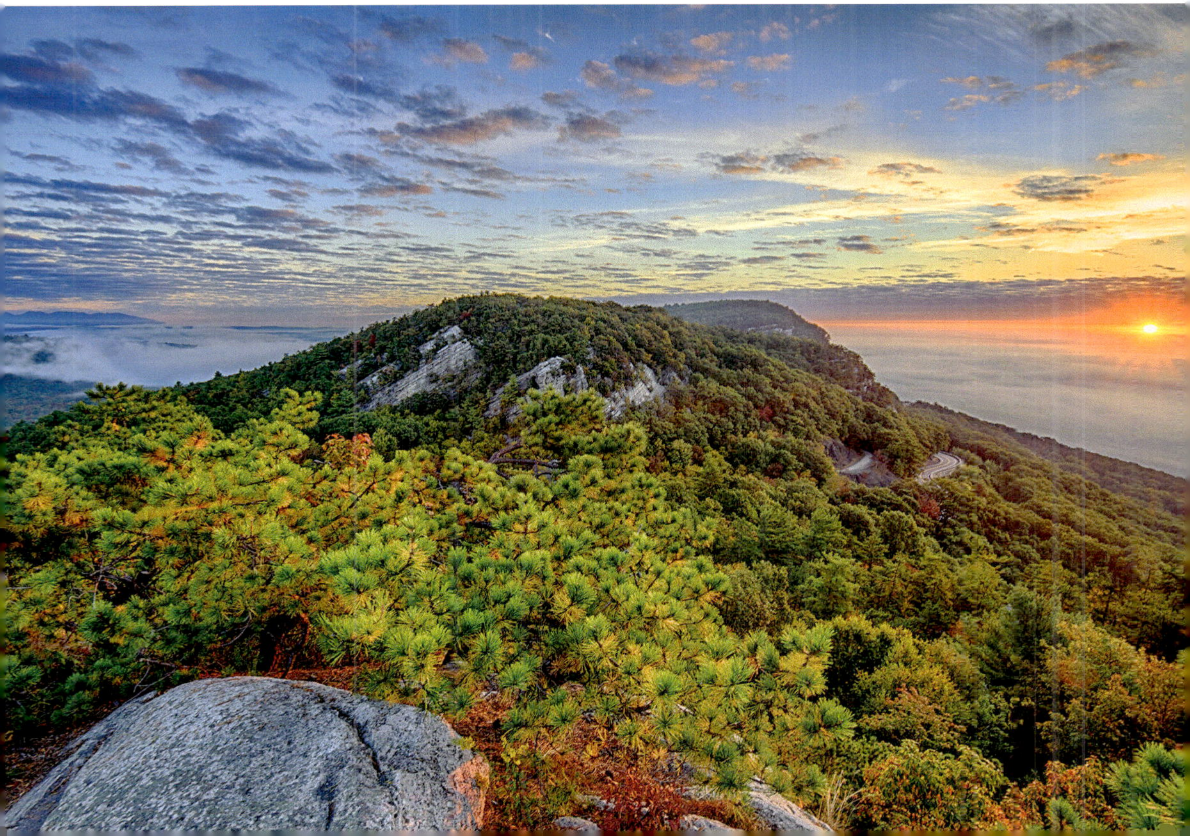

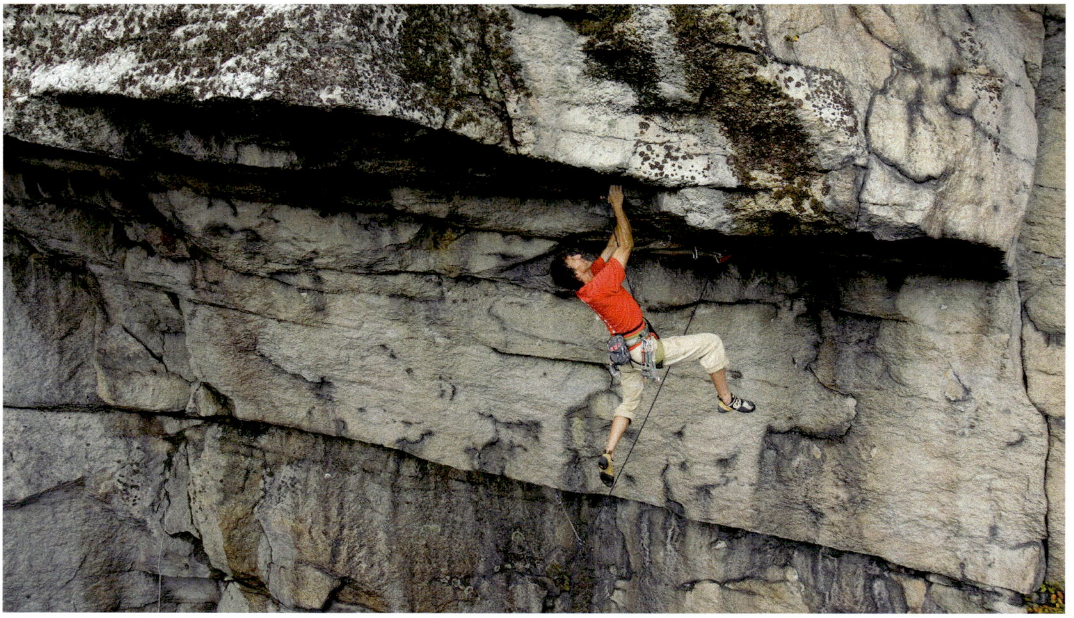

Above: World-class rock climber Russ Clune ascending Vandals, a 5.13 route described by him as "ugly, difficult and mentally taxing," which he and three others did the first ascent in 1983. Below Sky Top, Mohonk Mountain House, 2010.

Opposite page: View of the Shawanga (sic) Mountains (1865) sketched from Copes Lookout by John Hermann Carmiencke

Yet, as important as the rock was to the masons who fashioned millstones and continues to be for climbers, it was the discovery of the unique environments with clean air and unspoiled water of the Shawangunk Ridge that transformed the region into a destination for visitors from afar. Today, almost a half million hikers, rock climbers, skiers and others visit the region annually with tourism being the preeminent "industry" on the ridge and in the valleys.

Artists in the second quarter of the nineteenth century began to give shape to what has come to be called the Hudson River School, an art movement that depicted humans and nature in a romanticized symbiotic relationship. The establishment of the Catskill Mountain House in 1824, just twelve miles from the Hudson River on an escarpment with an awe-inspiring view, set in motion efforts to identify accessible sites for hotels such as the competing Kaaterskill Mountain House in the Catskills and others in the Shawangunks.

The grand old hotels in the Catskills prospered until the turn of the twentieth century and then tumbled into decline that lasted until the beginning of the Second World War. In 1963, the State of New York burned the dilapidated relic of the once proud Catskill Mountain House as the area became part of the state park. Within decades of the Second World War, all evidence of the once impressive grand hotels in the Catskills was gone.

In the southern Shawangunks, Thomas Botsford and subsequently his son put a spotlight on the impressive prospect overlook at Sam's Point in the 1850s. His first structure was a wooden observation tower that advertised "eatibles and drinkables," but repeatedly the winds brought the fragile towers down.

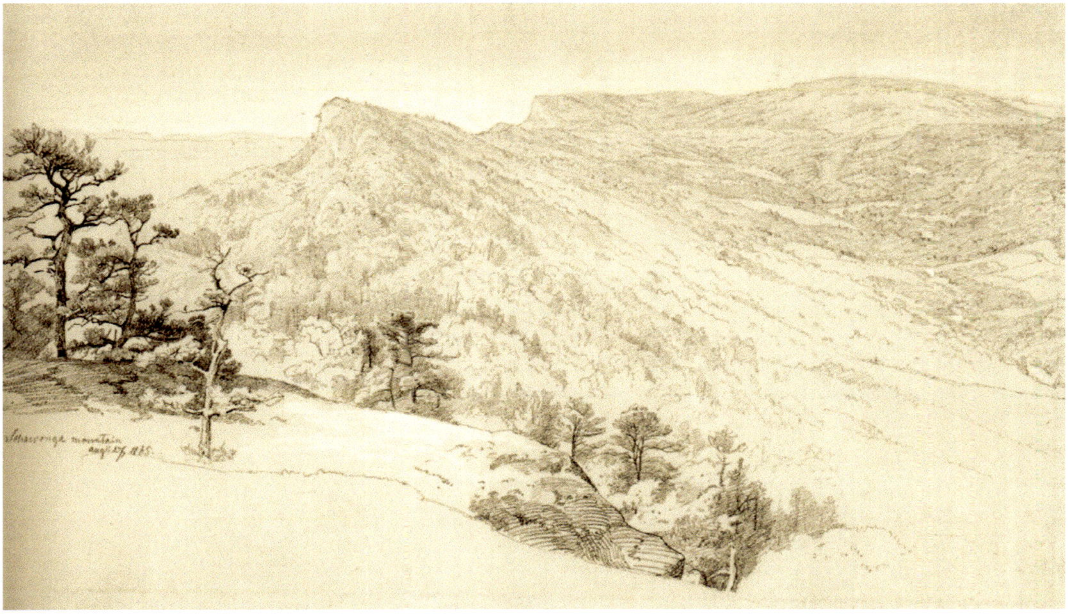

Their next effort in 1871 was a large, yet unadorned, three-story building called The Mountain House—the Thomas Botsford Dance Hall and Boarding House—that nestled just below the Sam's Point pinnacle. Unfortunately, it burned after only a few years and was never replaced.

As "the magnetic pull of the mountains for both transcendental value and aesthetic inspiration continued," according to the geographer Harvey Flad, three magnificent Victorian hotels were constructed in the northern Shawangunk Mountains in the decades after 1869. One was situated along Lake Mohonk and two rose on cliffs above Lake Minnewaska. Both of the Lake Minnewaska Mountain Houses were lost to suspicious fires a quarter century ago, and only the Lake Mohonk Mountain House continues into the twenty-first century.

In 1869, Albert Keith Smiley purchased Lake Mohonk in the Towns of Marbletown and Rochester as well as the tavern with ten bedrooms along its shore and 280 acres. Over the next forty years as a result of thirteen major construction phases, the Mohonk Mountain House we see today was assembled.

The Lake Mohonk Mountain House continues in the twenty-first century as a venerable historic hotel with new amenities, such as an award-wining spa, a low-key lounge serving alcohol, and a covered ice skating rink, among many others, that appeal to short-term visitors even as all guests sense that they are stepping back in time when they visit. Still, there are no televisions in the rooms although Internet access for smartphones and tablets allow those who want to be connected to be linked with the world outside.

Today, the Mohonk tag line is "The same, only better" a sensible statement that continues to echo efforts made over the past century and a half.

Expanding beyond Lake Mohonk, Albert's twin brother Alfred H. purchased and renamed Lake Minnewaska in the Town of Rochester, where he erected two large hotels—The Cliff House and Wildmere House—that faced each other across the lake. Over time, as farms and

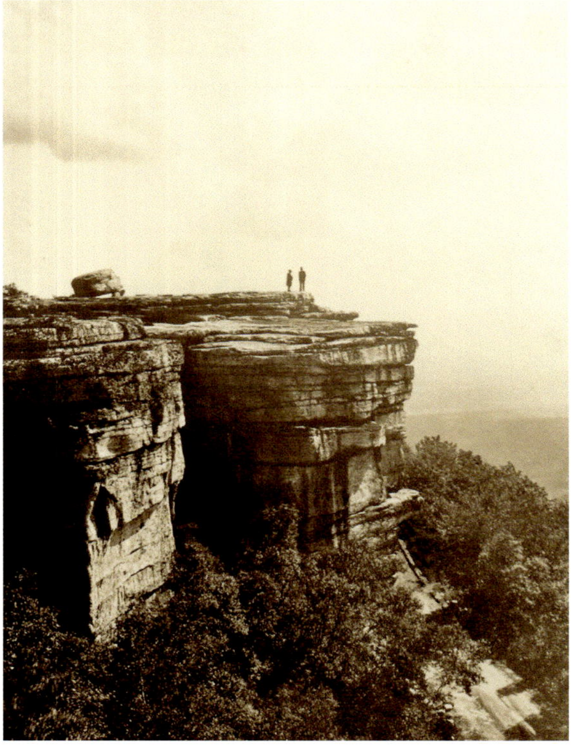

Windswept Sam's Point made it difficult to establish a hotel.

unspoiled acreage was acquired, the Mohonk and Minnewaska properties expanded beyond the towns in which their iconic buildings were located.

The two Lake Minnewaska hotels burned to the ground—The Cliff House in 1978 and Wildmere in 1986—erasing more than a century of hospitality. Subsequently, the property was purchased by the State of New York and incorporated into its park system.

The raw landscapes the Smileys encountered were viewed as artist's canvases that needed to be manipulated and shaped to inspire visitors by applying aesthetic principles to landscape design. Seemingly inexhaustible combinations of rough features with more gentle ones were brought together and made accessible for easy rambles on paths that led to strategically selected vistas or into the gardens.

Going farther afield, the construction of shale-covered carriage roads created a network that facilitated the transport of guests in horse-drawn carriages to more distant locations. These nineteenth century landscape designs continue to be enjoyed by visitors in the twenty-first century. According to Frederick Partington, "Getting the land may have been the hardest thing Mr. Smiley ever did—but taming it gave him the greatest delight of his life."

In the century and a half since these magnificent summer recreational spots were built, visitation to the region by those seeking quietude or active recreation has surged, eclipsing the principled desire of the Smileys who advertised their properties as places for "the refined and moral classes, where they could enjoy the splendid scenery without molestation from the fast and rougher elements of society."

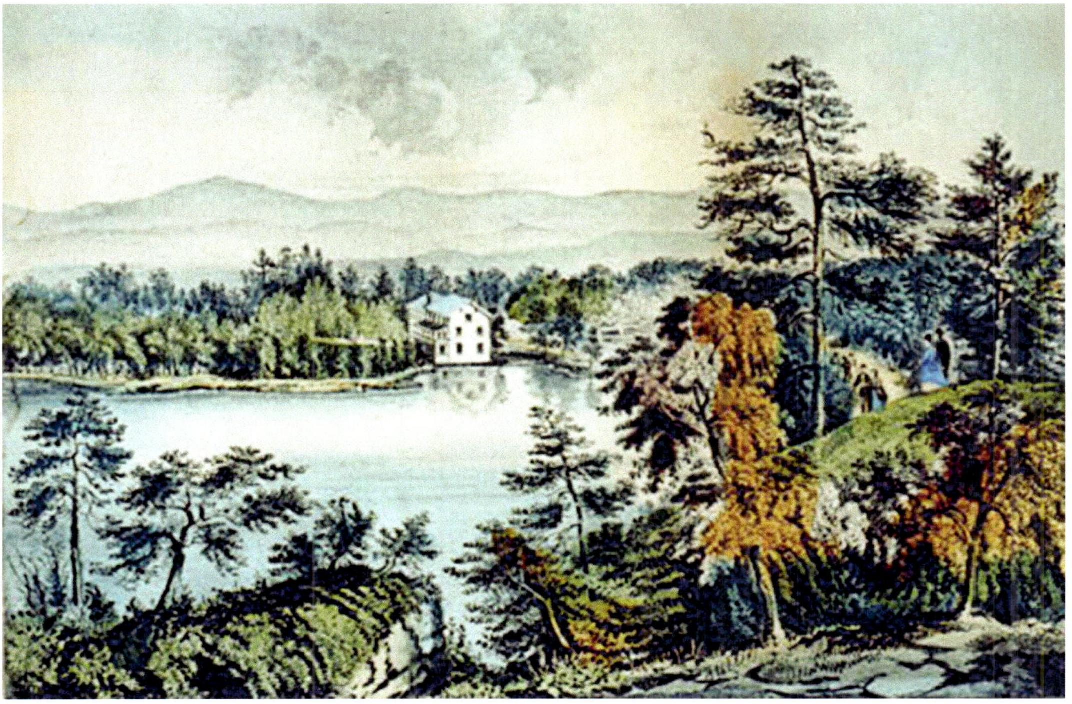

Lake Mohonk with Stokes Tavern along its western rim, Catskill Mountains in the background, 1860s, Currier & Ives.

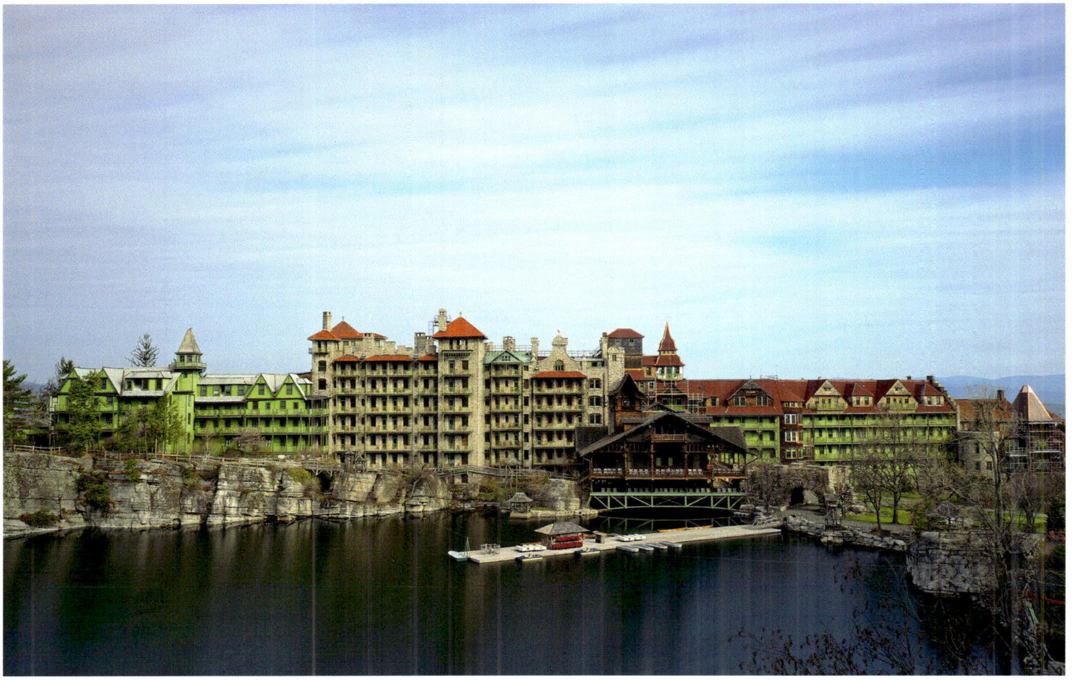

Mohonk Mountain House along Lake Mohonk, 2014.

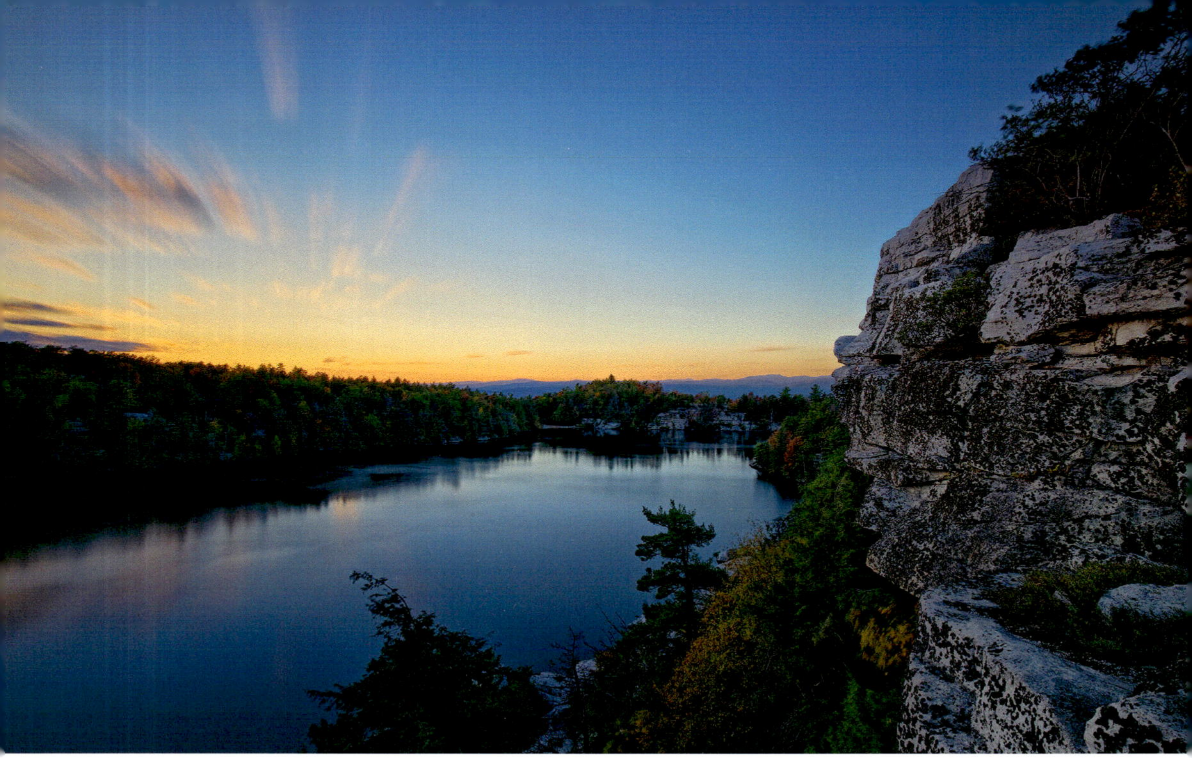

Lake Minnewaska, 2014.

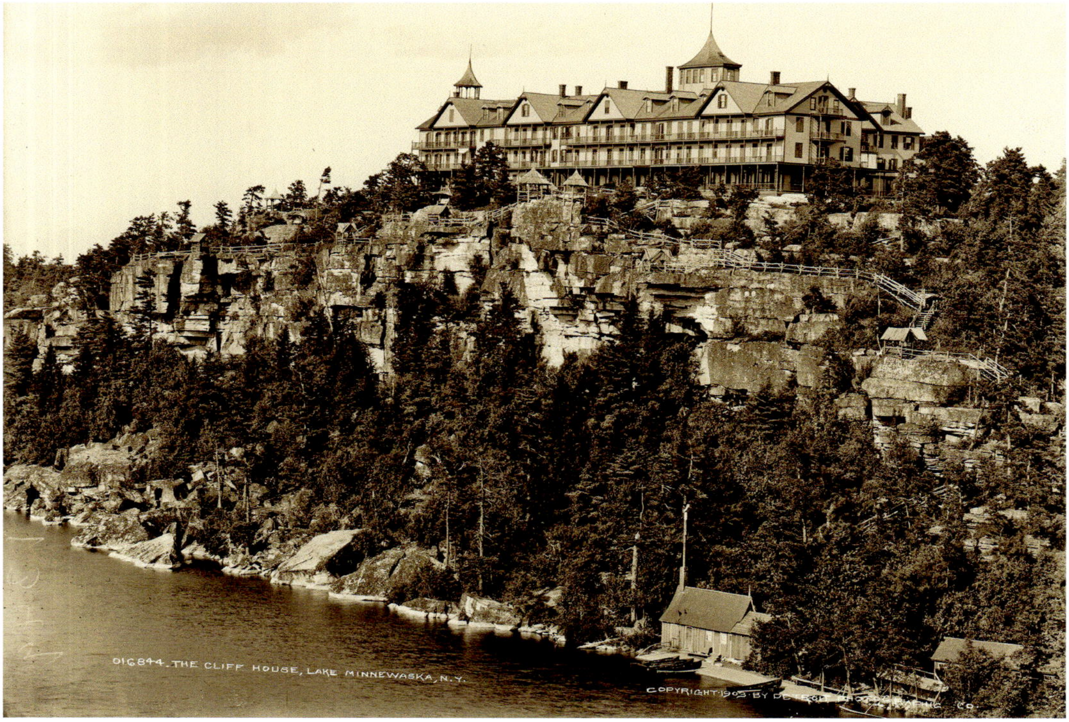

The Cliff House *c.* 1903.

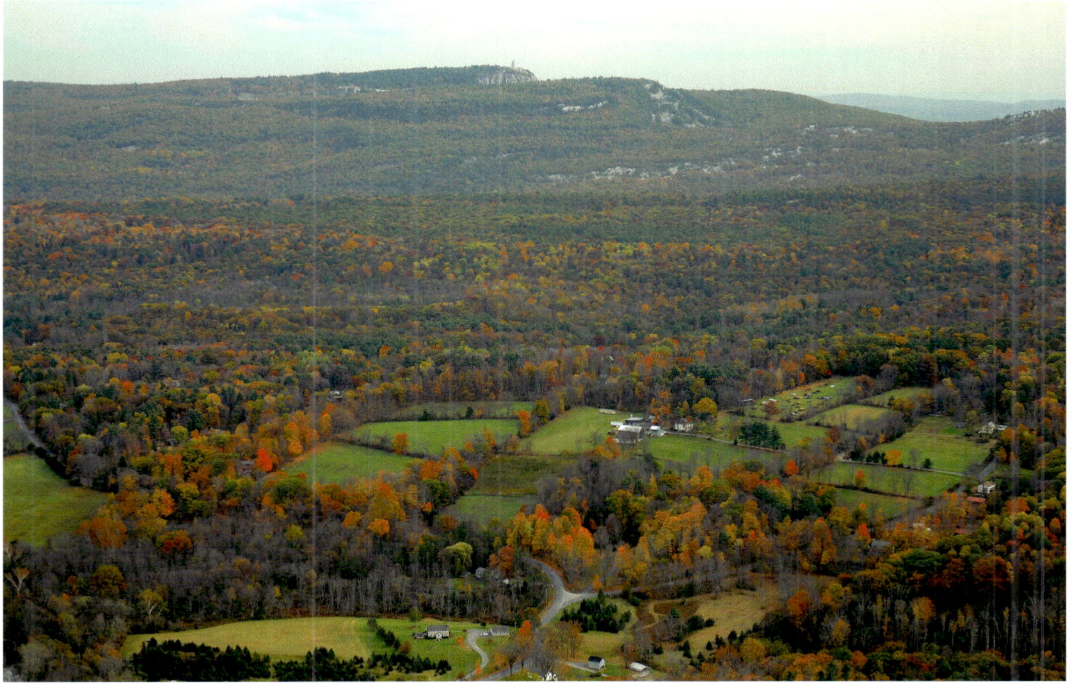

Aerial view of the Rondout Valley above Accord looking East towards Sky Top.

Even before the arrival of guests and tourists and the construction of hotels, mountain houses, inns, bungalow colonies, camps, and boarding houses that housed them, the Shawangunk region was the home of Native Americans and European immigrants. Archaeological and visible evidence of a Native American presence along the ridge can be seen at rock shelters as well as in the lines of early footpaths they traversed as the Native Americans moved between the valleys of the Wallkill River on the east and the Rondout Creek on the west.

With the establishment of New Netherland by the Dutch in the seventeenth century, three settlements along the Hudson River were established: New Amsterdam, now New York City; Beverwyck, now Albany; and Wiltwyck, now Kingston. Over the next century with Wiltwyck as a node, colonists from various areas of northwestern Europe travelled westward along the Esopus River and southward—upstream—along the Rondout Creek, both tributaries of the Hudson River.

Framing the Shawangunk Mountains are the valleys of the Rondout Creek along its western flank and its right-bank tributary the Wallkill River in the east—both north-flowing streams. Here one finds the thriving village and town of New Paltz as well as quaint hamlets like Gardiner and Rosendale. For the most part, these are lively, even cosmopolitan, places, a mixture of old families and newcomers, many of whom arrived as second-homers from New York City. The Shawangunk Grasslands National Wildlife Refuge, which is located in the valley below the ridge near the hamlet of Wallkill in the Town of Shawangunk, is one of New York State's most important areas for grassland dependent migratory birds. On the western side of the Shawangunks are Accord, High Falls, and Marbletown, as well as Ellenville, which are not covered thoroughly in this book because of the limits of space. All are in the viewshed of the Shawangunks as well as having the ridge as their own unique visual backdrop, each with its own history of development.

While each of these communities has a long history and its own charm, New Paltz lays claim to being "one of the oldest towns in America" because of the stone houses aligned along Huguenot Street. Huguenot settlers, who were immigrants from northern France in what is now southern Belgium, acquired a patent for elevated lands along the east bank of the Wallkill River in 1677. This patent ran from the Hudson River and included all of the current town of Lloyd, about two-thirds of what is now the Town of New Paltz, as well as areas to the north, such as one-third of what is now the Town of Esopus and one-fourth of Rosendale.

The original twelve patentees—called the Duzine—began to build homes the following year. At first, dwellings were constructed of easily available timber, but later by the eighteenth century were being constructed of stone in a style that is usually referred to as Dutch.

For much of the past, farming was the dominant activity with commercial activities concentrated in villages and dispersed in hamlets. The slopes of the Shawangunks were cleared of trees as areas were opened for both pasture and farming.

Throughout the first two-thirds of the nineteenth century, first streams, then roads with covered and uncovered bridges, as well as railroads and canals together helped shape an increasingly interconnected set of settlements in the valleys on both sides of the Shawangunk ridge.

On the east side of the Shawangunks, the Town of New Paltz was formally incorporated in 1785. In 1820, there were only 250 people living in the core area of New Paltz with the population reaching over 2000 in 1870.

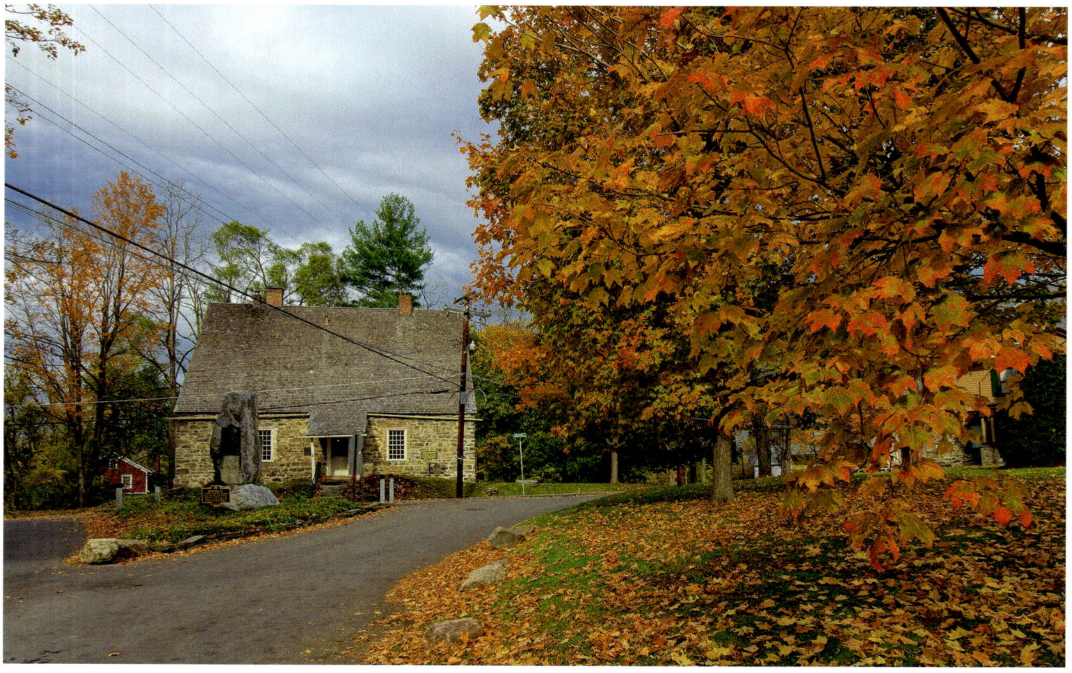

Jean or Jacob Hasbrouck stone house dates from the early 18th century.

As population increased in New Paltz in the nineteenth century, settlement spread farther east from the original Huguenot settlement and even to small satellite hamlets some distance from the village core. Homes and businesses were built on streets that radiated, first along what is now North Front Street and later on intersecting streets.

In 1828, a Classical School was established on North Front Street in the upper floor of what was the area's first purpose-built public school whose structure utilized stones—still visible today—from the settlement's church that dated to 1717. Increasing demand for education led in 1833 to the creation of the New Paltz Academy on the eastern embankment of the Wallkill River. According to Elizabeth and Robert Lang's *In a Valley Fair*, the Academy advertised that "it is in the midst of a romantic, fertile and healthy country, retired from the noise and confusion as well as the temptations incident to thickly settled places" with a "supply of fresh water piped directly from the Wallkill River." In 1884, the Academy's structure burned and, after much discussion in Albany, was recast and rebuilt as the first state-supported Normal School in southeastern New York State. These institutions are heralded as the precursors of today's State University of New York, New Paltz.

The commercial center of New Paltz developed along Main Street, first servicing farmers in the surrounding areas, then providing goods and services for townspeople. With the establishment of the Lake Mohonk and Lake Minnewaska hotels as well as smaller inns and boarding houses on the ridge and in the valleys, New Paltz soon thrived as a transit hub shuttling guests to and from their vacation abodes.

Meanwhile, over the years, the once expansive extent of New Paltz was reduced in size as sections were taken to form Esopus in 1843; Rosendale in 1844; all of Lloyd in 1845; and part of Gardiner in 1853. Each of these incorporated political units has its own unique story of development.

In 1870, when the Wallkill Valley Railroad arrived at New Paltz with the tracks running north and south along the east side of the Wallkill River below Huguenot Street, commerce was further stimulated . The Village of New Paltz was incorporated in 1887 as the commercial core for the more rural Town of New Paltz that surrounded it.

In addition to train service New Paltz acquired trolley service in 1897 that led to the steamboat and ferry landings at Highland on the banks of the Hudson River, extending the range of visitors even to New York City. For a while the line reached Poughkeepsie, which had been chartered as a city in 1854, via a route across the railroad bridge. By 1925, after twenty-eight years of service, the streetcar line folded. Passenger service on the railroad continued until 1937 with freight continuing into the 1970s. By the later quarter of the twentieth century, the village of New Paltz catered more to college students and tourists than locals whose needs were increasingly met by the shopping malls that proliferated on upper Main Street on the way to Exit 18 of the New York State Thruway.

Parallel with these developments east of the Shawangunks was the creation of an extraordinary engineering enterprise—the Delaware & Hudson Canal on the west side. Inspired by the already successful Erie Canal that had been completed in 1816, this new interstate canal, which was constructed between 1825 and 1828, linked the coal mines of northeastern Pennsylvania with the Hudson River at Rondout near Kingston, New York, with coal transshipped onward to New York City and beyond via larger barges. Along the canal

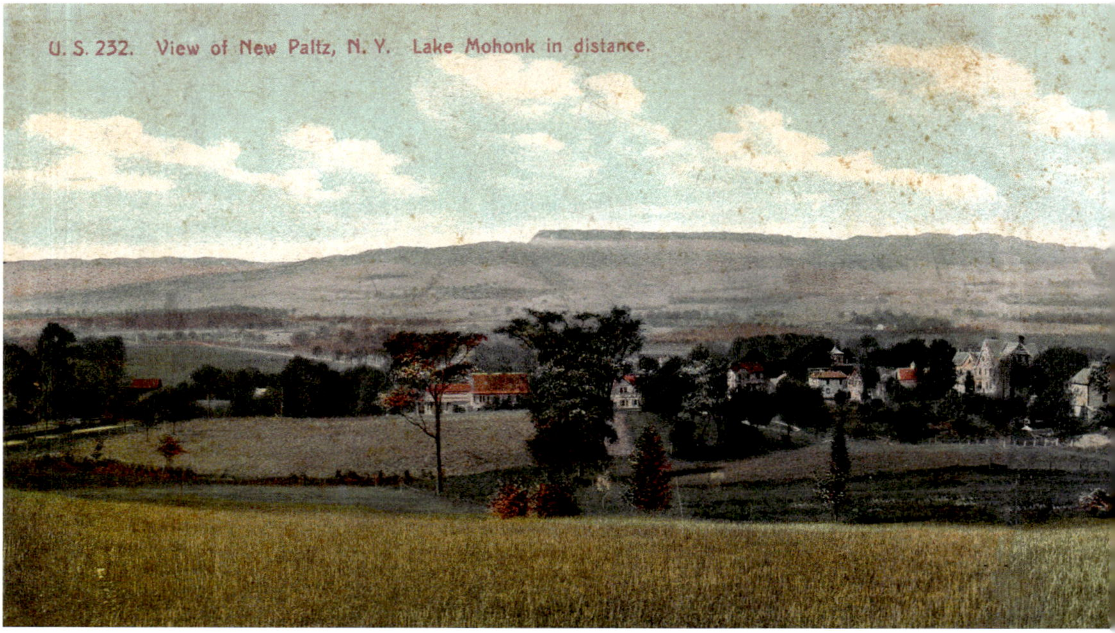

route in New York, once small settlements in the valleys on the west side of the Shawangunk Ridge like Ellenville, Accord, High Falls, and Rosendale began to thrive as canal towns.

The bucolic countryside along the Rondout Creek began an industrialized metamorphosis with the arrival of the D&H Canal and the establishment of cement works. High Falls-Rosendale especially emerged as important industrial sites with the discovery of dolostone—natural cement—during the excavation of the canal. Used initially as mortar in the construction of locks and canal walls, Rosendale Cement quickly became a generic term and the most famous American cement during the latter half of the nineteenth century. This easily transportable cement was used in construction all along the eastern seaboard, including national landmarks like the Brooklyn Bridge, Statue of Liberty, and the U.S. Capitol.

Cement kilns and mills increased rapidly along the canal-side hills in the environs of Rosendale, bringing with it rapid prosperity that was eventually eclipsed around 1900 with the discovery of faster setting Portland cement. With declining prosperity, tragedy struck the village of Rosendale in 1895 due to a fire that consumed many of the wooden businesses and homes along Main Street. By 1910, the Delaware & Hudson Canal ceased operation. Floods along the Rondout in 1928, 1938, and 1955 further impacted livability in Rosendale.

Since the 1970s, Rosendale has undergone a renaissance of sorts as abandoned underground cement mines were repurposed as dark areas in which to grow mushrooms, as well as to provide secure document storage. The arrival of artists and others seeking low rents and affordable properties resulted in the purchase of old residences and businesses. Today, Rosendale is bustling.

Farther west, High Falls, Marbletown, and Accord have attracted second homers from the New York metropolitan area. Only Ellenville has lagged, as its industrial and tourist facilities closed one after the other, leaving the village a shell of its once vital life.

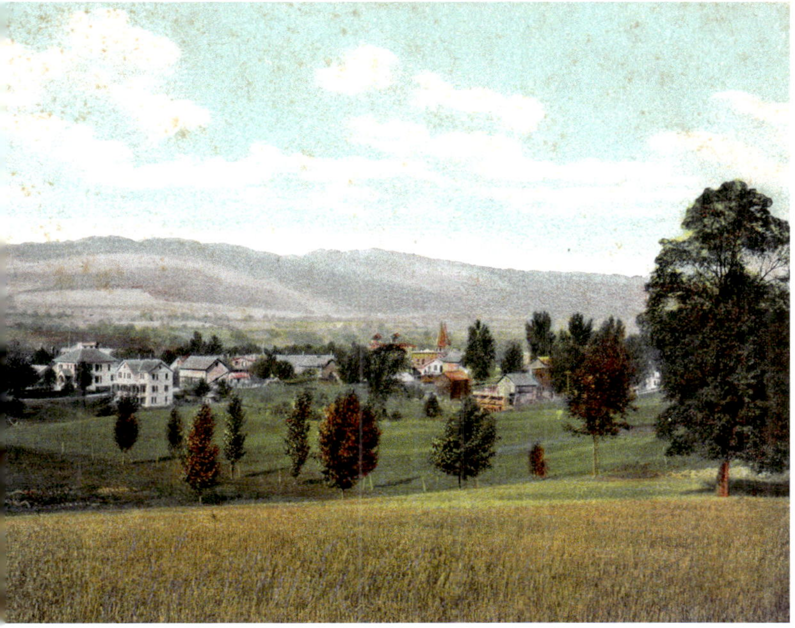

Left: View overlooking New Paltz towards the Shawangunk Mountains, 1920s.

Below: The Delaware & Hudson Canal passing under the Rosendale Trestle sometime around 1902.

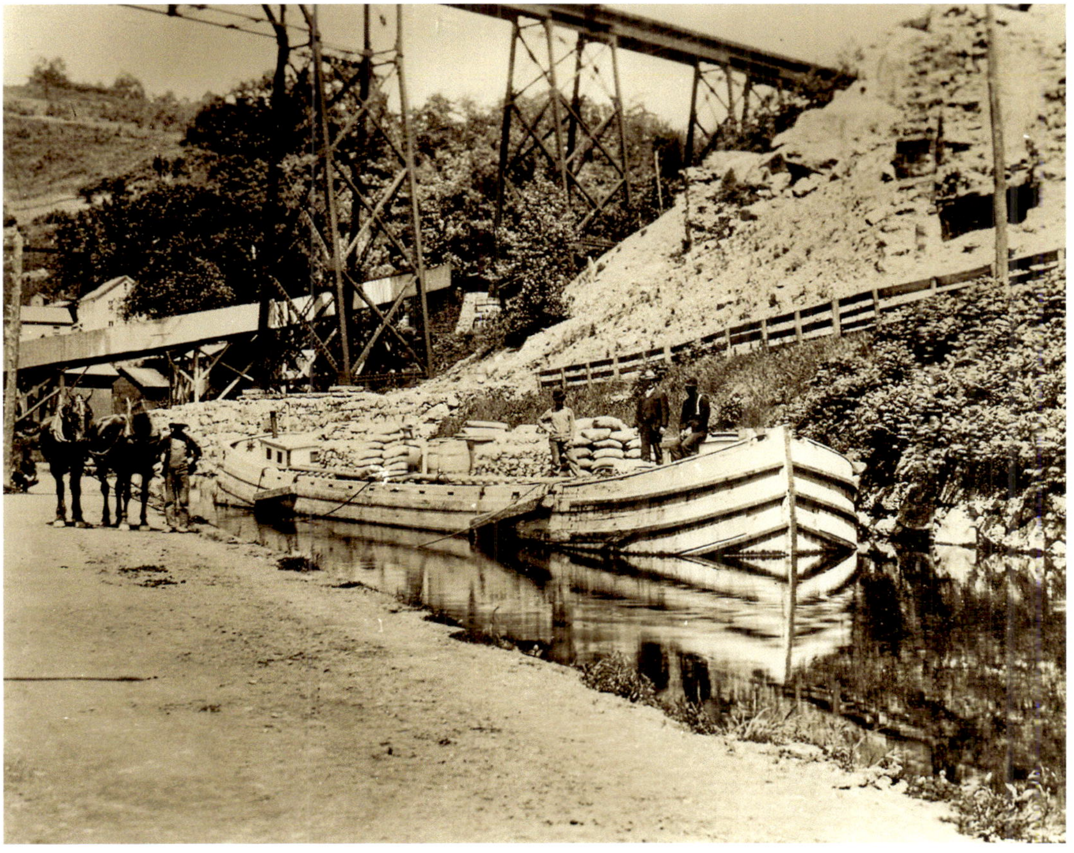

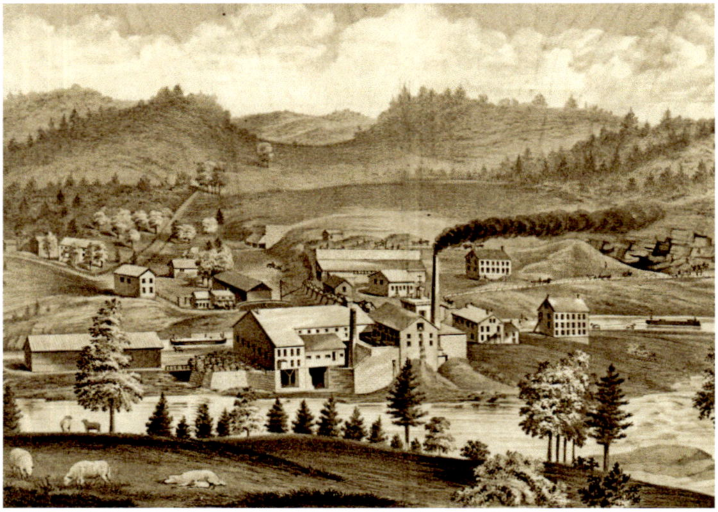

Located less than two miles west of the present village of Rosendale, the Lawrenceville Cement Works was among the first to exploit the natural cement found within the adjacent hills.

Still, even with the denial of a license to open a casino resort at the former Nevele Hotel in winter 2014, there is much optimism that Ellenville will have a rebirth as it focuses on re-developing a robust four-season tourism economy centered on a sportsplex resort with video lottery terminals at the once grand Nevele Hotel.

Today, whether on the ridge or in the valleys on either side, there is only limited residual evidence of the industrialized landscape of the nineteenth and early twentieth century out of which three of America's great engineering achievements—the Delaware & Hudson Canal, mentioned above, the Rosendale Trestle, and the Catskill Aqueduct—emerged. Each of these is presented in the images that follow. All three were considered engineering wonders when they were constructed.

Virtually all of the boarding houses and inns as well as the two Mountain Houses at Minnewaska are but dim memories held by old timers. Only the venerable Mohonk Mountain House, which will celebrate the 150 anniversary of its founding in 2019, provides evidence of nineteenth century leisure.

New residents and visitors alike often view the forested slopes of the Shawangunks as primeval havens when in fact they are relatively new growth that underscores the resilience of nature as it recovers from the onslaught of human action that a century ago transformed, even disfigured the landscape, for agriculture, mining, and the pursuit of water. While the D&H Canal as well as the Wallkill Valley Railroad and the Ontario and Western Railroad are now mere memories with their lands repurposed to meet contemporary needs, residents in New York City as well as valley villages continue to draw on a reliable source of water made possible with the construction of the Catskill Aqueduct a century ago. The landscapes of the Gunks region on the ridge and in the adjacent valleys continue to evolve as visitors and new residents arrive in increasing numbers, many establishing fresh roots as they join with others whose descendants have been here for many decades, even centuries. Those here a short time and those longer still struggle with how much transformation is tolerable even as they recognize that change is necessary and inevitable within a landscape that still evokes a seeming timelessness.

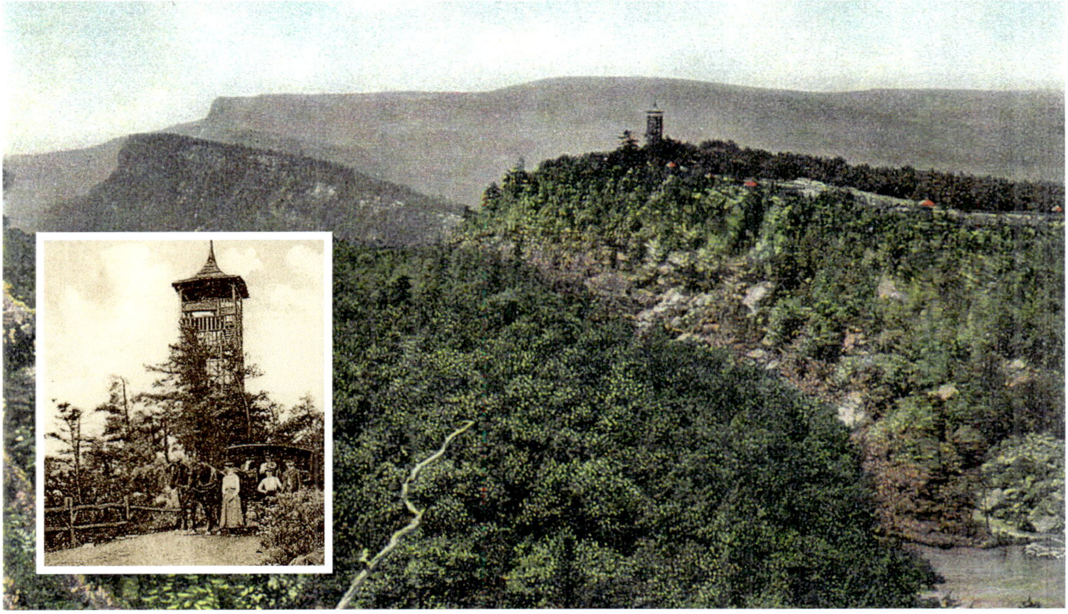

Eagle Cliff, The Trapps, and Beyond, Marbletown & Gardiner

This view south along the ridge from the Sky Top Path captures the continuing vegetative richness that has endured for more than a century. Below right in both images is a narrow sliver at the southern tip of Lake Mohonk. Nearby woodland thrives with denser cover than in the past. Eagle Cliff, which is reached by one of Mohonk Mountain House's most popular carriage roads, once had an observation tower near its southern tip. Constructed in 1880, this wooden tower complimented the Sky Top Tower that had been erected in 1872. Today, with the Eagle Cliff tower gone, walkers take in their views from well-sited summerhouses aligned along the edge of the carriage road.

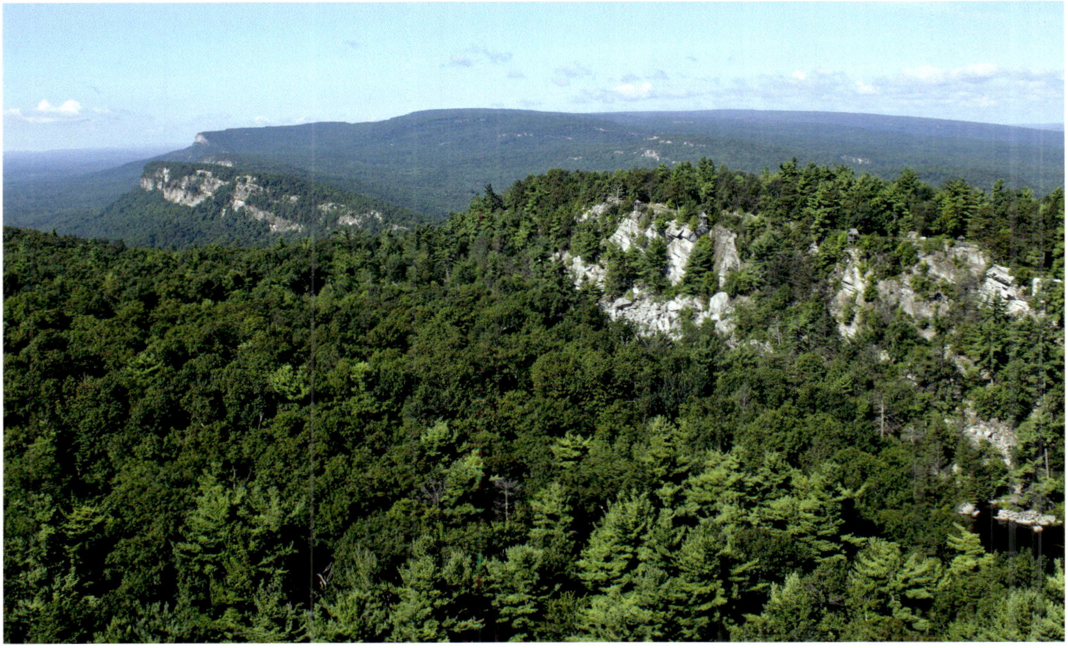

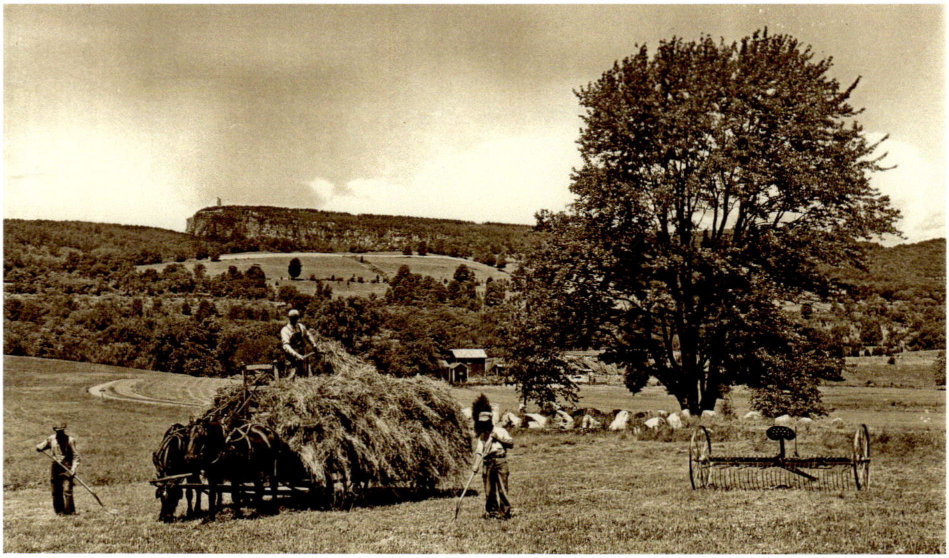

Brook Farm and Sky Top: The Ridge as Backdrop, New Paltz

From most any vantage point in New Paltz, the sweep of the Shawangunk Mountains, which locals simply call "the ridge" and its striking prominence called Pfalz or Paltz Point with Sky Top Tower rising above, provides a backdrop celebrated in photographs and paintings. Many—locals and visitors—proclaim that the view across the farms towards the ridge is iconic, indeed emblematic of New Paltz.

One of six working farms formerly managed by the Mohonk Mountain House that once encircled the Mohonk Mountain House resort, Brook Farm provided hay for feeding its stabled horses, bedding in the stables, and insulation for its stored ice, as well pasturage for livestock.

Today, except for Chapel Farm, these farms are owned by the Mohonk Preserve. Brook Farm and adjacent Pine Farm to the north are the site of the Hudson Valley Farm Business Incubator, a project of Glynwood in collaboration with the Open Space Institute. The Incubator project's purpose is to work with beginning farmers that will lay the foundation for establishing up to 15 new sustainable food and farming businesses in the Hudson Valley before 2020.

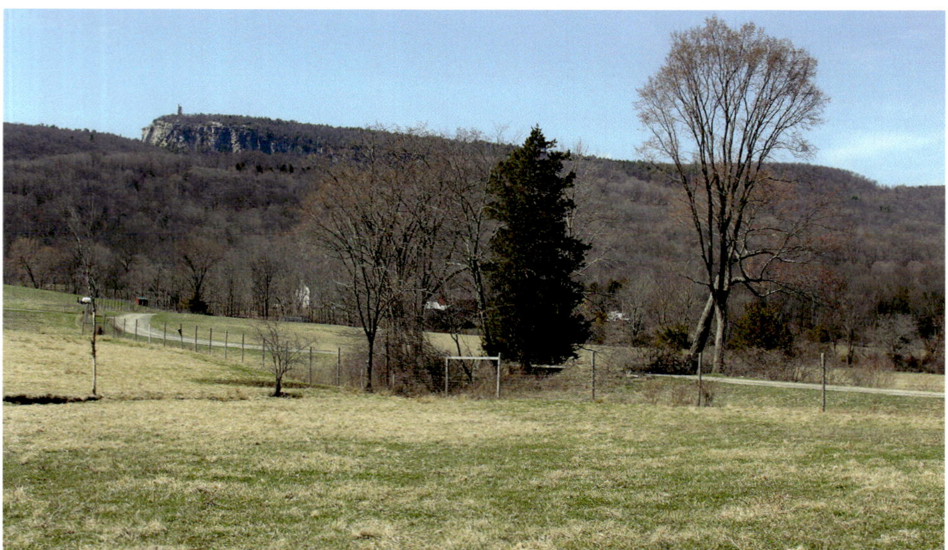

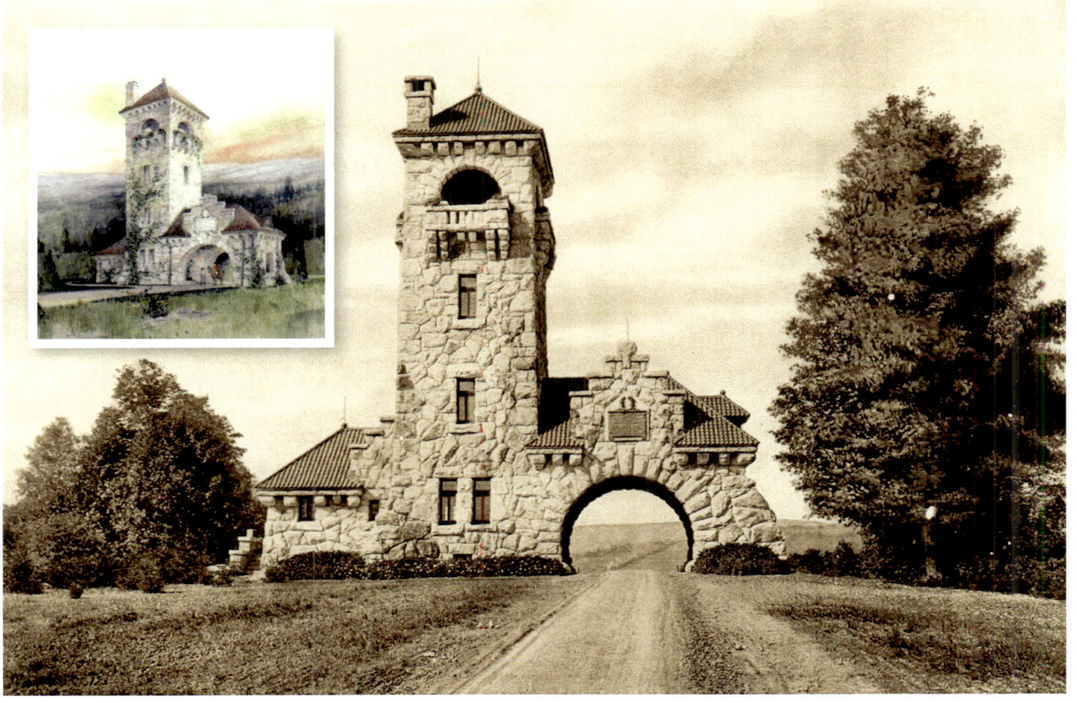

Testimonial Gateway to the Mohonk Mountain House, New Paltz

This imposing structure is the Testimonial Gateway. Designed by James E. Ware & Sons and dedicated in 1908, it created a grand entrance to the Mohonk Mountain House as guests traveled from the train station in New Paltz up the mountain via a series of carriage roads with unrivaled vistas until arrival at their secluded holiday spot along Lake Mohonk. Constructed to commemorate the 50th anniversary of the marriage of Albert K. and Eliza Smiley, the Testimonial Gateway includes a four-story tower with a loggia at the top and a basement beneath. After climbing the stairs, guests could rest briefly in a sheltered space that offered glimpses of the magnificent Shawangunk ridge in the distance and the farmlands between, areas that they would traverse as they climbed the mountain. The commemorative plaque over the archway declares *Quare Monumentum Circumspice* "When you seek a monument look around."

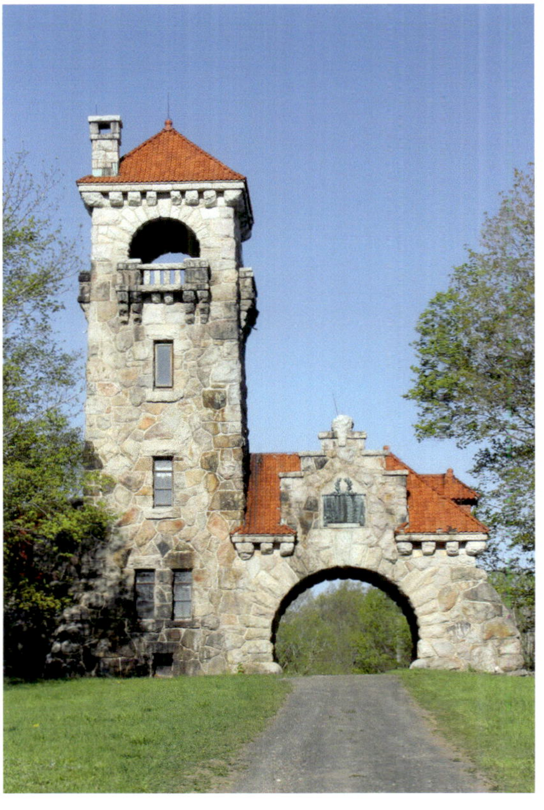

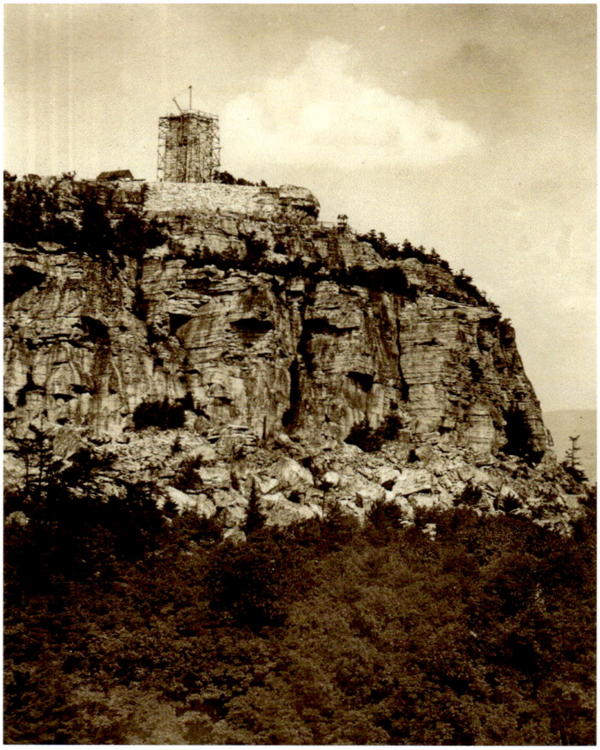

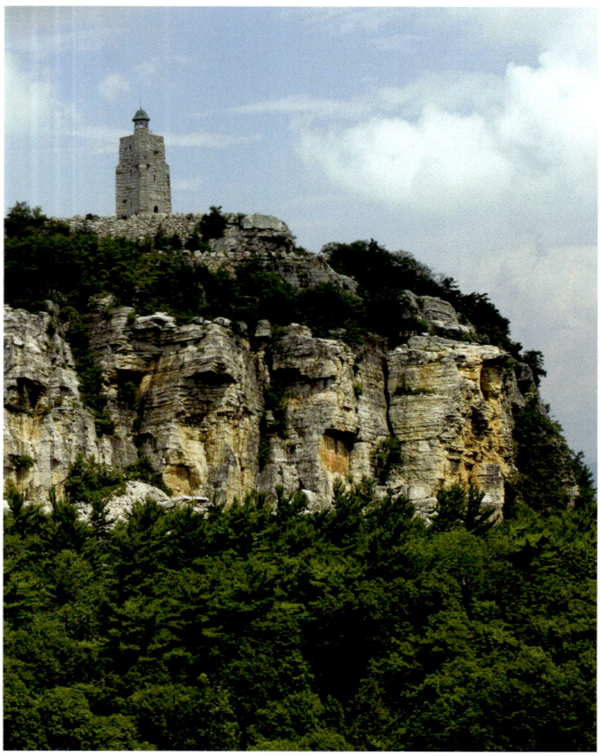

Sky Top: Albert K. Smiley Memorial, Marbletown

The promontory Sky Top with its tower dominates the northern Shawangunks and is viewable from throughout the Wallkill River valley. From the valley below, Sky Top appears as a rugged mass of glistening milky-white conglomerate rock projecting upward with a prominent southern exposure.

At the summit of Sky Top with a prominent cupola atop it is the Alfred K. Smiley Memorial Tower. Completed in 1923 of stone quarried nearby, the tower served as a fire lookout by the New York State Conservation Department until 1971.

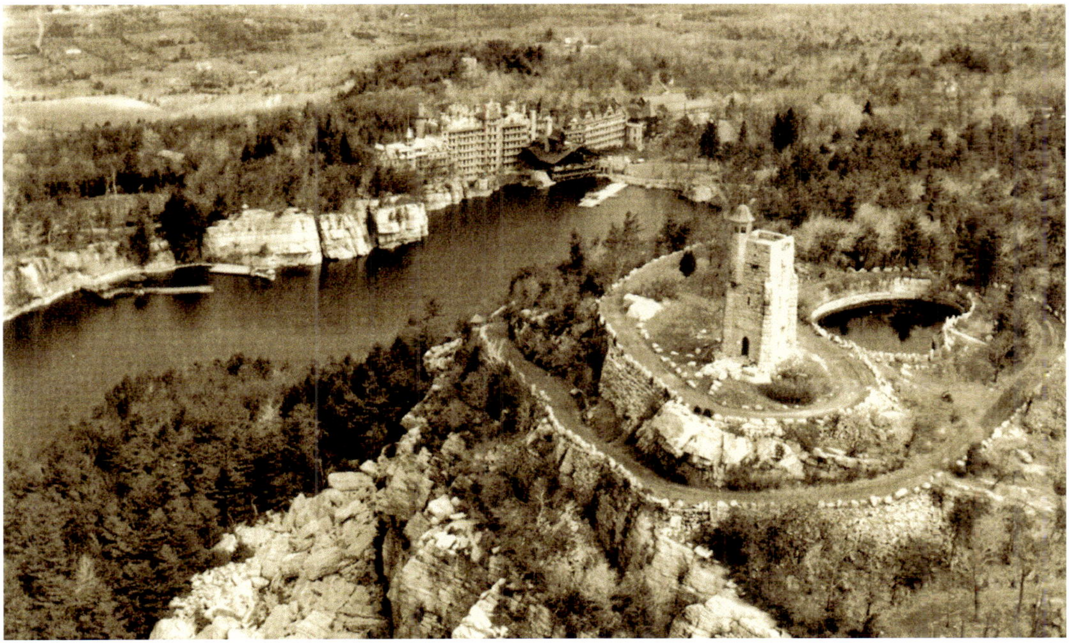

Today, hikers climb its 100 steps to the observation platform beneath the cupola. From the top of the tower, there is a 360 degree panoramic view of the nearby valleys as well as six states, including the silhouettes of the mountain ranges in Vermont, Massachusetts, Connecticut, New Jersey, and Pennsylvania.

On the western side is the fabled Labyrinth with its Lemon Squeeze, a challenging yet manageable rock scramble and climb that has been enjoyed by families for more than a hundred years. The route begins at a path along Lake Mohonk and terminates some 300 feet higher at the base of Sky Top.

Reachable via a challenging rock scramble through the Labyrinth and Lemon Squeeze, the route forces even the most agile to grapple with a helter-skelter assemblage of talus, navigate through narrow crevices, and climb steep ladders.

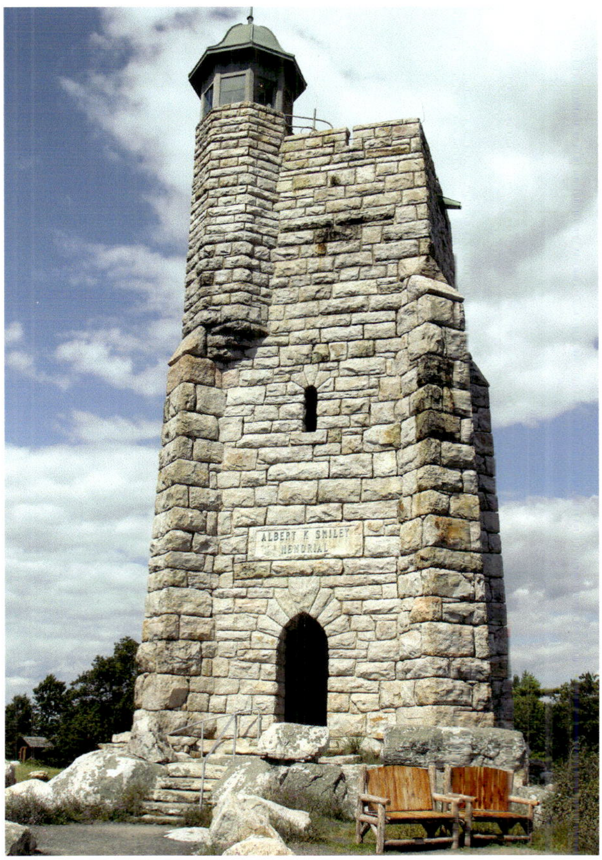

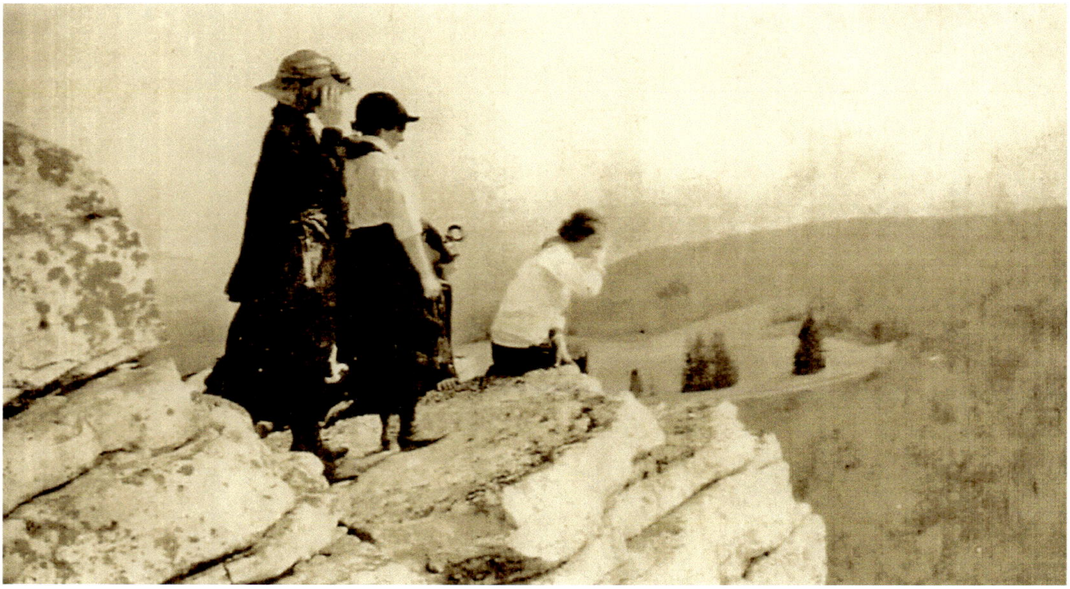

View of the Wallkill Valley from Sky Top, Marbletown & New Paltz

While climbing to the pinnacle of the impressive Albert K. Smiley Memorial Tower is the goal for many who hike to the summit, many also climb out onto the inclined rock where they are treated to spectacular vistas in all directions. The impressive views of the valley below as well as exhilarating windswept sense of danger have beckoned Mohonk Mountain House guests and others for nearly a century and a half.

Although some enjoy the challenge of the tortuous ascent through the labyrinth, others take the easier and gentler route to the crest via Sky Top Carriage Road either on foot or in a horse drawn carriage.

The undated early photo shows a group of students from the New York State Normal School at New Paltz on an outing enjoying the wind-swept view of Home Farm, one of the six farms once maintained by the Mohonk Mountain House. The latter photograph reveals not only the heavily wooded slopeland and Home Farm, but also the Wallkill River Valley and beyond to the east.

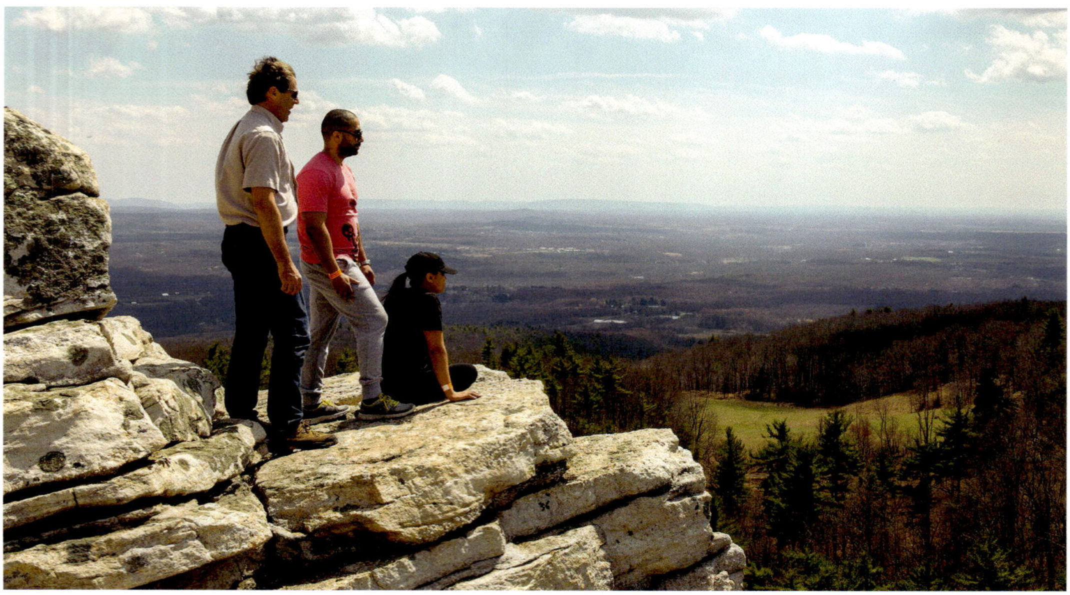

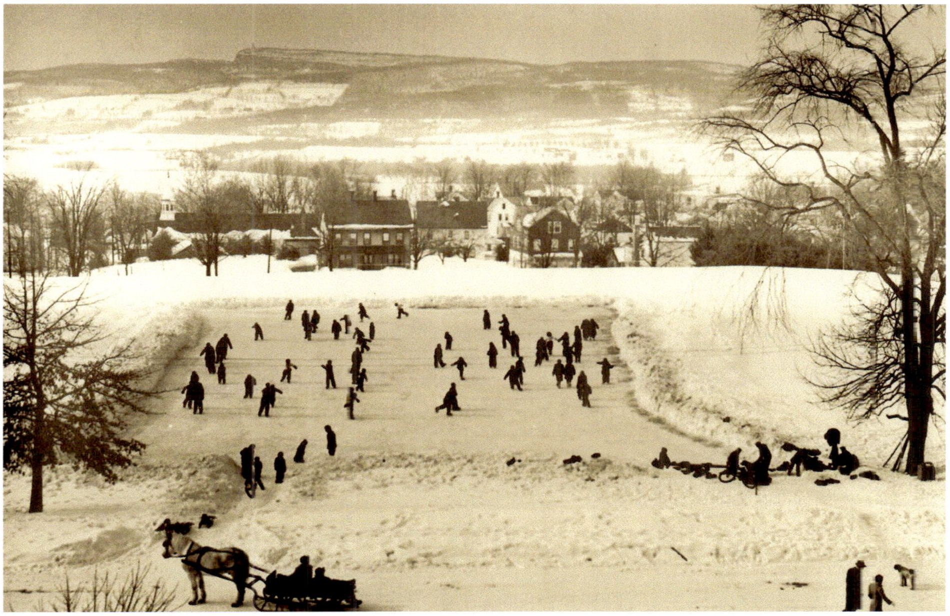

The Shawangunk Ridge with Distant Sky Top, New Paltz

As one moves east across the Wallkill River, the landscape rises in a series of terraces, two of which are occupied by the State University of New York, where students and faculty enjoy stunningly beautiful views of the Shawangunk Mountains.

This view west is from what was constructed in 1930 as the Lawrence H. van den Berg School of Practice, a training center for new teachers that many still call "The Campus School," and now the van den Berg Hall housing the School of Business. During a cold winter day in 1945, ice skaters enjoyed the cleared section of the school's open fields, a recreation not enjoyed for many decades here. Today, periodic fairs and festivals as well as a children's play area and team sports fill the area.

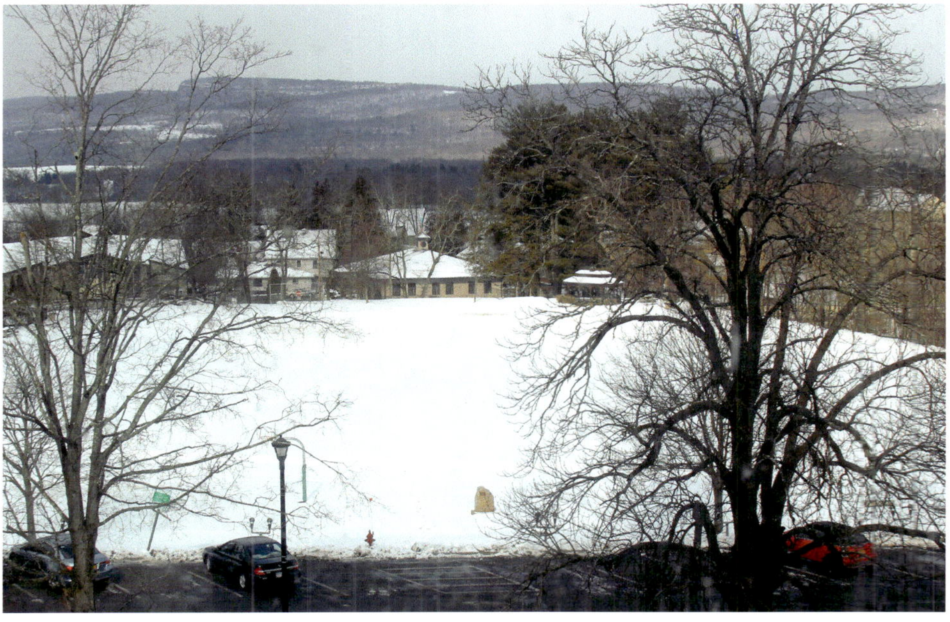

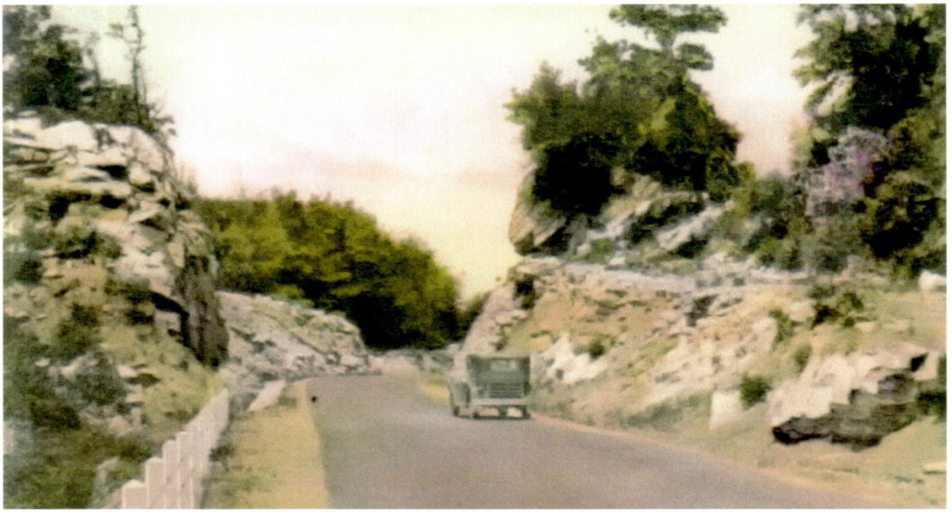

MINNEWASKA TRAIL, APPROACHING THE STEEL BRIDGE AT THE TRAPPS, GARDINER

Passage across the ridge has a history that dates to a Native American footpath that passed through a gap and linked the valleys. In 1856, a toll road with a dirt surface, supplemented with planking in wet areas, was laid out from New Paltz in the Wallkill Valley to Wawarsing in the Rondout Valley. The intent was to create a cost-effective turnpike route so that the products such as axes and iron, tanned leather, and glass from workshops on the west side of the ridge could be transported reasonably to markets to the east. Tolls were to be collected at the gap atop the ridge. However, in 1861 the turnpike went bankrupt and fell into disuse as an unimproved public road that was called the Minnewaska Trail once that complex was developed. Remnants of the New Paltz/Wawarsing turnpike are still evident in the Mohonk Preserve where sections have been repurposed as a parking area.

In the 1920s, a state highway was proposed to cross the ridge, partially along the line of the old New Paltz/Wawarsing Turnpike, but deviating where modern equipment made it feasible. This highway, now called US Route 44/55, was completed in 1929. Its line was just to the south of Mohonk carriage roads. Except for some "shaving" of the rock outcrops and increased vegetation, the *Then* and *Now* images are quite similar.

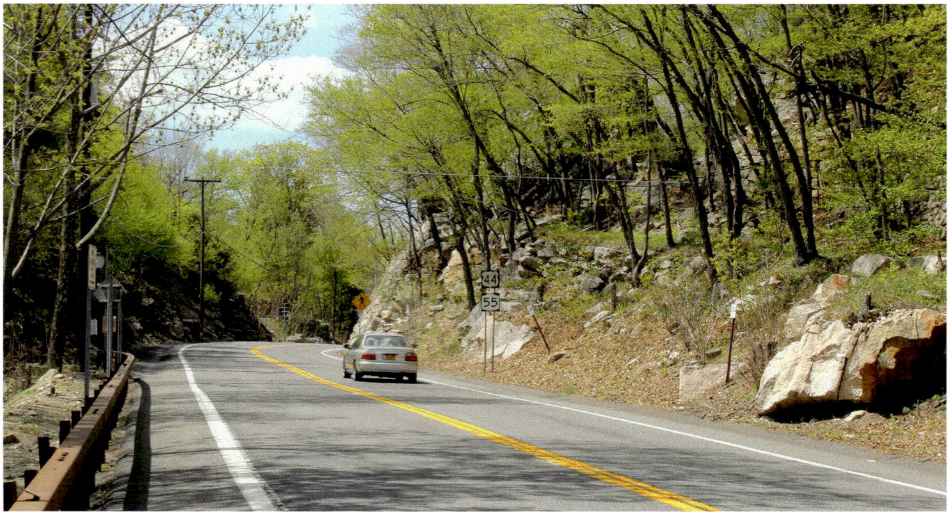

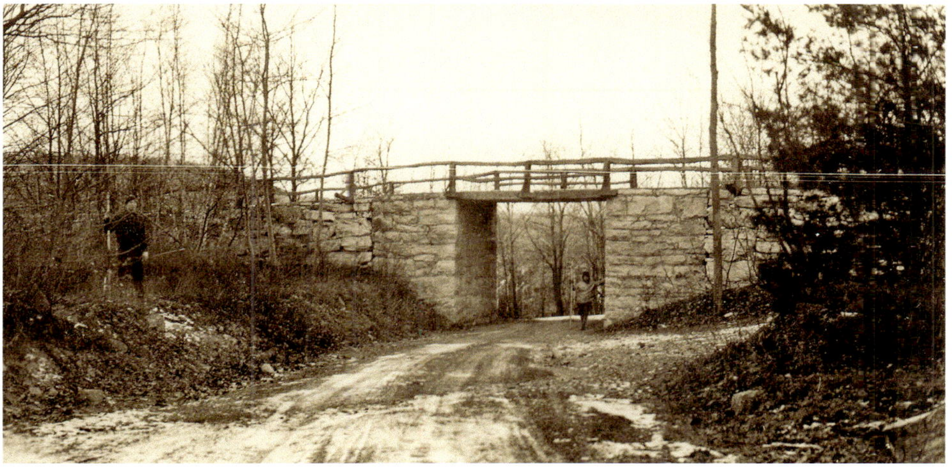

Trapps Bridge—"The Steel Bridge," Gardiner

The ever improving highway over the Shawangunk Ridge that lay between New Paltz on the east side and Wawarsing and points west was a critical factor in the region's development.

Moreover, because Alfred Smiley of Lake Minnewaska and Albert Smiley of Lake Mohonk wanted their guests to enjoy reciprocal rights at each other's hotels, they determined early on that a bridge was needed to span the highway so that horse-drawn carriages could travel easily. From the beginning, it was called Trapps Bridge.

The first bridge as seen in the *Then* photograph, which was installed in 1907, was a modest stringer or beam bridge constructed of timber over a single lane dirt road. Abutments and approaches were constructed using locally available cut conglomerate.

By the time the highway was improved in the 1920s, the state agreed to absorb the costs of a longer and more durable steel bridge to link the carriage roads. Over the years, an access road was cut from the highway that led up to the steel bridge. Nearby, a rustic campsite for climbers was established and more recently handicapped parking that provide easy access for those with mobility problems to the carriage road network.

At the beginning of the 21st century, inspectors deemed the steel bridge, which was opened in June 1930, deficient and called for its replacement.

Both the names Trapps Bridge and Steel Bridge are used by visitors to the Mohonk Preserve to mark this well-known geographic landmark.

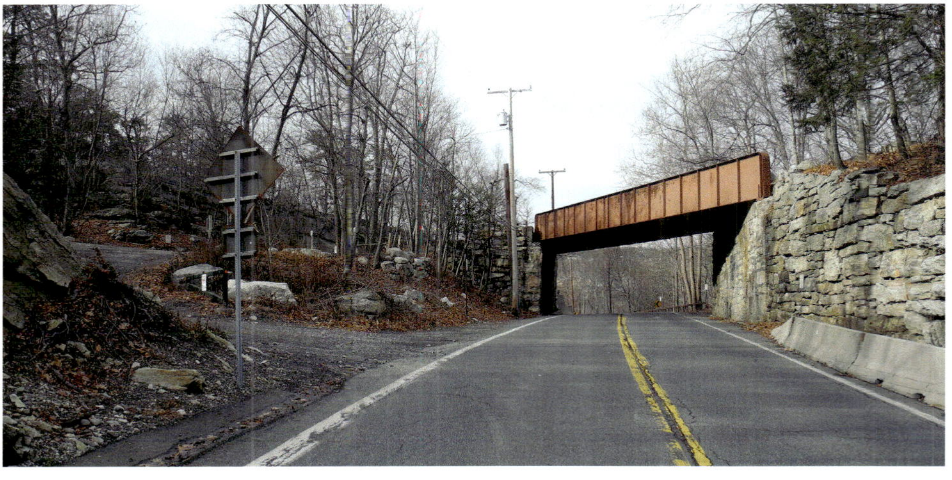

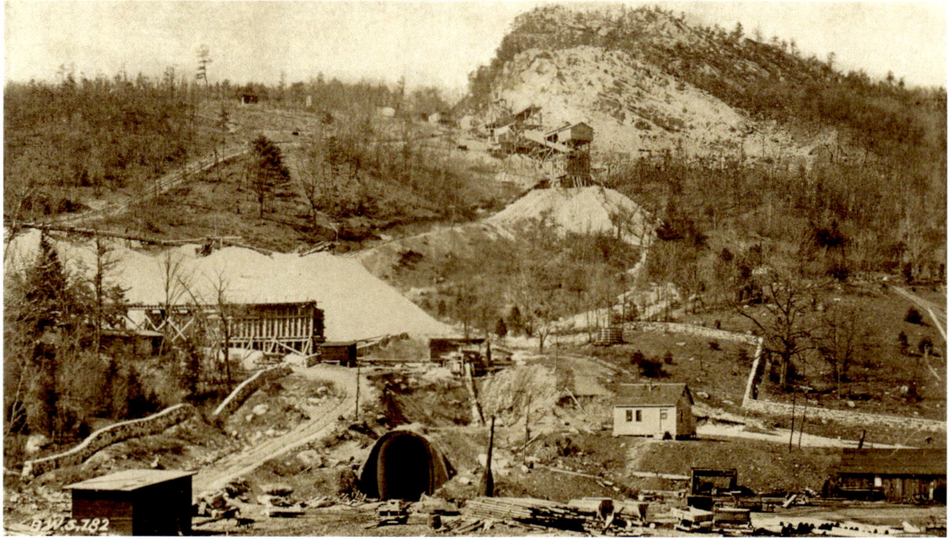

Catskill Aqueduct, Bonticou Tunnel, New Paltz

Between 1908 and 1912, the eastern slope of the ridge from Bonticou Crag in New Paltz through Gardiner was extensively transformed during the construction of the Catskill Aqueduct with the purpose of providing water for New York City. On its northwestern side near High Falls a 7,350 foot long tunnel pierced the ridge and emerged on the eastern side of Bonticou Crag. From this point, the tunnel became a cut-and-cover aqueduct structure called the Freer Cut. As the 1912 photograph reveals, there was extensive removal of tree cover to provide timbers that were milled to facilitate the construction of buildings to house workers and managers. A quarry and stone crushing plant were set up at the base of the crag with a rail line laid to ease the movement of voluminous amounts of stone.

Today there is essentially no surface evidence of the destruction a century ago. The cut-and-cover portions of the aqueduct here and elsewhere along the ridge are broad lines that until 9/11 were favorite places to hike or ski. Since 2001, New York City's Department of Environmental Protection has restricted public access to the aqueduct. Wherever trails and roads cross the aqueduct, there are signs that advise the public not to stray onto the adjacent areas.

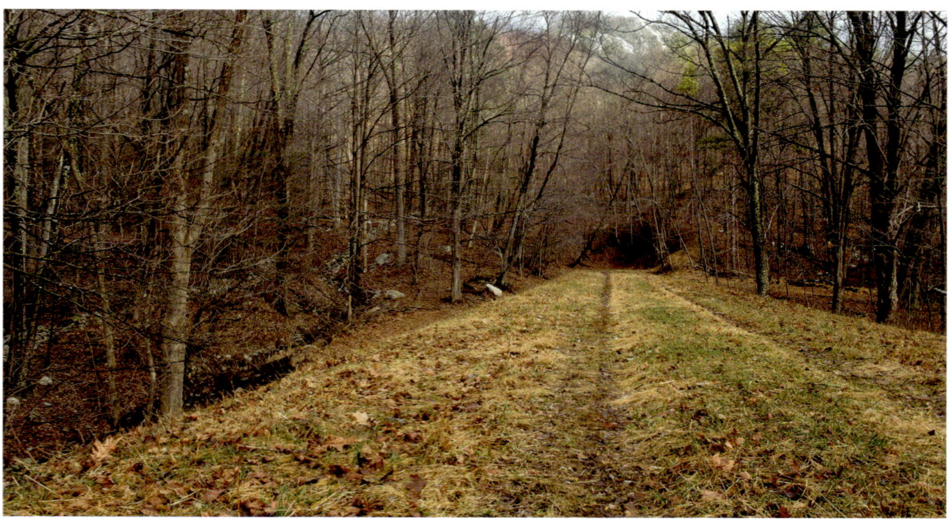

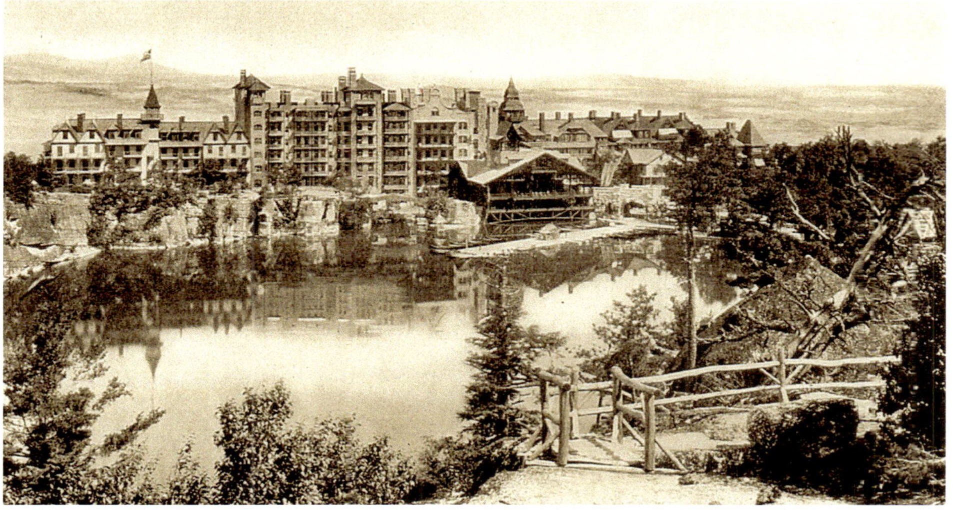

THE MOHONK MOUNTAIN HOUSE & LAKE MOHONK, MARBLETOWN

The full sweep of the nearly eighth of a mile long Mohonk Mountain House from its 1879 Rock Building on the left to the grand Dining Room on the right poses a striking silhouette, a feature clear in both photographs. In a remarkable architectural feat of coexistence, a spa wing, whose wood and stone evoke earlier times, was completed in 2005 to the south of the Rock Building, the first major addition in a hundred years. Evident in these photographs are the variety of architectural styles and mixture of building materials.

Peaked roofs, tile-capped towers, and multiple balconies still present a scenic assemblage that echo comments made by an unnamed *New York Times* writer's "Life among The Rocks" at Lake Mohonk on August 14, 1882 well before the bulk of the hotel was completed: "One house is perched high on a rocky hill; others are built on the slope; another stands boldly out over the water at the base of the hill, and yet others nestle among the trees in the background. ... needless to say that the Lake Mohonk Mountain House is picturesque." In 1882, the hotel accommodated 300 guests while today some 600 often fill the house.

In 1986, the Mohonk Mountain House and many of its surrounding buildings as well as much of the original estate of some 7,500 acres, was designated a National Historic Landmark

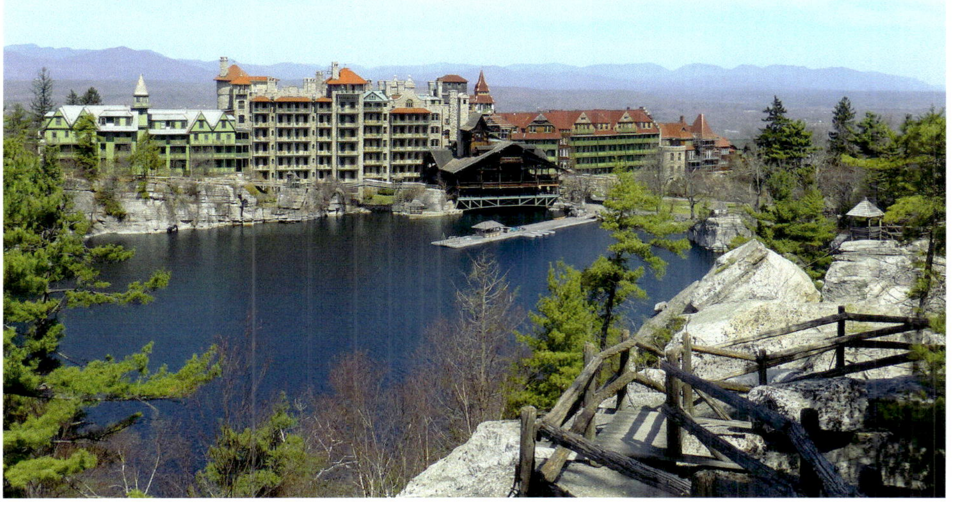

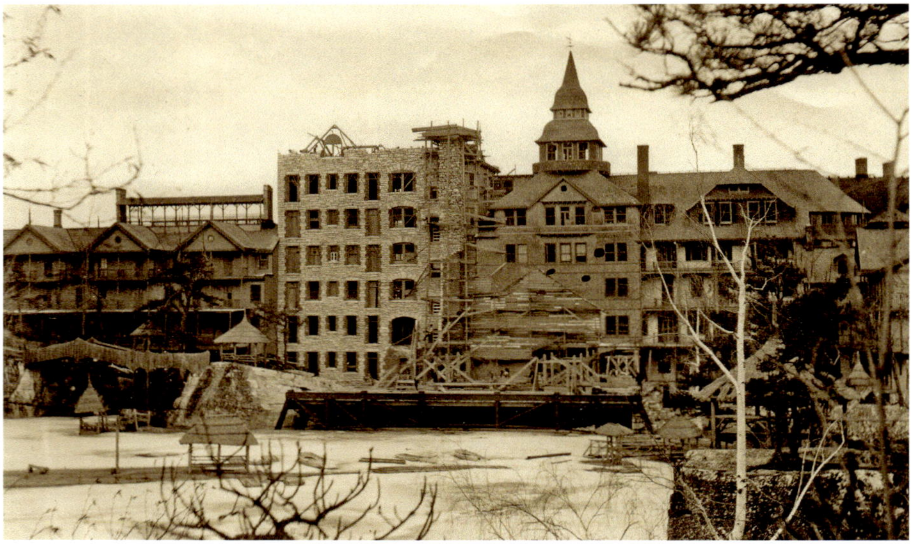

TURN OF THE 20TH CENTURY CONSTRUCTION, MOHONK MOUNTAIN HOUSE, MARBLETOWN

The turn of the twentieth century brought with it dramatic changes to the evolving Mountain House building that we appreciate today, an eclectic assemblage of styles and materials. The *Then* photo shows the original Central Building on the right with the adjacent towered Stone Building. The Stone Building rose in two stages, first the vertical six-story building in 1899 and then to its south the horizontal structure that replaced the triple-gabled wooden building on the left, completed in 1902, whose elements are seen better in the *Now* photograph. Beyond to its south and connected by a labyrinth of corridors is what is the multi-gabled Rock Building, a wooden structure built on rock in 1879, which was fully renovated to modern standards in 1997.

The Parlor Wing, with its wide and soaring gable structure constructed over the edge of the lake, which reminds many of a Swiss chalet, was completed in 1899. Its dominating presence is clear in the *Now* photograph revealing both the expansive porches and tucked-in balconies that have afforded more than a century of guests places to relax on rocking chairs and enjoy the placid lake and stunning scenery.

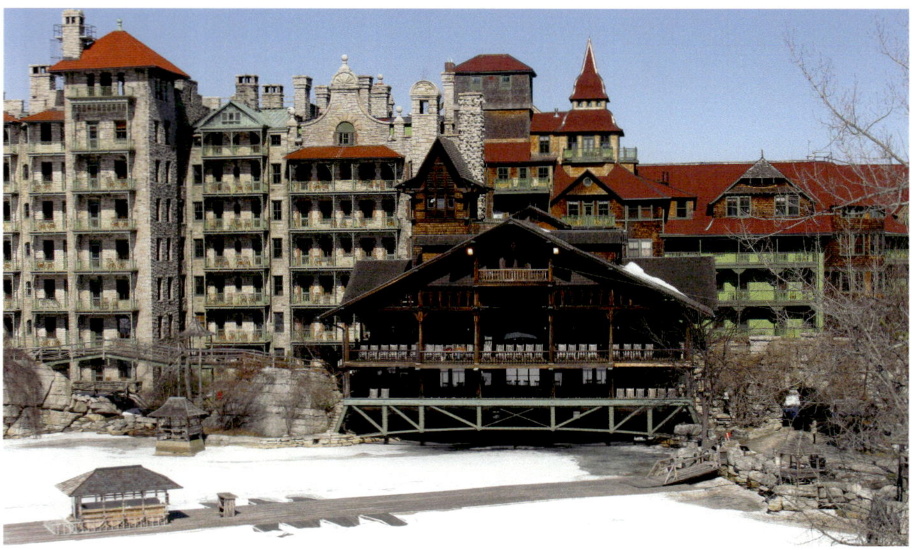

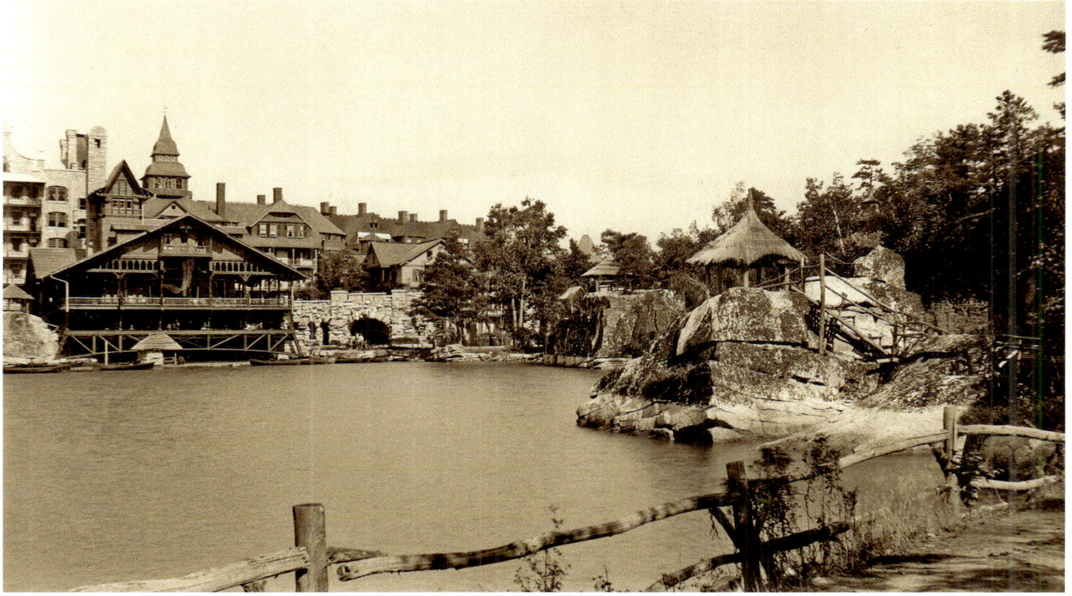

View across Lake Mohonk & Summerhouses, Marbletown

Even in 1882 when the *New York Times* reported on the quaint character of the still-young Mountain House, the manipulation of nature was underscored: "Under Mr. Smiley's fostering care the country about Mohonk is beginning to resemble a great English demesne" with the addition of carriage roads, footpaths, open vistas, gardens, and summerhouses. By the end of the century in 1897, Benjamin F. Trueblood in the *New England Magazine* declared, "If one were commanded to pick out the most civilized and civilizing spot in America, he would not go far wrong if he selected Lake Mohonk."

"Fine carriage roads wind around the bluffs, and to every point at which a fresh view is to be had footpaths lead to the same spots by the most circuitous and picturesque routes." The routes along the lake and to promontories that overlooked the lake were the first to be created for the enjoyment of those on foot.

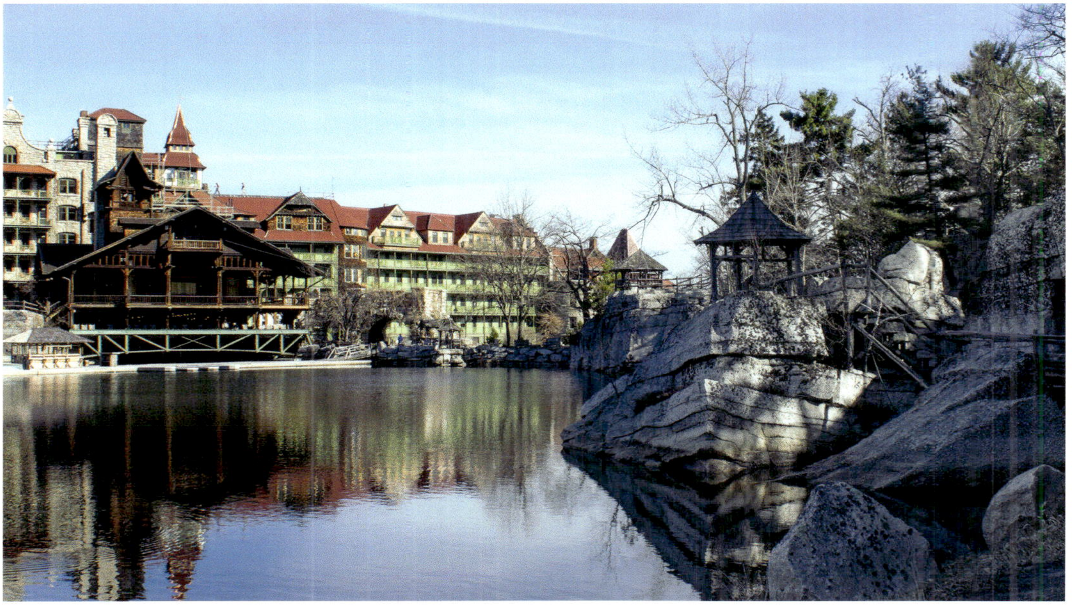

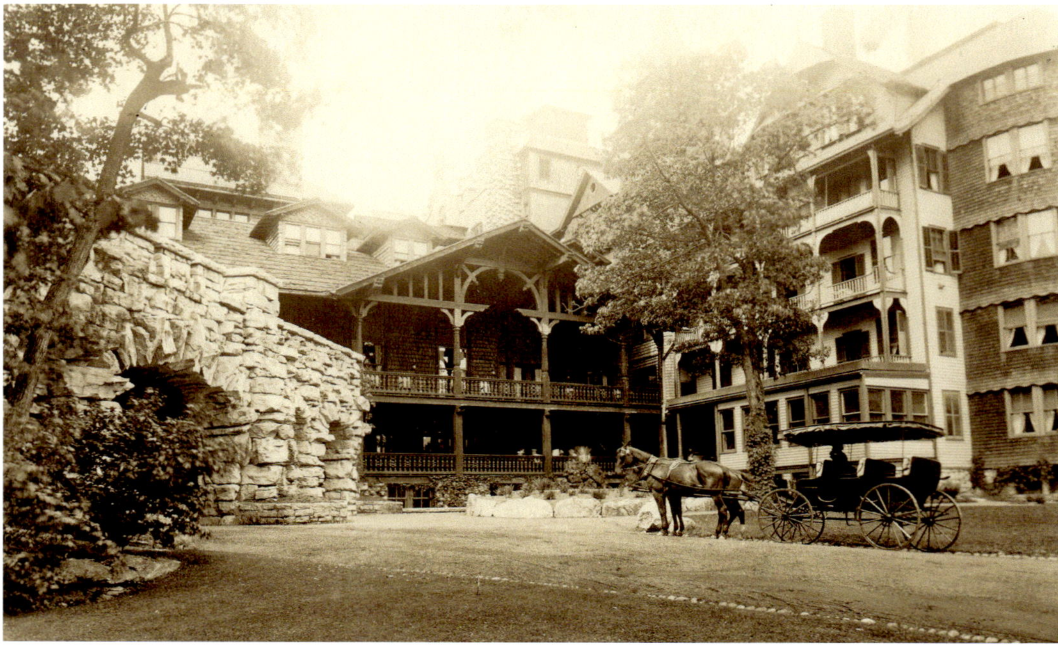

Porte Cochère Area Alterations, Marbletown

With a carriage approaching the massive stone porte cochère on the left, the *Then* photograph shows the early twentieth-century entrance to the Mountain House. This covered entryway was completed in 1899, along with the extraordinary Parlor Wing with its generous public spaces, including reception as well as quiet pursuits such as prayer, conversation, chess, letter writing, and reading. In 1966, the main entrance was shifted to the west side of the building while the porte cochère still offers those on foot an imposing entry and exit reminiscent of the Victorian era.

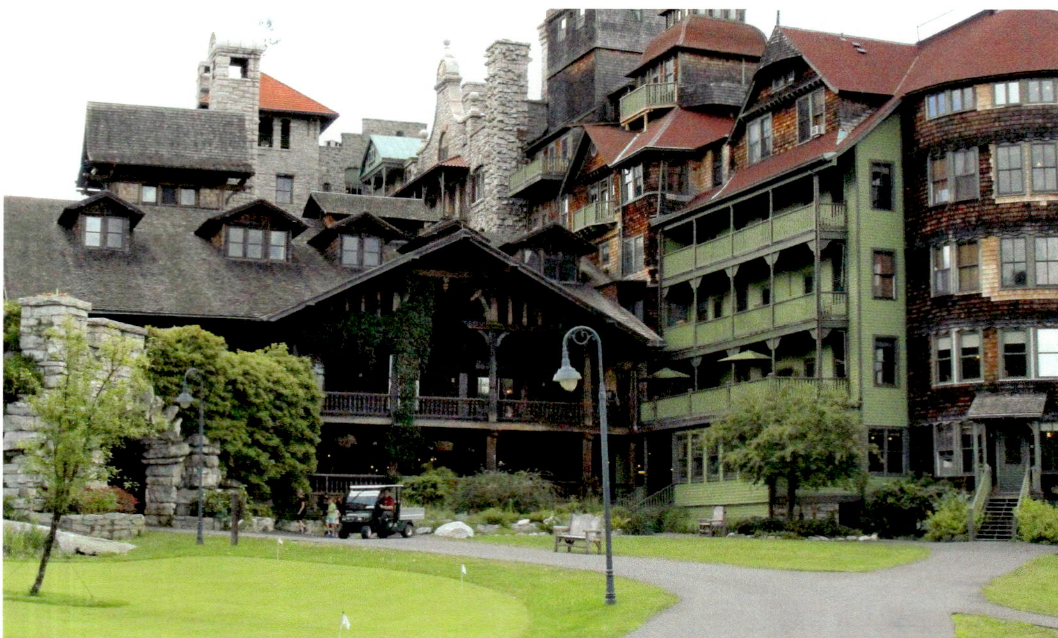

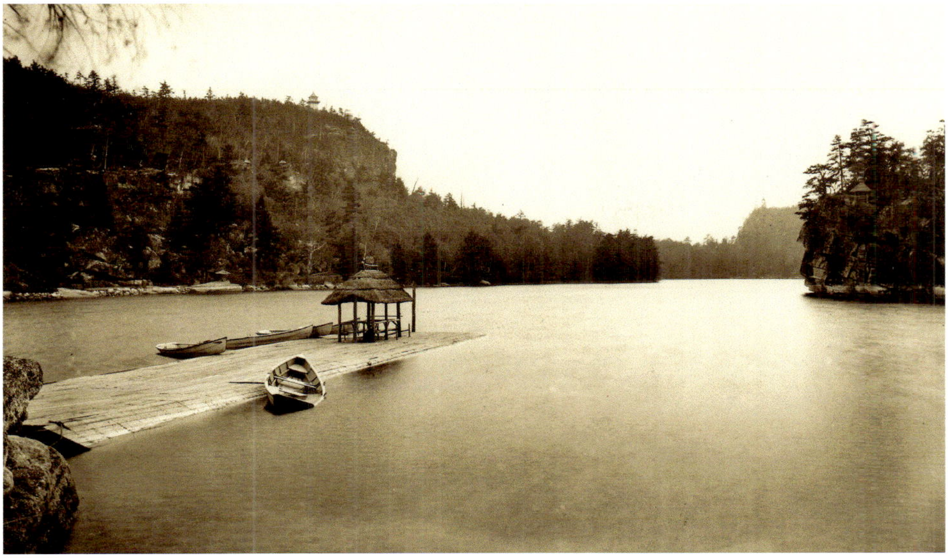

Boat Wharf, Lake Mohonk with Sky Top, Marbletown

Although quiet, even ethereal, in the early morning, the Boat Dock on the northern margins of the half-mile long Lake Mohonk has long been the site of busy activity. Mountain House guests at the turn of the twentieth century rented one of forty-five flat-bottomed St. Lawrence River skiffs, which were suitable for the timid, those wanting to relax without effort, and those wearing long dresses, as well being quite stable and safe. Over time, canoes, kayaks, and paddleboats were added for the more adventurous. Fishing equipment, including rods and bait, have long been available on the wharf.

While ice skating was also a traditional winter pastime, more important was the ice harvesting that took place during the coldest days of winter once the ice was ten to eighteen inches thick. From the 1870s onward, a horse-drawn single-blade saw cleaved the blocks of ice, but this method was replaced later by a more efficient power saw. Ice cutting did not end due to warmer winters, but ended in 1964 due to the availability of improved ice making machines and staffing changes. When the *Then* photo was taken, the slopes of the Sky Top promontory were quite bare.

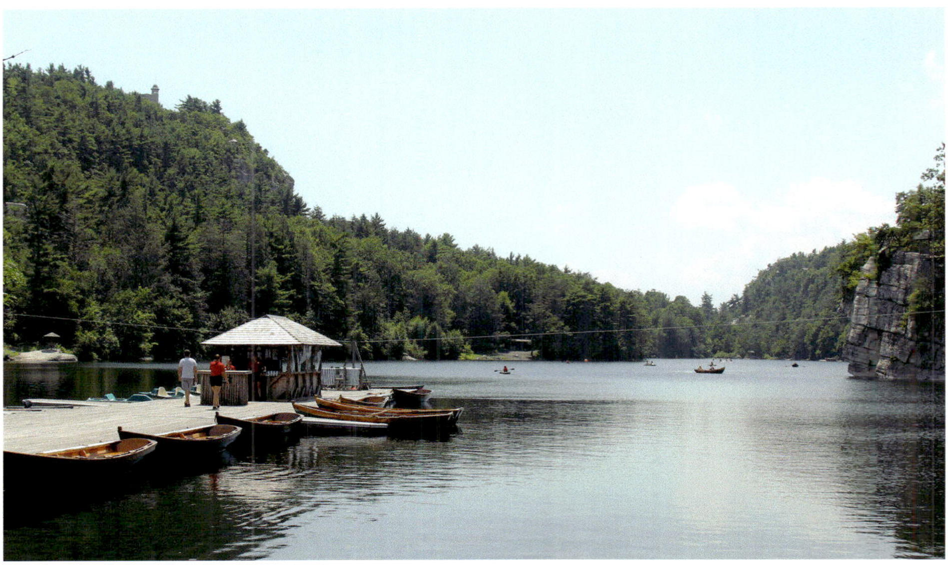

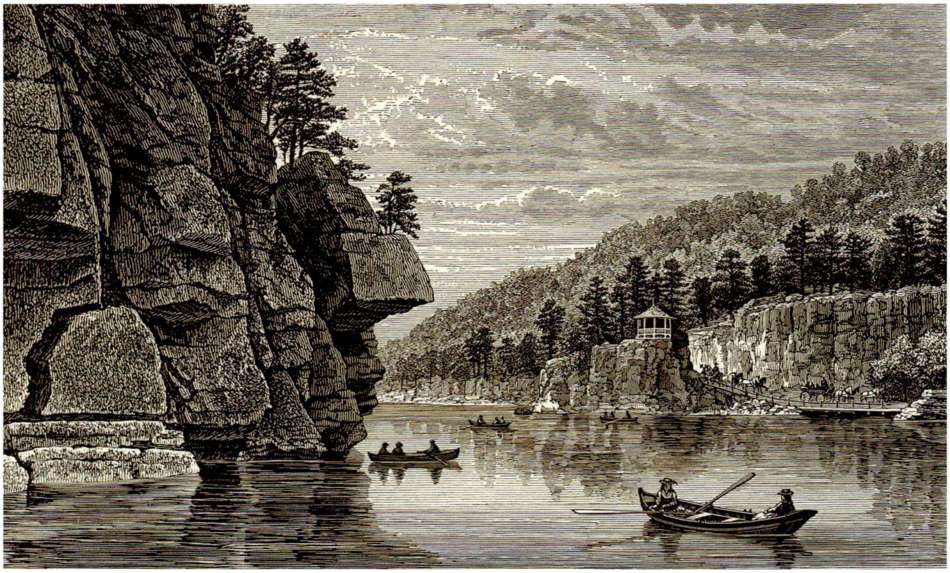

Lake Mohonk and the Face of Pine Bluff, Marbletown

The romanticized *Then* etching and the *Now* photograph suggest that little has changed even as the etching reveals some artistic license in what is depicted on the right rear section. The patterns of fractured stone, trees, even summerhouses express the timelessness of Mohonk.

Yet, the third image showing a couple seated on a rustic bench beneath an overhang reveals that the vertical face of the rock was blackened while the contemporary photograph shows a glistening white surface. Over the past 100 years, there has been a dramatic decline in the presence of lichens—a composite living organism comprising a fungus and a photosynthetic partner that thrive together in a symbiotic relationship—on the vertical surfaces of rock around Lake Mohonk, a subject studied by the naturalist Daniel Smiley and his colleague Carl George with many photographic pairs. The reasons for the decline are not clear, although air pollution and periodic drought have been speculated as causes.

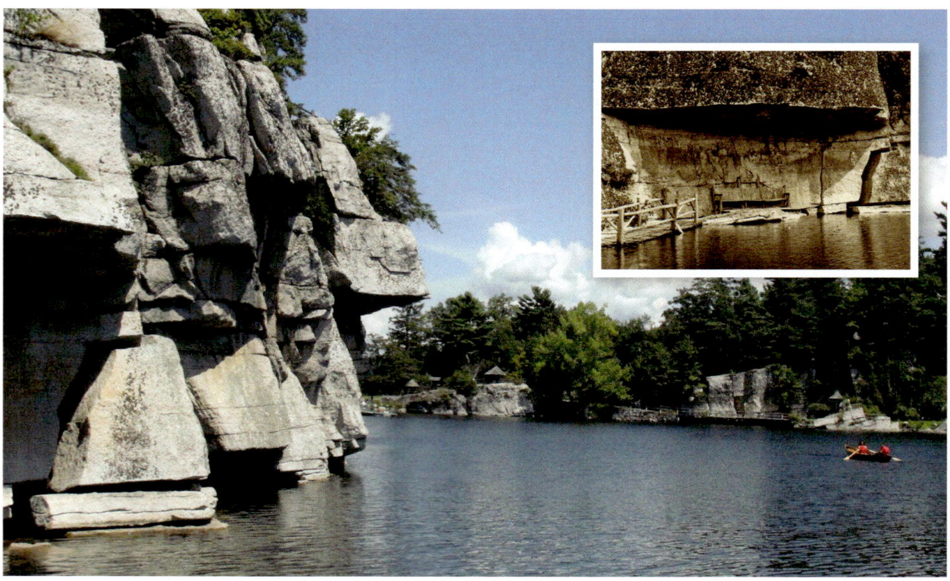

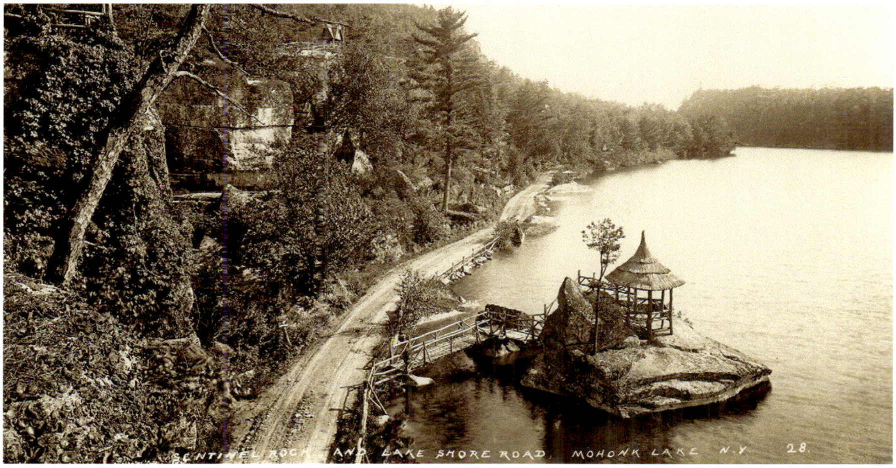

Start of Carriage Road to Lake Minnewaska, Marbletown

When Arnold Guyot, the Princeton Professor, visited the Shawangunks in 1877, his remarks highlighted the trails already in place around the Mohonk Mountain House, especially encircling Lake Mohonk. During the ensuing decades an extensive network of carriage roads and foot paths were laid out that stretched for miles beyond the lake. These extensions were sometimes lined with rustic rails where there was danger of falling. They were accompanied by the careful placement of gazebos, called summerhouses. At distances away from the lake, vistas were cleared to highlight noteworthy and panoramic views. Today these look much like they did in the past.

In time, carriage roads reached to more distant locations including to the Mountain House at Lake Minnewaska, some seven miles away, which was constructed by Alfred H. Smiley, the twin of Albert K. Smiley who managed the Mohonk property. Horse-drawn carriage rides for leisure as well as to carry guests from Minnewaska to Mohonk or the reverse were facilitated by the fact that guests at one resort could dine at the other.

Carriage roads were a device for bringing guests into nature where they could experience the craggy character of the terrain and come unbelievably close to nature, all the while riding in a horse-drawn buggy. In those early years, when women wore long dresses and shoes not meant for long-distance hiking, a carriage ride immersed them with unforgettable experiences. By 1897 some forty miles of carriage roads extending out from the Mountain House in all directions had been constructed on the ridge by the Smileys.

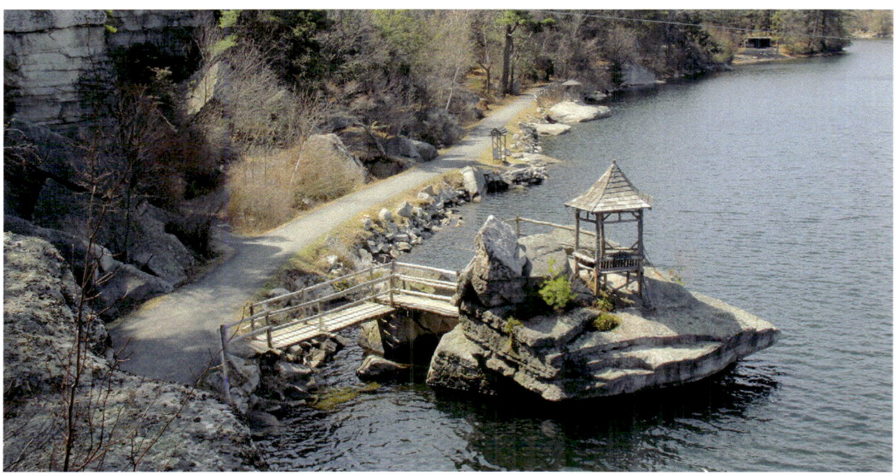

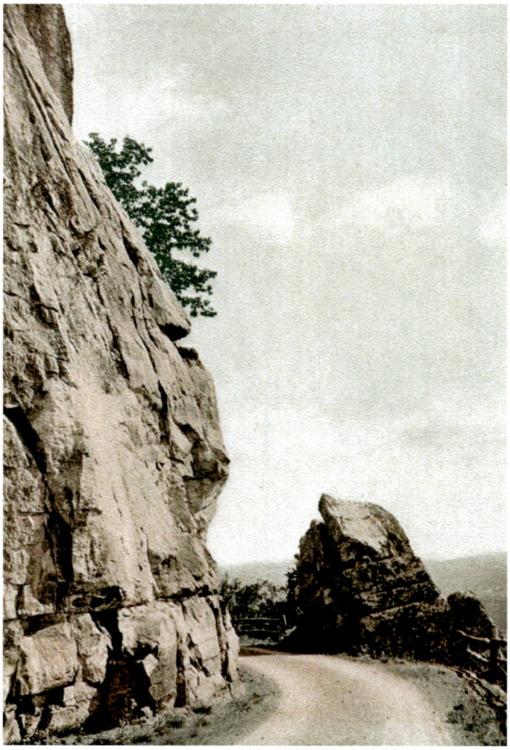

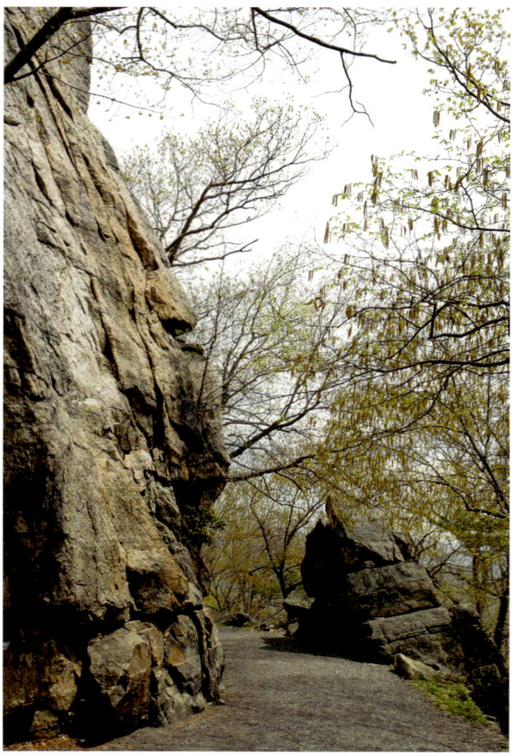

Undercliff Carriage Road, The Trapps, Gardiner

During the late nineteenth and early twentieth century, new carriage roads radiating out from the Mountain House were constructed for horse-drawn carriages. Viewed not simply as utilitarian routes, each of the carriage roads was seen as having aesthetic qualities that led visitors to tarry and admire the vistas.

Rock outcrops were shaved, abutments and walls were shored up, and bridges were constructed where necessary. Local and immigrant stoneworkers and carpenters, wielding simple tools and utilizing horse drawn equipment, were employed to tame the "wilderness of boulders and cliffs."

The Undercliff Carriage Road was cut through the rock in 1903, leaving a prominent boulder to the side.

While part of the Undercliff—Overcliff Carriage Road loop, it also provided a through route between the Lake Mohonk and Lake Minnewaska hotels whose guests enjoyed reciprocal access.

While it is not common to see horse-drawn carriages today, the carriage roads are still enjoyed by hikers, bikers, as well as cross-country skiers and snowshoers during winter. A short distance from this spot visitors can glimpse on the left the world-famous sites for rock climbing and on the right the Wallkill Valley below.

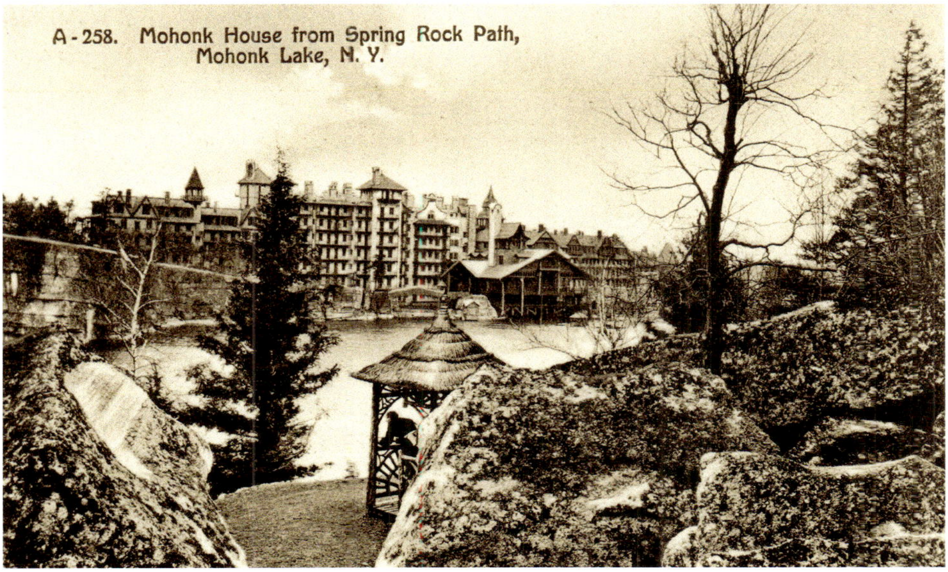

Spring [Rock] Path, Marbletown

The *New York Times* reported in 1882, "Summer houses of rough wood and neatly thatched roofs, of all sizes and shapes, are perched like birds' nests on every overhanging rock and in every retired nook. One or two even stand out in the water, securely founded on sunken rocks serving both as buoys and as retired places for picnickers. There are something over 90 of these houses scattered at different points ..." Called by some "rustic gazebos," the summerhouses, increased in number to about 155 early in the twentieth century. Today, they still total an impressive 117 at the last inventory. Only one summerhouse is found on Mohonk Preserve land, on a ledge at Cope's Lookout. Each was carefully sited to provide an artful view as well as a tranquil spot for contemplation, conversation, and reading whether it was clear or foggy. Thatching, which required ongoing maintenance and frequent replacement, was substituted with shingles beginning in the 1960s. All thatching was ended in the 1980s.

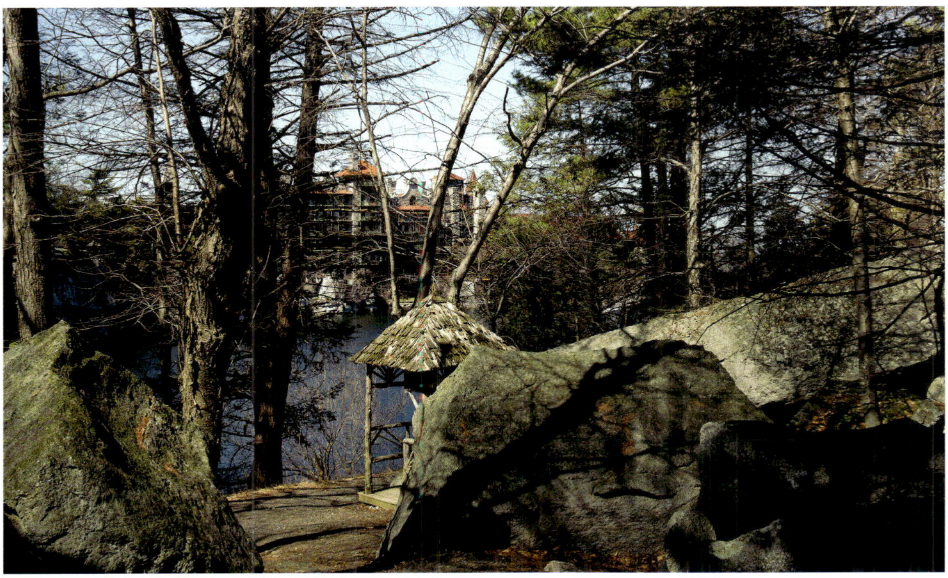

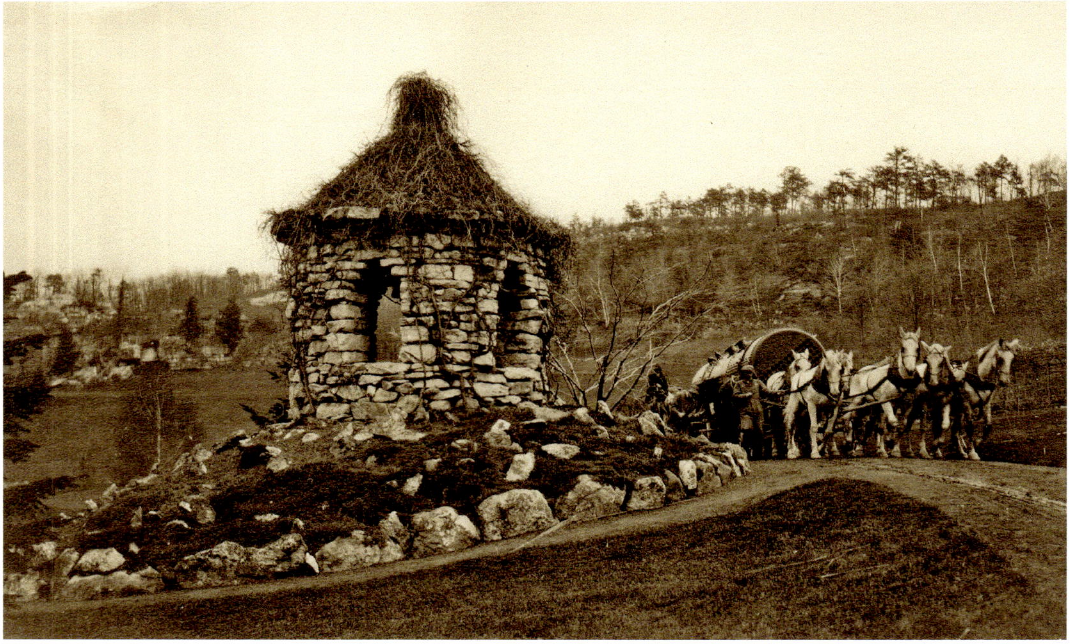

Stone Summerhouse, Marbletown

One unique summerhouse was constructed in 1890 of sturdy stone along Garden Road. As depicted in this 1917 view, six horses haul a cylindrical boiler that was to be fitted into the Powerhouse adjacent to the hotel so that steam radiators could be installed in rooms rather than wood burning Franklin stoves.

While the *Then* and *Now* photographs are not surprisingly similar, it should be noted how sparse the tree cover on the hillslope was a century ago. Natural and selected plantings have softened the view as has the paved road made winter time travel easier.

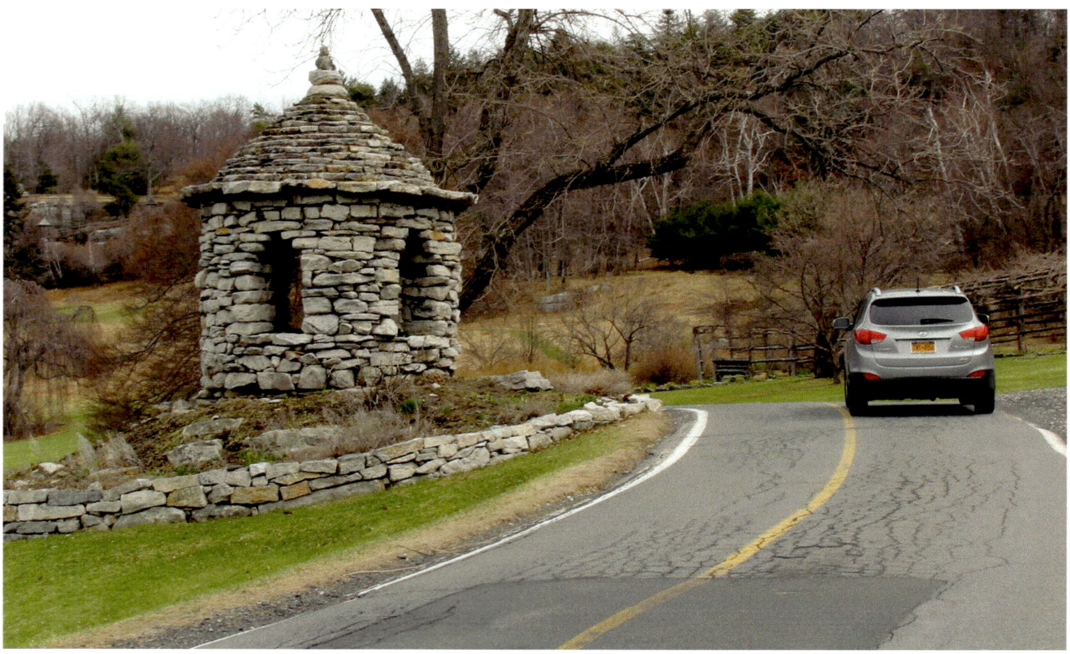

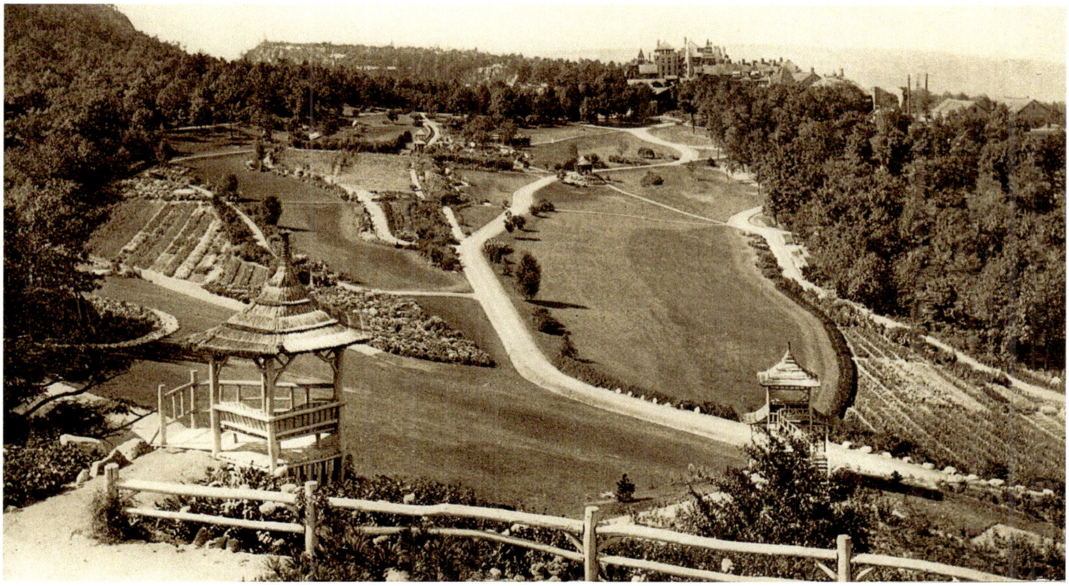

Mohonk Mountain House Gardens, Marbletown

This distant 1906 view looking southwest towards the Mountain House reveals that the Mohonk Gardens were once more extensive than they are now. Close examination discloses that the linear patterns were berry bushes, which were attentively groomed to provide fresh and flavorful fruit in the dining room. The last of the berry canes were taken out in the 1970s to lessen the burden on the gardeners.

Establishing the gardens was onerous because of natural obstacles: thin soils underlain by a rock substrate. Frederick Partington's 1911 description provides a good summary: "There was not a square of a hundred feet where anything but ferns and lichens could hold on—and it had taken some of the lichens a hundred years or more to cover a few inches."

Some sections of the early gardens have been converted to lawn. Center right is the imposing weeping beech tree that was planted in 1898.

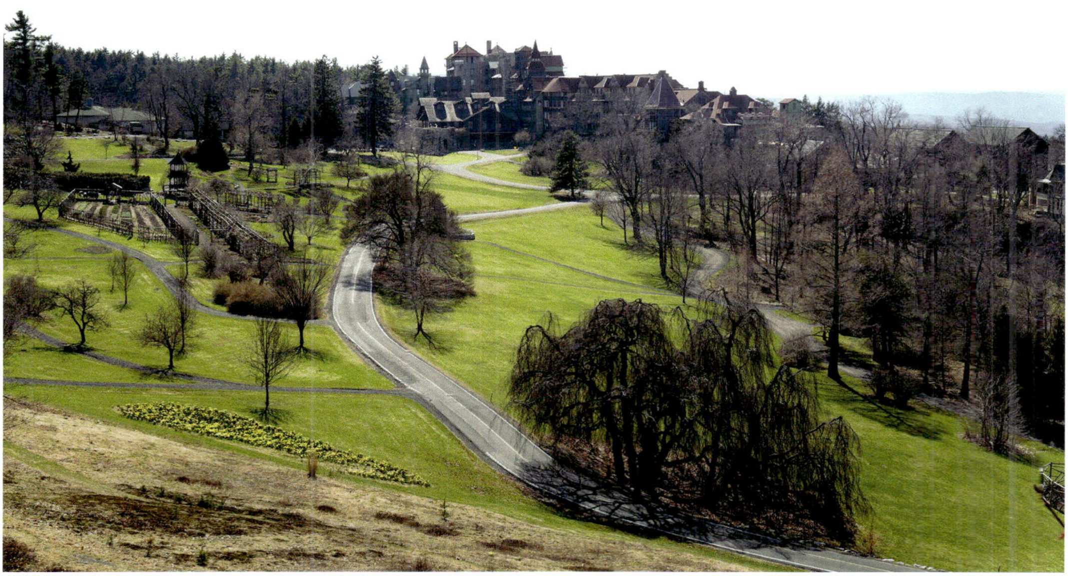

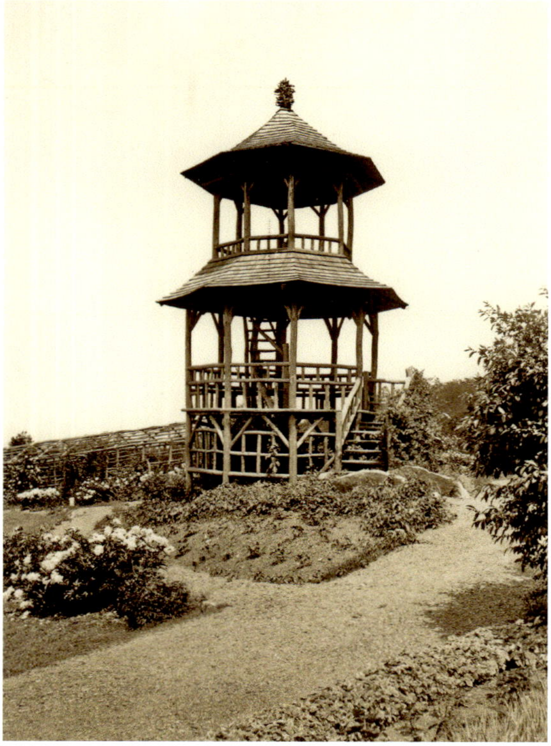

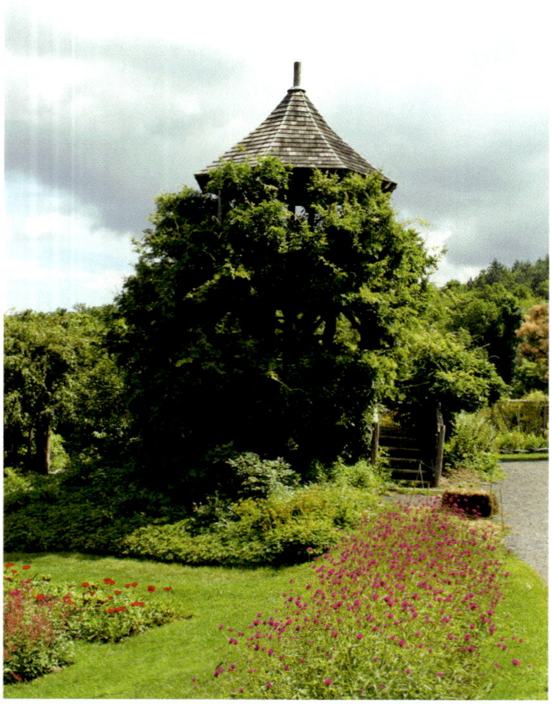

Two-story Summerhouse, Marbletown

This two-tiered rustic summerhouse constructed of cedar is said to have been suggested from a sketch by Andrew Jackson Downing. The 1906 *Then* photograph reveals a newly constructed arbor beyond, which are still quite open. Located within the Mohonk Gardens, these wooden structures continue to be focal points amidst Victorian-style beds of flowers, each with masses of single or contrasting colors.

In recent years, themes based on color and geography have permitted the gardeners to introduce new elements that are appreciated by returning guests. In addition to rose and herb beds, there are a children's garden, heirloom plants, and more recently a Victorian maze that was added in 1998.

Today, the award-winning Mohonk Gardens retain the characteristics of a picturesque, though sometimes formal, composition—irregular layouts and vibrant colors varying seasonally—that continue to evolve.

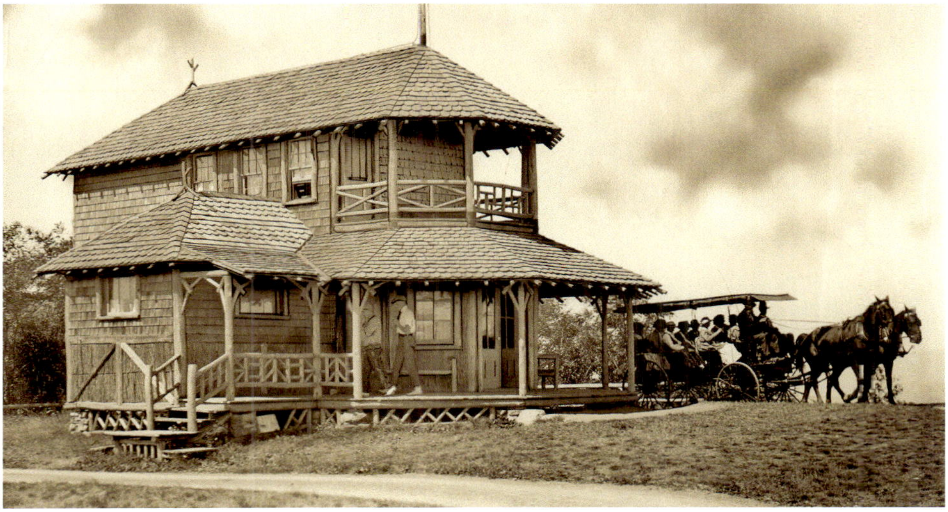

Mohonk Club House/Golf Cottage, New Paltz

A classic late-nineteenth century Scottish-influenced golf course was laid out at Mountain Rest in 1897. Designed initially with 9 holes and later expanded to 18 holes, the nine-hole course on a steep slope was eliminated in the 1920s. What remains of it is one of the oldest in the United States. More recently the course was certified as part of the Audubon Cooperative Sanctuary program and on Earth Day 2012 was selected as one of "Top 10 Environmentally Friendly Courses" in the country by *Links Magazine*. This Green course is open to the public as well as hotel guests.

Constructed in 1903 on a prominence on the edge of the golf course just off the second tee, the striking Mohonk Club House in the *Then* image served well for 77 years until the function was moved to the Farmhouse, a larger building across the road that had parking for cars. During early days, golfers arrived via horse-drawn carriages after a two-mile ride from the Mountain House. Subsequently, the two-story Golf House was renovated as Golf Cottage, one of a handful of venerable structures that appeal to adults and families who do not want to live in a hotel room yet desire modern amenities in a unique outdoor environment. Golf Cottage now is a three bedroom and 1.5 bath building with a wraparound porch. The upstairs porch overlooks the golf course.

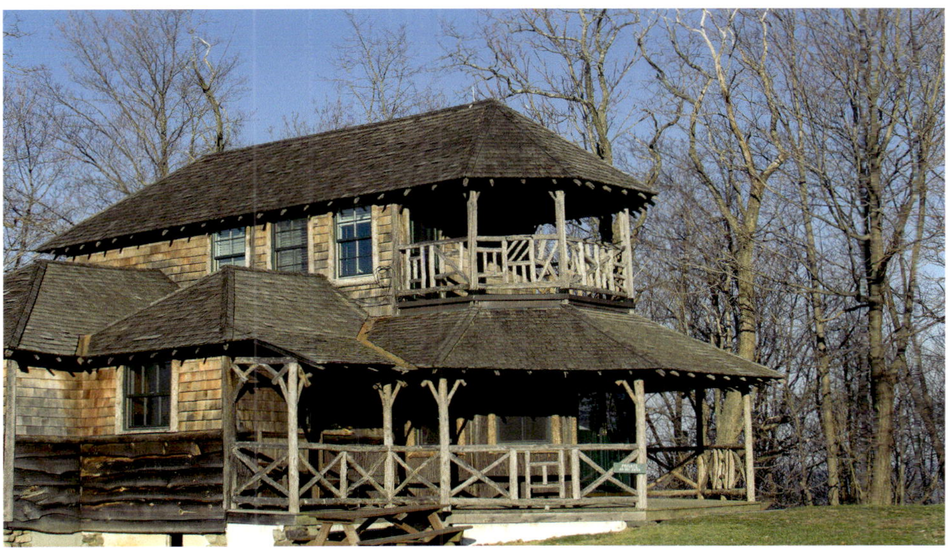

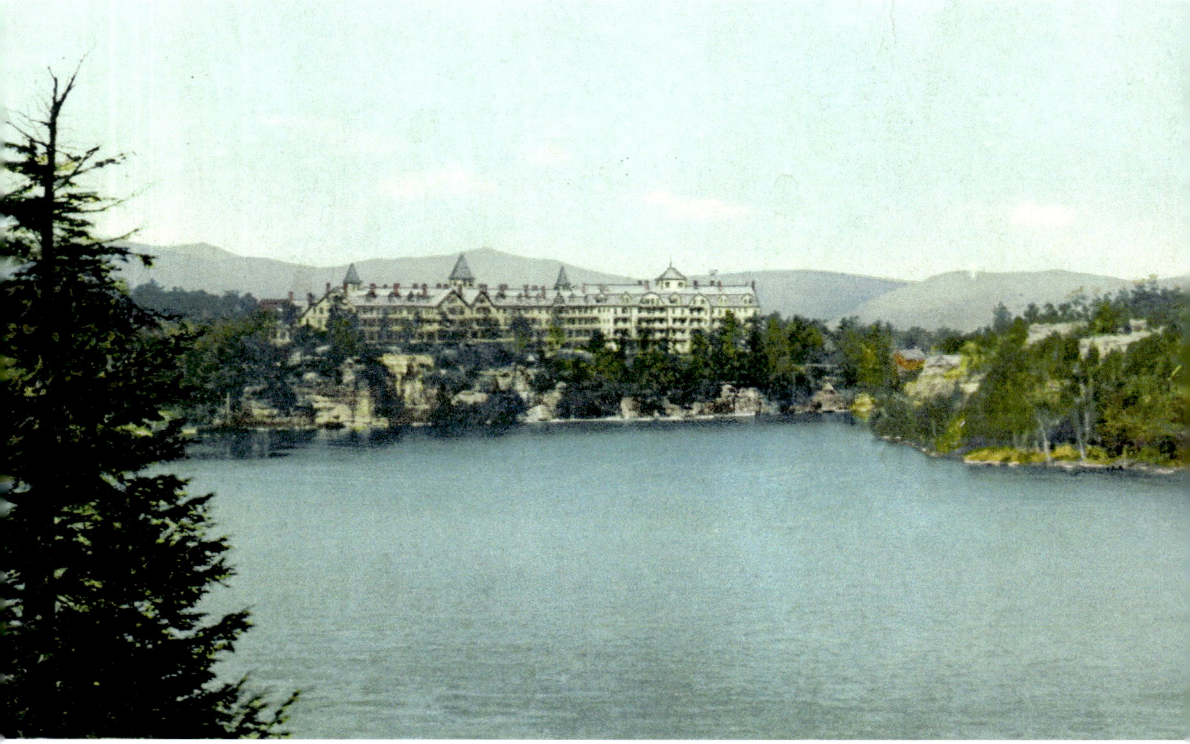

WILDMERE AND THE CLIFF HOUSE FROM ACROSS LAKE MINNEWASKA

During the decade after the purchase of Lake Mohonk in 1869 and the initial development of a hotel there, Alfred H. Smiley, one of the twins, scouted out property to the south.

In 1875, he purchased 2200 acres around and including what was then called Coxing Pond and renamed it Lake Minnewaska. In 1879, he opened the Lake Minnewaska Mountain House in the Town of Rochester with a four story building that subsequently gained renown as The Cliff House on the east side of the lake, then enlarged it in 1881 to accommodate 250 guests. At an elevation greater than that of the Lake Mohonk Mountain House, The Cliff House boasted even more expansive valley and mountain views.

When viewed separately, Wildmere and The Cliff House each has distinctive characteristics. When paired as buildings across the expansive waters of Lake Minnewaska, they are even more remarkable as a grouping of natural and cultural features unparalleled in New York State.

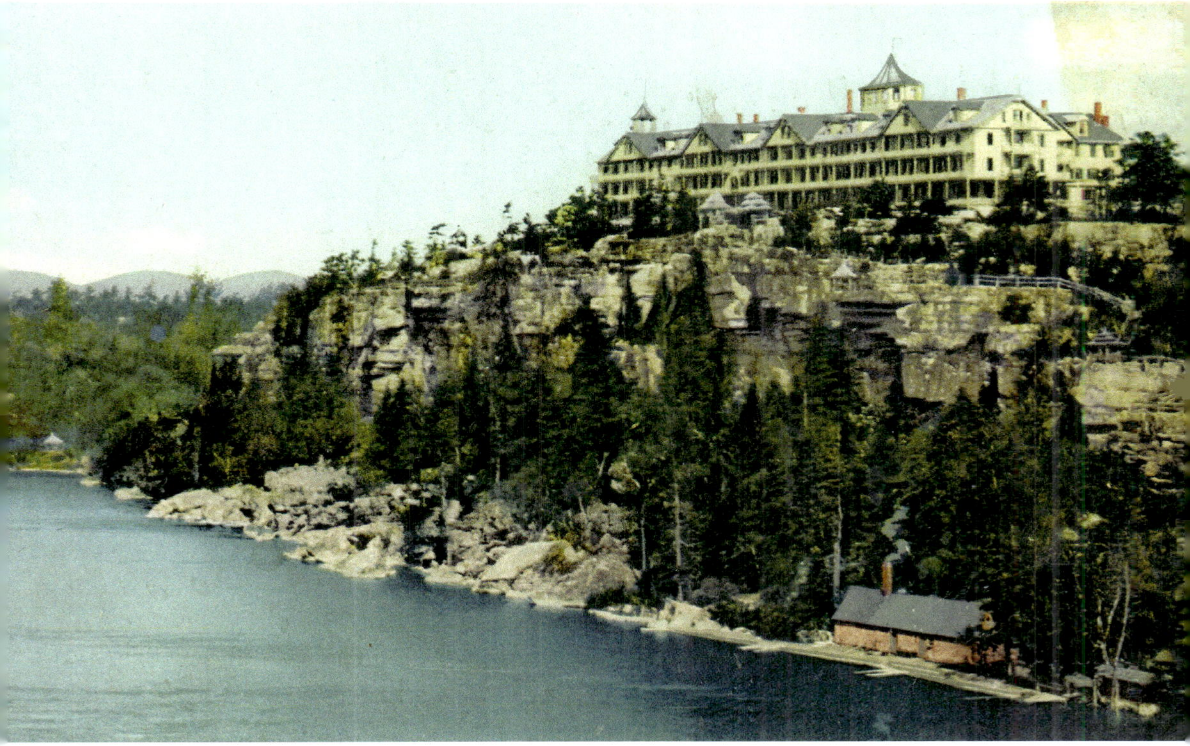

Records shows that some 200,000 board feet of oak were transported by canal, streams, and wagons pulled by oxen and horses from Honesdale in Pennsylvania to build Cliff House. Local mills and carpenters fashioned finishes out of nearby harvested hemlock, cherry, chestnut, and maple. As a result of two disastrous fires, one consuming Cliff House in 1978 and Wildmere in 1986, both of these enormous wooden structures were reduced first to smoldering embers and rubble, then ashes and fragments of metal and stone. Today, except for old photographs and memories, there is little evidence of their existence.

Beginning in the final decade of decline in 1969 and continuing to 1987, portions of the Minnewaska property were acquired by the State of New York and transformed into the Minnewaska State Park Preserve, a natural jewel without many of the man-made elements that served it so well for more than three-quarters of a century.

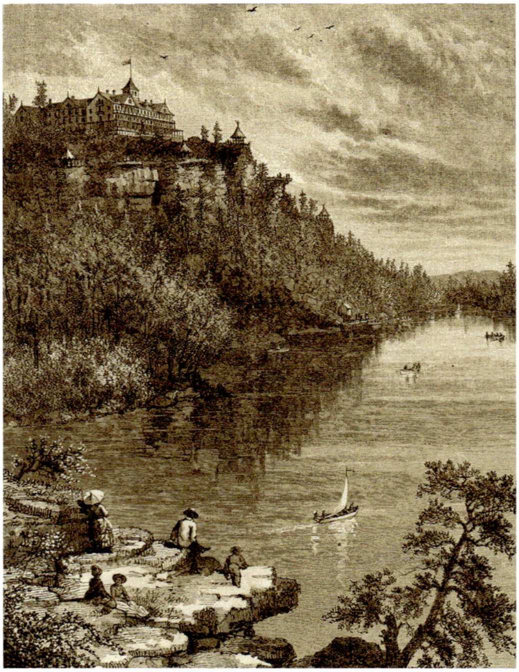

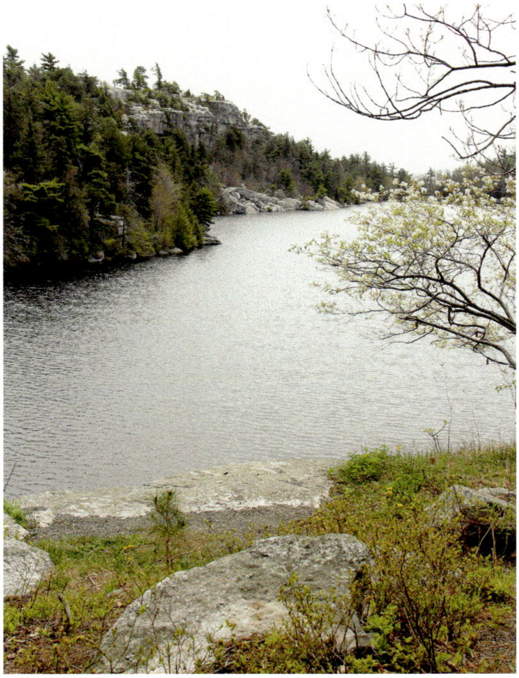

The Cliff House and Absence, Lake Minnewaska, Rochester

The 1887 *Then* image does not include the 125 foot long addition to the building, but underscores the commanding height "on a crowning ridge" 150 feet above the lake and at an elevation of some 1800 feet. The brochure boldly and competitively added "nearly as high as the Catskill Mountain House" with "private balconies." "The bracing and restoring quality of the atmosphere," "strange and picturesque places," "extraordinary bluffs," and "piles of tumbled rocks," as well as boating and rock ledges on which to tarry were some of the enticements offered prospective and returning guests.

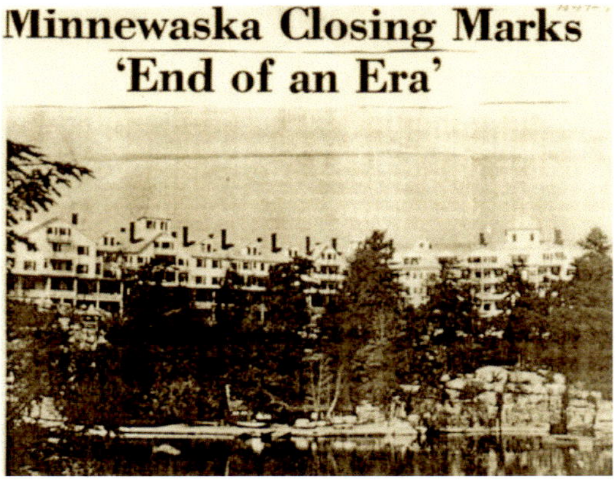

With the extension of the New York, Ontario & Western Railroad to Kerhonkson on the west side of the Shawangunks in 1902, it was no longer necessary to take the longer route via New Paltz. Guests could purchase tickets and have luggage checked through directly from New York, Brooklyn, and as far as Philadelphia.

After a long decline, Cliff House was abandoned in 1972 due to disrepair and soaring maintenance costs. Subsequently, the owner Kenneth B. Phillips, Sr., who had acquired the property from the Smiley family in 1955 and had struggled with innovations to make it profitable, was in bankruptcy. At the New Year in 1978, Cliff House burned to the ground in a spectacular fire that according to news reports brought "shock and regret" to those in the valleys who had valued the venerable resort. In October, 1979, newspapers announced that the hotel would close its doors on November 4 to be replaced with a new structure as a component of a Marriott resort. Although this plan had some supporters, a coalition of environmental groups disapproved of the Phillips-Marriott project, and by Spring 1985 the deal was dead. On June 13, 1986, Wildmere burned to the ground. A year later, the State of New York purchased the property with the intent of establishing a State Park Preserve open to the public.

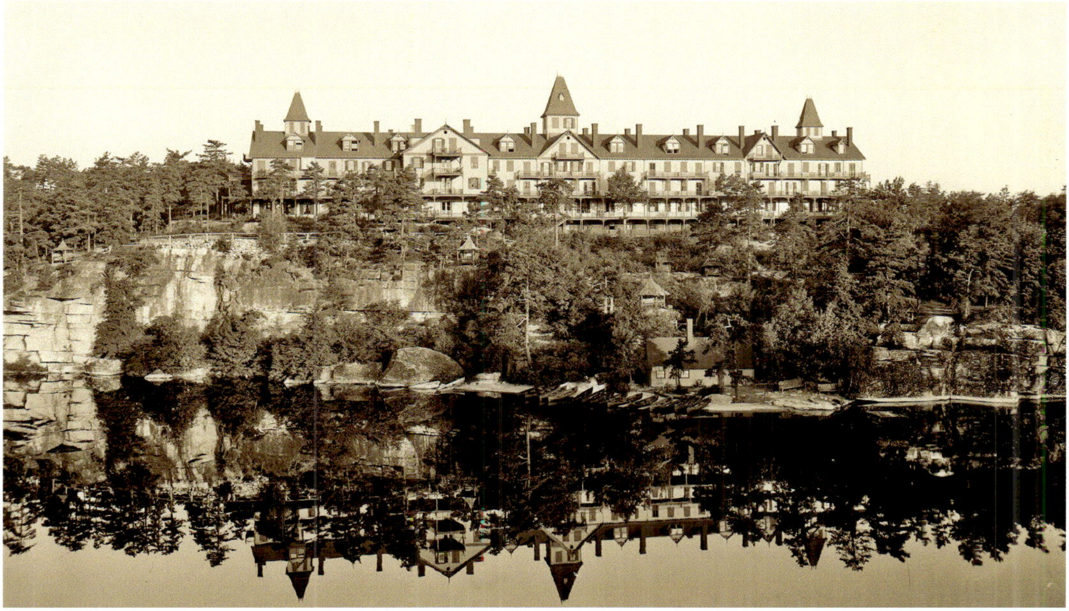

Wildmere and Absence, Lake Minnewaska, Rochester

With visitation to Lake Minnewaska expanding rapidly, Alfred H. Smiley decided to build a second hotel, Wildmere, on a rocky escarpment above the lake on the western rim facing the renamed Cliff House. Opening in 1887, only eight years after Cliff House, its silhouette mirrored to some degree the facing structure, but differed in terms of the placement of its gables and cupolas. The New York Times on May 25, 1890 reported that the Smiley properties in the Shawangunks "are almost exclusively patronized by persons of quiet and religious tastes," clearly insufficient numbers to support a thousand hotel rooms.

Without knowing there once was an imposing structure atop it, the lake, wooden shore, and glistening vertical rock today still bring enjoyment to visitors.

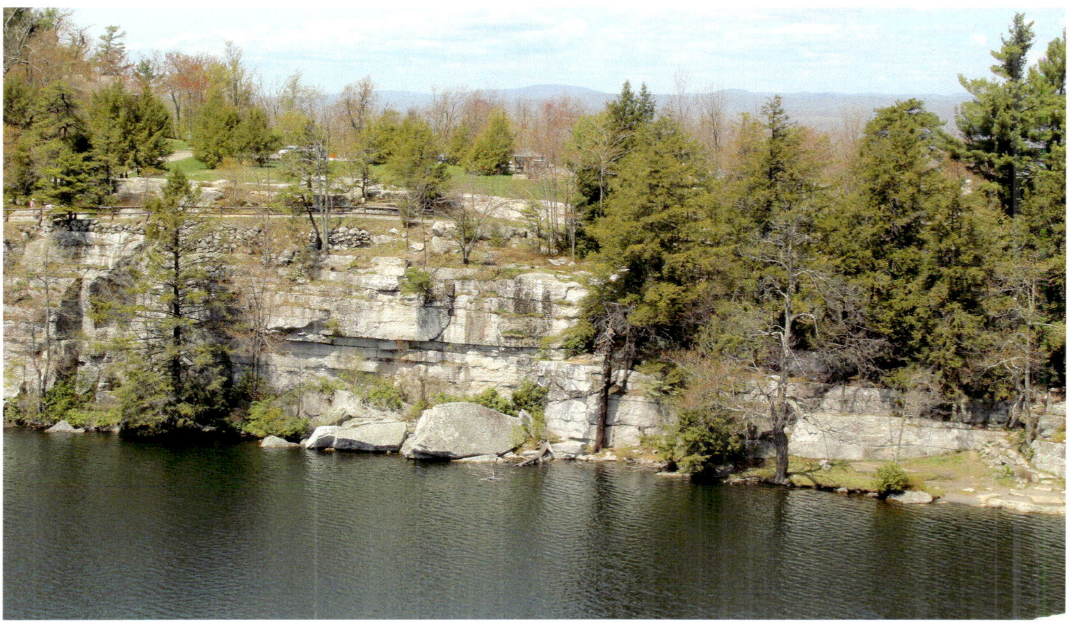

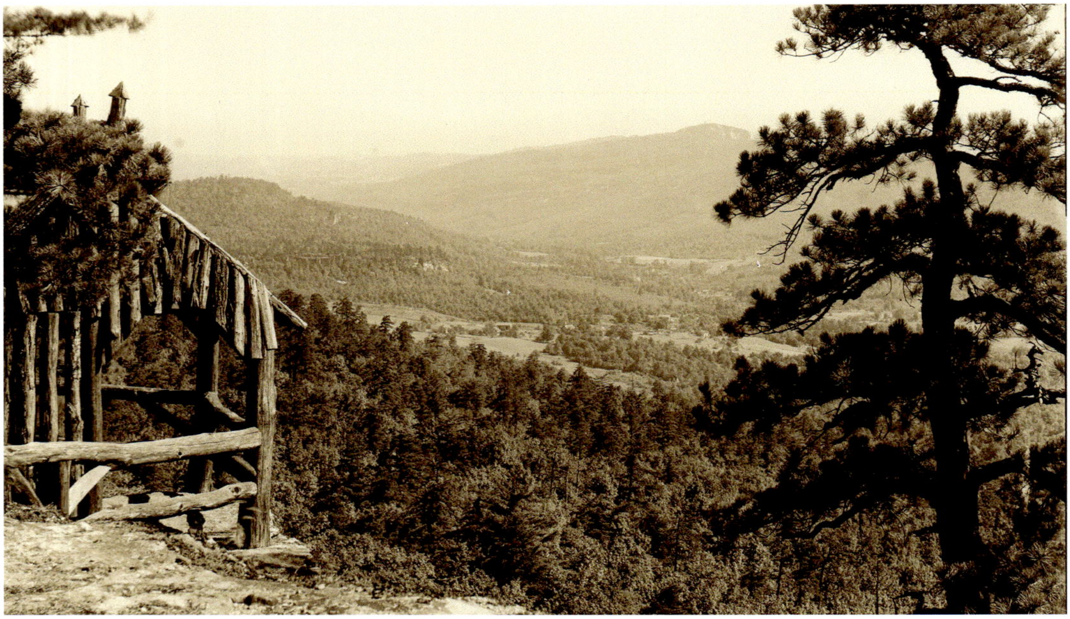

Sky Top Viewed from Lake Minnewaska, Rochester

An outcropping along Pine Cliff Path provided hikers a chance to sit in the rustic summerhouse and view the farms and fields that are part of the Trapps Mountain Hamlet, and the slopes leading down to the Wallkill River Valley to the east as well as the protruding Sky Top prominence at Lake Mohonk in the distance. Separated by seven miles, both the hotels at Lake Minnewaska and Lake Mohonk encouraged guests to take horse-drawn vehicles along the carriage roads that linked the twinned hotels where they enjoyed reciprocal privileges. Today, the summerhouse is gone but visitors are still able to sit on the outcrop and glimpse one of the most spectacular sites at Minnewaska State Park Preserve, one of the most unique and beautiful parks in New York. Some 300,000 visitors arrive each year.

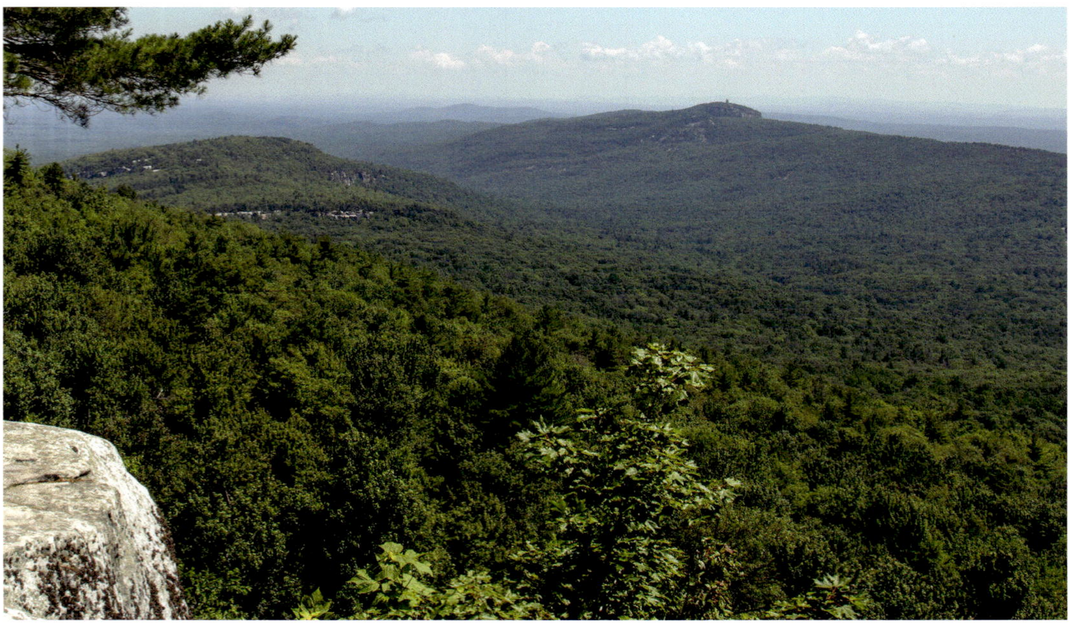

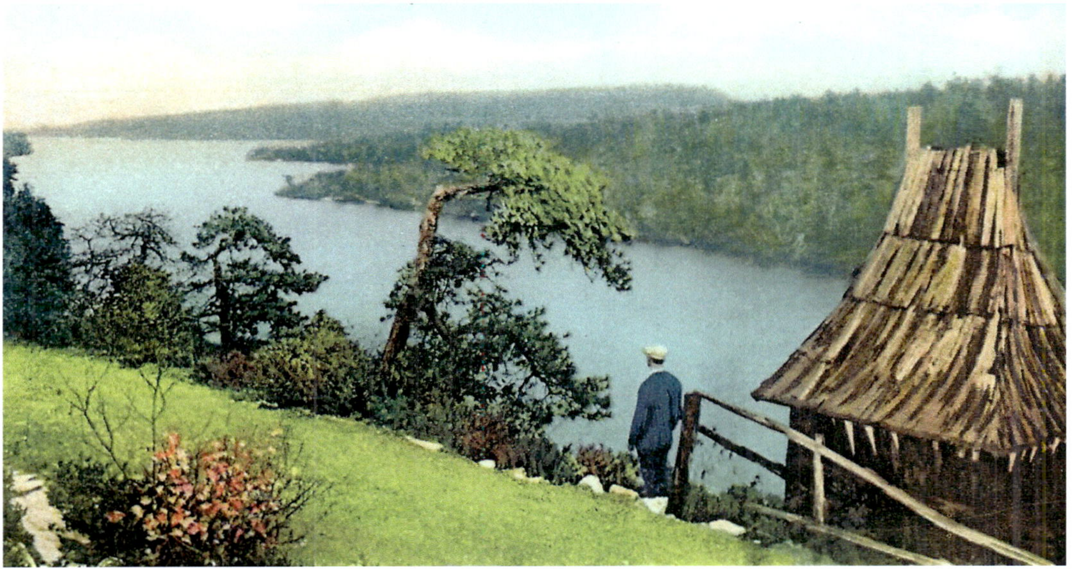

LAKE AWOSTING, WAWARSING

Lake Awosting, four times larger than Lake Minnewaska and the largest lake on the Shawangunk Ridge, is one of five rain-fed "skylakes" running from north to south: Mohonk Lake, Lake Minnewaska, Lake Awosting, Mud Pond, and Lake Maratanza.

Some nineteenth century maps called the impressive water body Long Pond or Big Pond, names that hardly did justice to its extensive nature. Before the Lake and its surrounding acreage were purchased by Alfred H. Smiley in 1879, a real estate flyer called it Lake Aioskawasting. The original name 'Aiaskawassing' was first used in 1664 in an Esopus Indian land deed to Governor Thomas Dongan. According to hotel brochures, this difficult to spell and pronounce name was transformed to Lake Awosting, a more romantic, even evocative, name and one certainly easier to write. In the *Then* colorized postcard, what appears to be a grassy pathway was in fact a shaled carriage way The absence of a both a rustic summerhouse and overgrown vegetation in the *Now* image is striking.

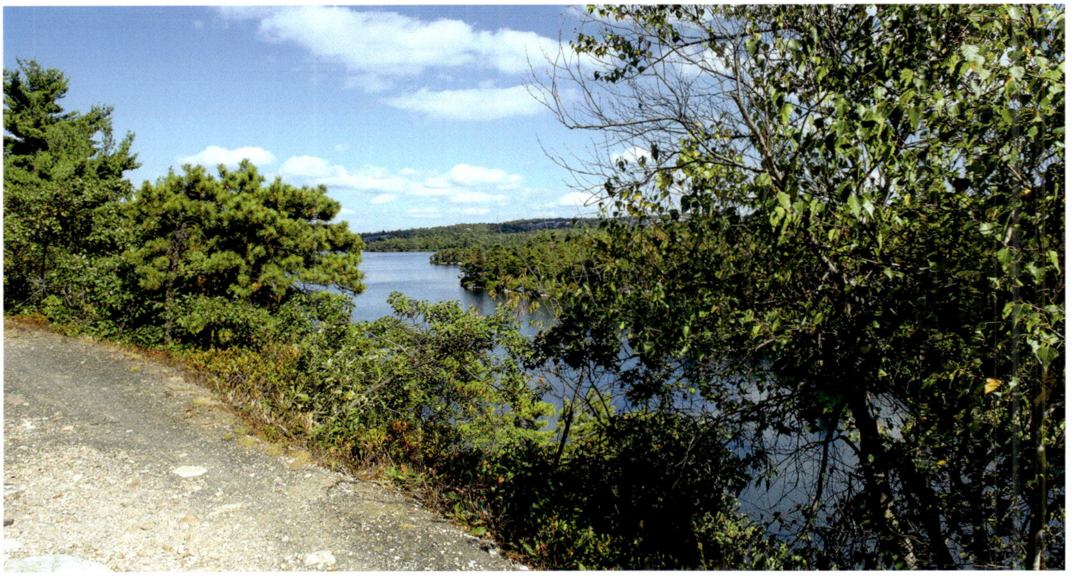

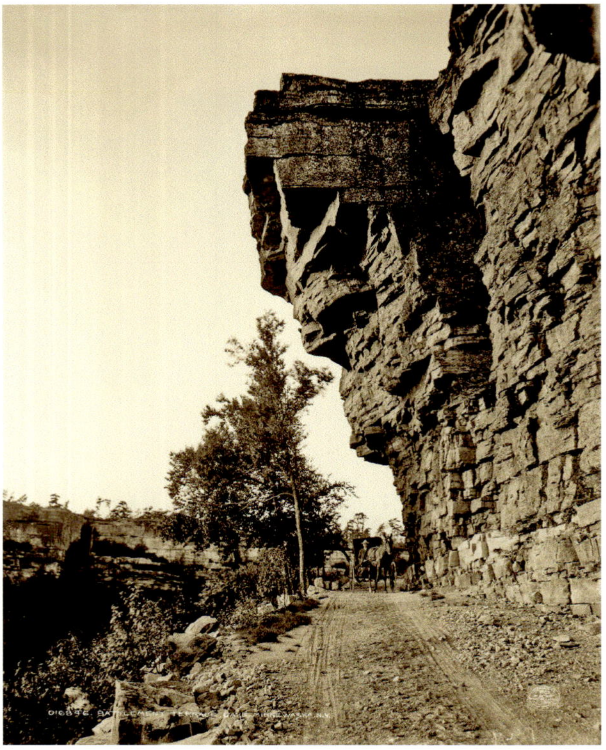

Battlement Terrace, Wawarsing

The much painted and photographed Battlement Terrace is a lofty overhanging ledge of rock. Most published views are from this direction, and was also often featured in turn-of-the-twentieth century postcards, some in stark black and white.

Located along the Castle Point Carriage Road, the imposing escarpment is sometime referred to as “castellated cliffs” because sections suggest the battlements and turrets of a castle. The c.1903 *Then* image portrays a rugged, somewhat precariously overhanging rock formation with a horse drawn carriage passing beneath it on a rubble strewn carriage way.

Until recently, the foliage was overgrown and passage a bit precarious. Extensive Carriage Road restoration work was carried out in 2013–14. Crushed bluestone was employed to create a smooth surface for the enjoyment of hikers, runners, bikers, horseback riders, and skiers. Retaining walls along the edge were strengthened. Foliage was cut back and the vistas open.

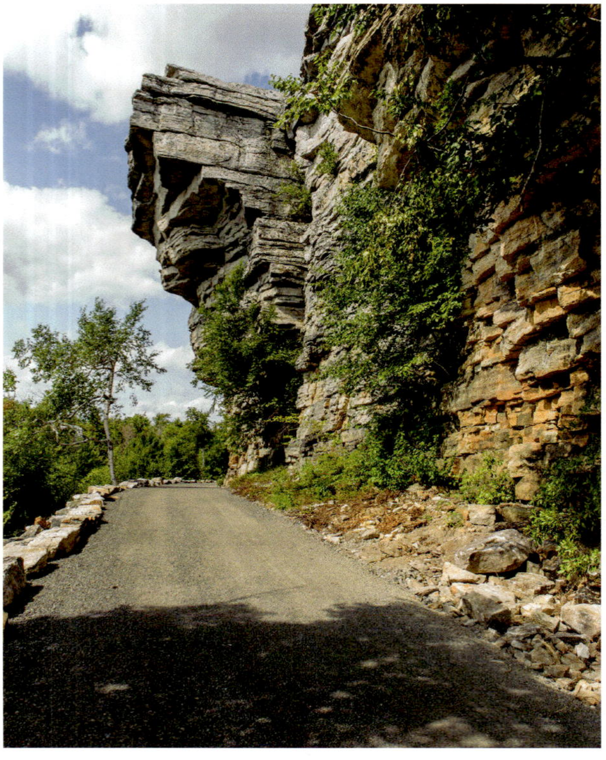

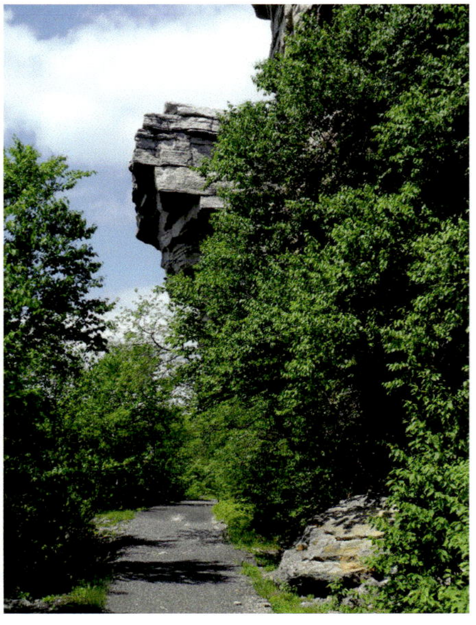

Awosting Falls, Rochester

Several water falls are within a mile of Lake Minnewaska, including the ever-popular Awosting Falls whose pouring sound alerts hikers from quite a distance away.

Falling over a cliff of conglomerate, the Peterskill drops into a deep pool of water that was for nearly a century a favorite swimming spot. Today swimming is not permitted.

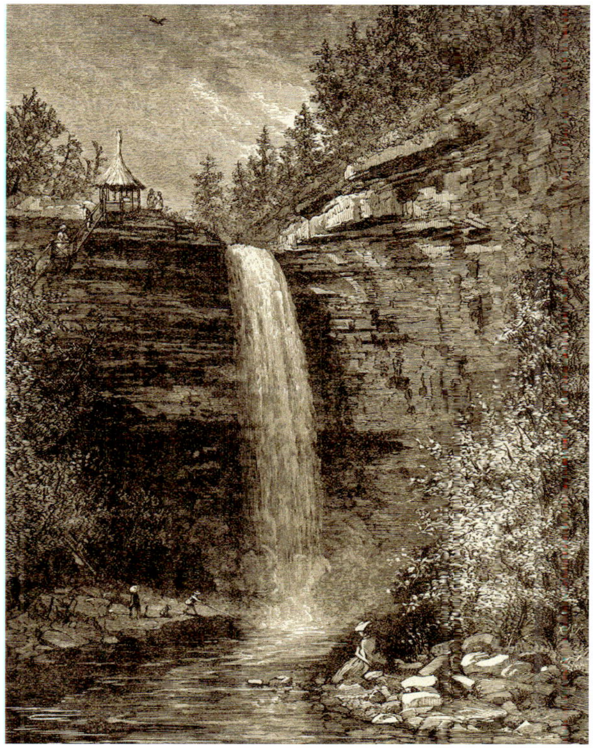

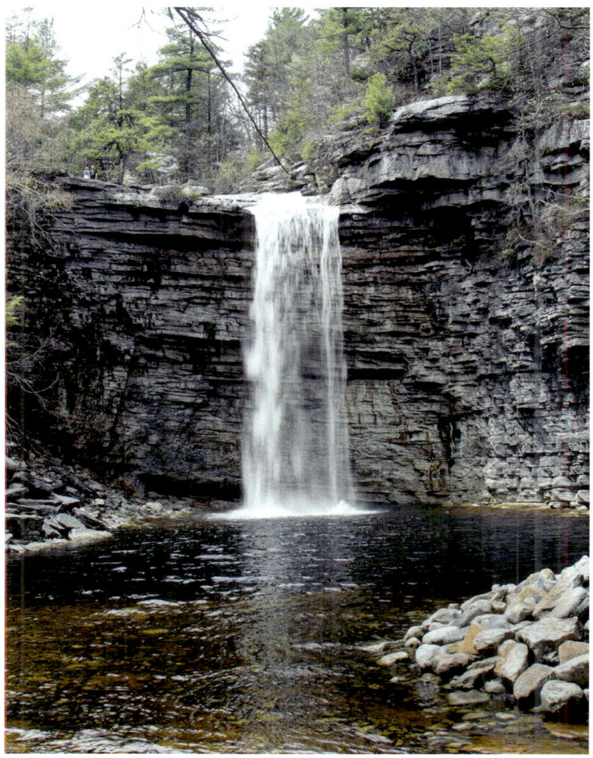

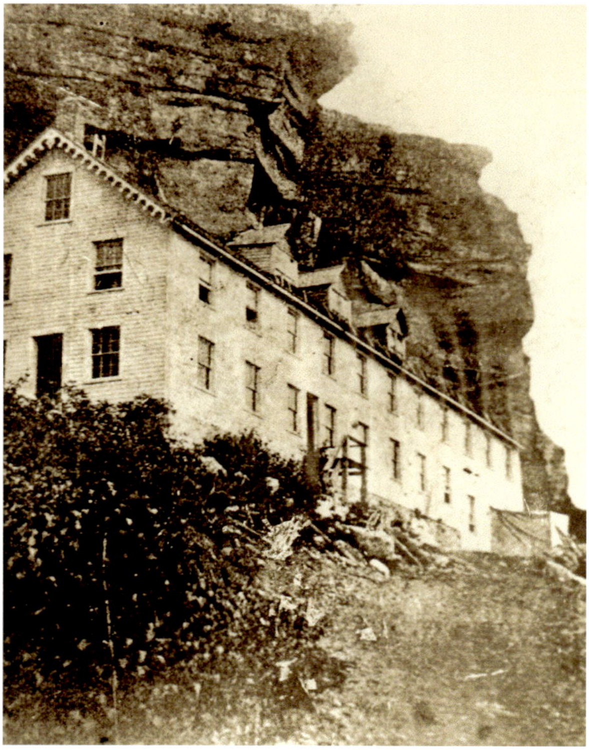

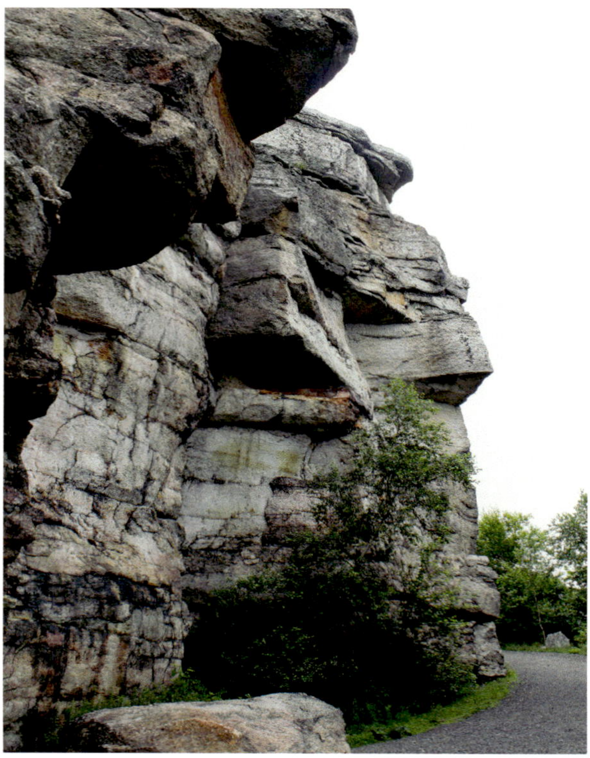

Sam's Point, Wawarsing

The imposing hotels at Lake Mohonk and Lake Minnewaska came to dominate the "refined" trade that sought to escape the discomfort of urban centers from New York City to Philadelphia.

Significant numbers of other summer visitors, usually of less means, found accommodations in boarding houses and inns on and off the ridge.

Especially entrepreneurial in the southern Shawangunks was Thomas Botsford and subsequently his son. Their first establishment was a tower atop Sam's Point that promised "eatibles and drinkables." However, the windswept ridge top proved to be an unsatisfactory site for his wooden towers that repeatedly were blown down. In 1871, they overcame this by constructing a three-story building called The Mountain House—Thomas Botsford Dance Hall and Boarding House—that was tucked in below the Sam's Point pinnacle. Unfortunately, it burned after only a few years and was never replaced.

Between Cragsmoor and Ellenville in the south and around New Paltz in the north, summer guest houses increased significantly as the century came to an end.

Just as the Wallkill Valley Railroad in New Paltz benefited visitors who stayed at hotels, boarding houses, and inns in the north, the New York, Ontario & Western Railroad with a depot in Ellenville and Kerhonkson on the west side of the ridge facilitated access to both Lake Minnewaska and other smaller accommodations.

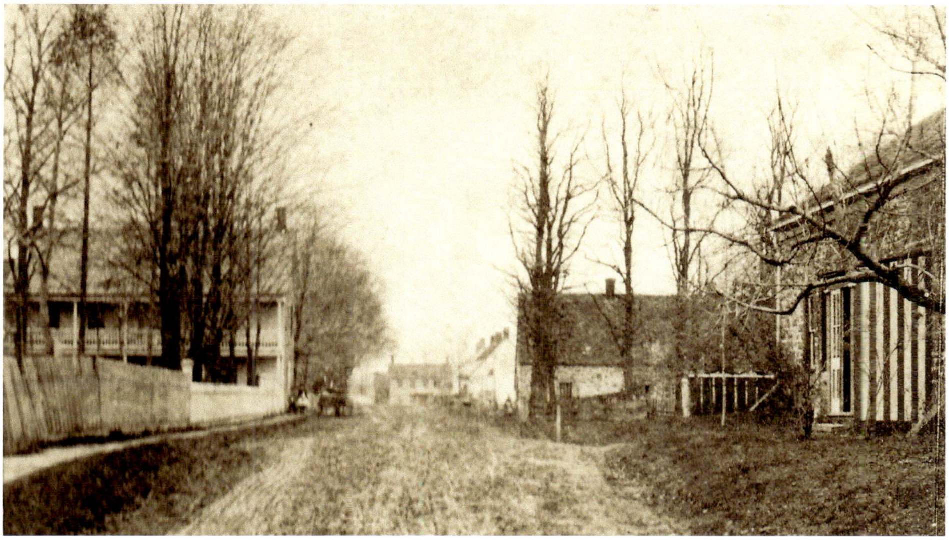

Huguenot Street, New Paltz

Huguenot Street, as it is known today, runs along the rise on the east bank of the north flowing Wallkill River at an elevation high enough not to be flooded. It is one of the oldest continuously inhabited settlements in the United States. Twelve French-speaking Huguenots—early on called Walloons—met with Esopus Indians on May 26, 1677 to purchase what became the New Paltz Patent for "40 kettles, 40 axes, and lots of wampum."

When the *Then* photo was taken in 1890, the area was considered *old* but not *historic*. It was only with the establishment of the Huguenot Patriotic, Historical and Monumental Society in 1894 that a transformation took place. Subsequently, family associations comprised of descendants of the original Huguenot founders acquired most of the stone houses in the district.

Today, five stone houses dating from the early eighteenth century and several other structures from the nineteenth century still stand along the street in a ten acre National Landmark Historic District. All of the properties as well as an archive are owned by the venerable Huguenot Historical Society, now renamed Historic Huguenot Street (HHS).

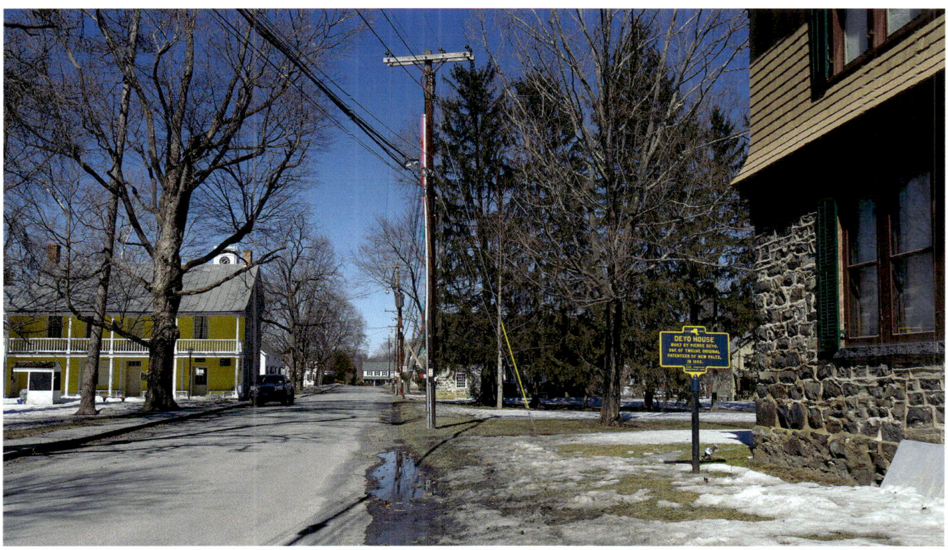

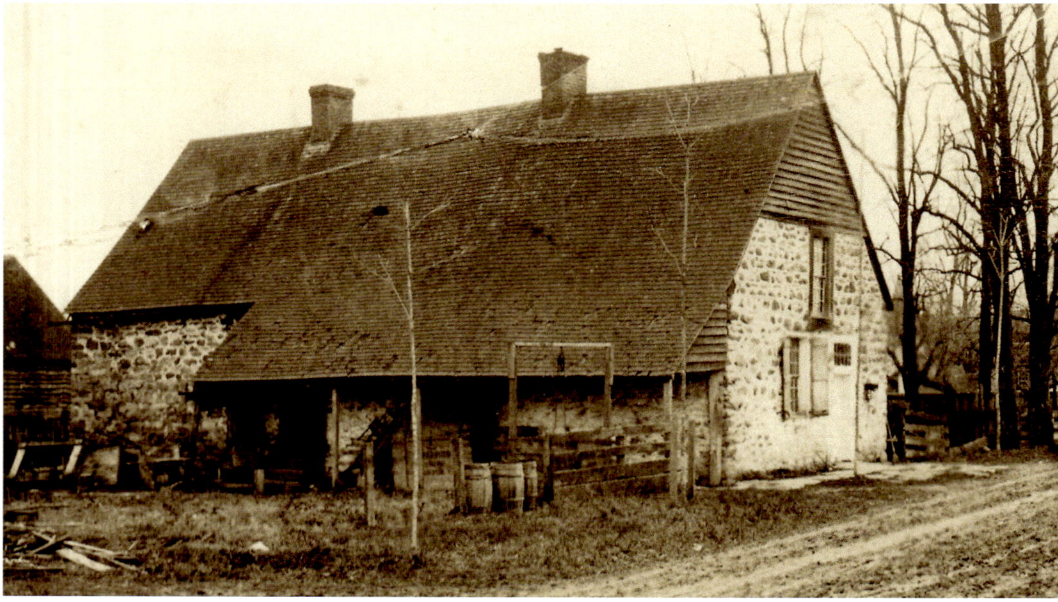

Bevier-Elting House, New Paltz

Constructed and expanded circa 1692 for Louis and Marie Bevier and their son before being sold to Josiah Elting in 1761, whose family retained it until the home was donated in 1963 to the Huguenot Historical Society, the residence is formally known today as the Bevier-Elting House. Its original form was a modest stone structure with a basement and entry through the door on the gable end facing the lane. Presumably the basement also served as slave quarters. Two rooms subsequently were added one after the other towards the east. The overhanging porch adds a distinctive element as does the rebuilt stone-lined dug well, now curbed in stone where once, as shown in the *Then* photo, it was framed with wood. Water was drawn from the well using a bucket that was raised and lowered via a rope and pulley. The cellar provided space for cooking as well as the sleeping quarters for slaves.

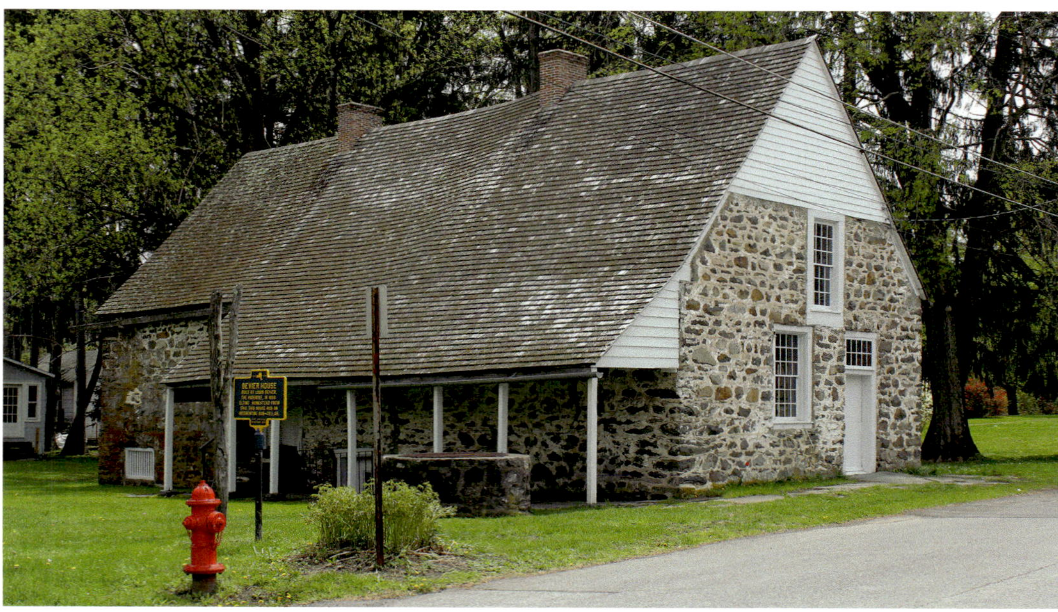

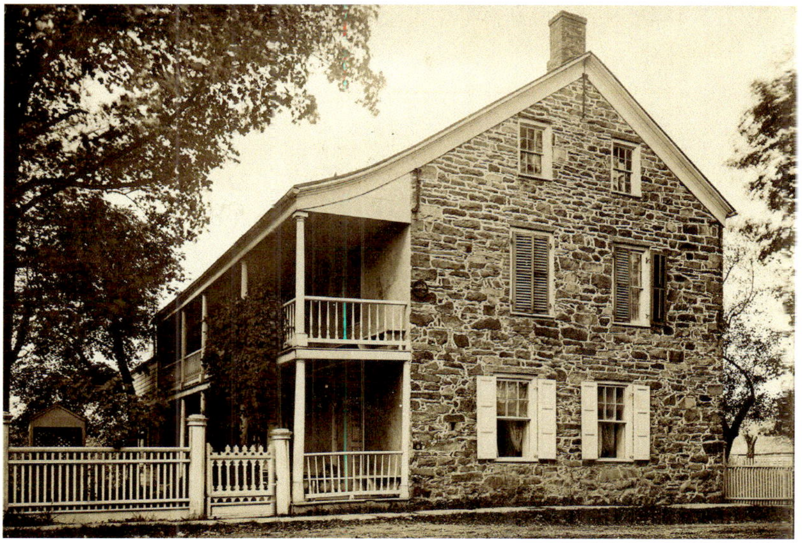

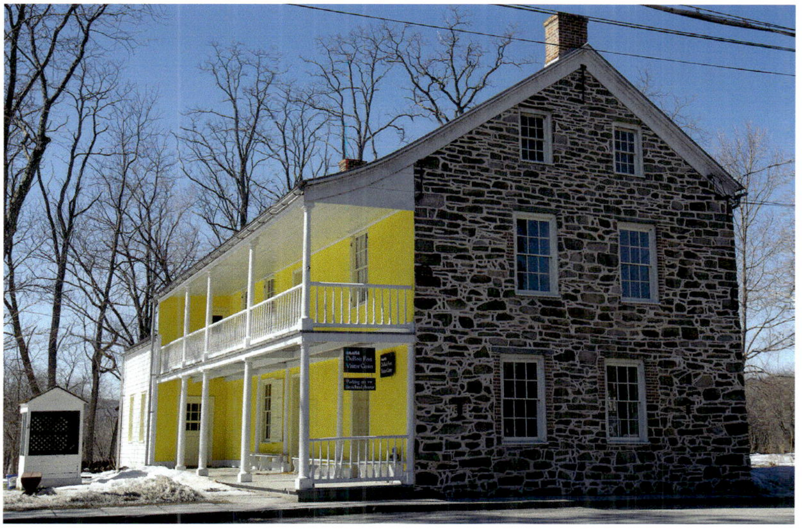

DuBois Fort, New Paltz

The so-called DuBois Fort was first constructed around 1705 by the sons of Louis DuBois, one of the original patentees, as a small 1½ story stone building facing south with the gable end fronting the dirt road and may have served as a fortified space for the community although not necessarily as a "fort" as the gun ports suggest. The building was enlarged and took its current appearance in the late 1830s with the addition of a second story with an extended overhang that resulted in a south-facing two-level set of porches.

For the most part over the years, the building served as a residence for the DuBois family. However, in the twentieth century it became first an antique shop and then a tea room. Beginning in 1937 and for more than a half century until 1990, the structure was transformed into a popular restaurant called "The Old Fort" that offered rooms to let upstairs.

With funds from the DuBois family, the Huguenot Historical Society gained title to the property in 1968 and with the demise of the restaurant transformed it into the Historic Huguenot Street Visitor Center.

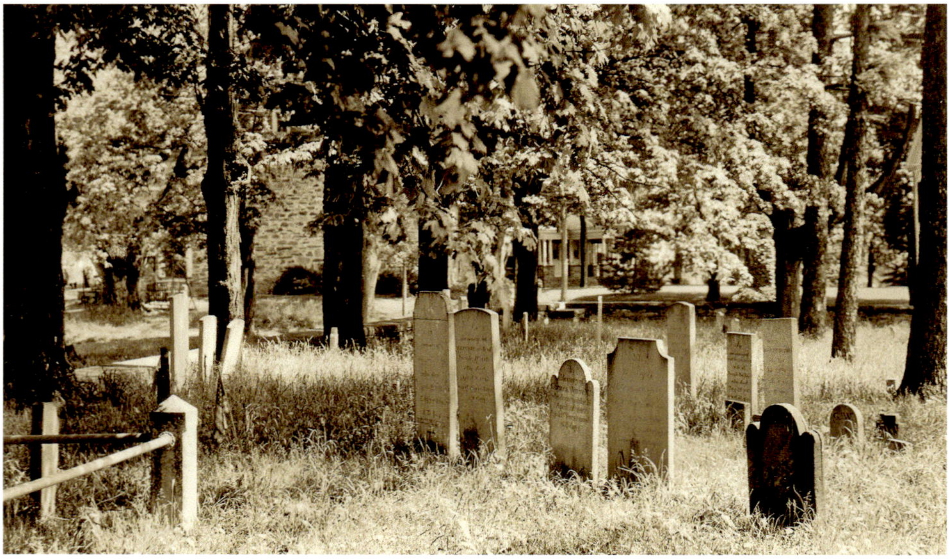

Huguenot Burial Ground, New Paltz

The burial ground adjacent to the Crispell Memorial French Church, which is a reconstruction completed in 1972, has the earliest graves found in New Paltz. The first church on this site, probably a log structure, was constructed in 1683 and replaced by a square stone building in 1717 and rebuilt in stone in 1773. In 1839, services were moved to the newly constructed Reformed Church.

While the earliest graves probably only had wooden markers that disintegrated over the years, some were replaced by carved headstones with names and dates only while others had adornments. Those of Joseph and Elsie Hasbrouck, for example, are side-by-side and made of different material, yet both feature carvings of wings. Elsie's is an angel. Ten of the original twelve patentees are buried here, except for Louis DuBois and Antoine Crispell. The earliest headstone is that of Andries LeFevre, a patentee who died in 1714. Although it is often said that the last burial in this modest cemetery was in 1864, another took place in 2013, the ceremonial burying of the remains of an unnamed African-American who may have been a slave in the community.

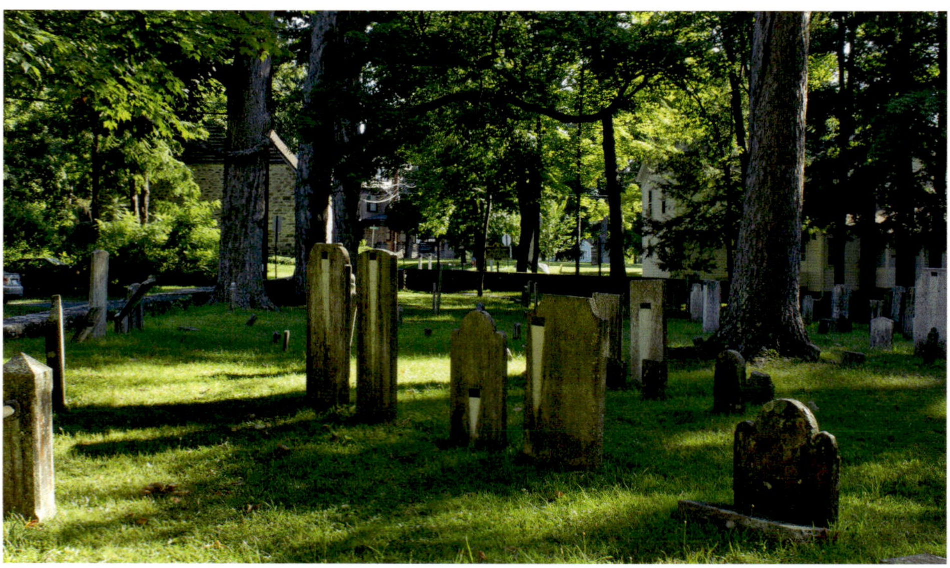

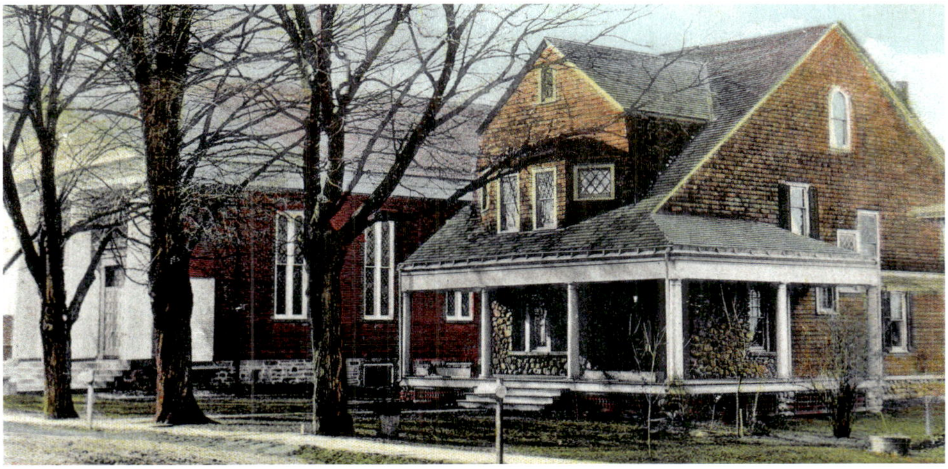

Parsonage and Reformed Church, New Paltz

The roots of the Reformed Church on Huguenot Street in New Paltz go back more than 300 years to 1683, just five years after the Huguenots arrived along the banks of the Wallkill. Over the years, a succession of church buildings were constructed, beginning with "stone house of prayer" in 1717, later lost, and which was reconstructed in 1972.

The present church was erected in 1839 with an addition of transepts on the western end in 1871–72. Early discussions focused on whether stone, brick, or wood should be the major material used. Stone, while readily available, was deemed too expensive and wood was seen as impermanent, thus a red brick church was built. With four white Doric columns supporting a substantial pediment, and a prominent two-stage cupola—all painted white—the church became quickly a prominent landmark that still is judged as stately. Over the years, interior renovations have honored the historical forms that echo the original classical elements while acknowledging the needs for changes.

The original parsonage, a wooden frame structure was erected to the south of the church in 1848, serving that purpose until 1909 when a more commodious home for the pastor and his family was constructed on the north side of the church on the site of recently demolished horse sheds. As seen in the *Then* image, the new structure was spacious with cobblestone walls below and wooden shingles above. The porch with its four front columns complements that of the adjacent church. Over time, the two large trees in front were removed and a driveway laid out.

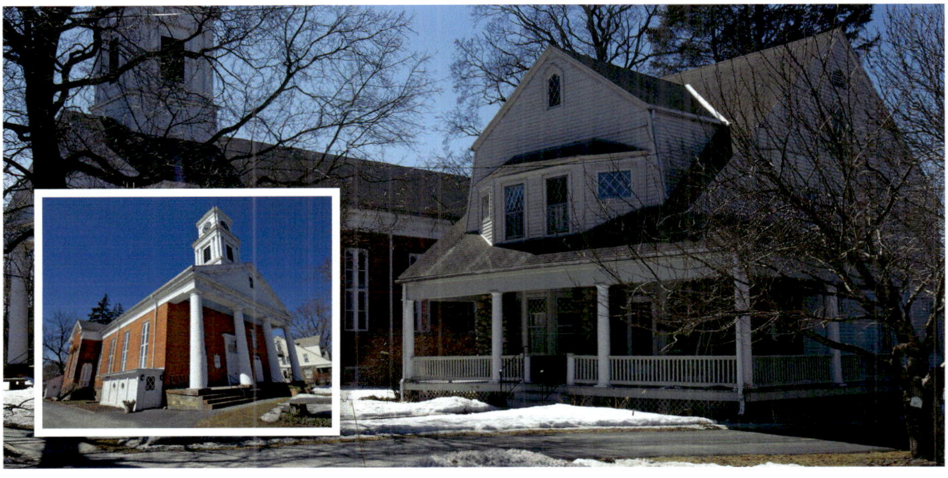

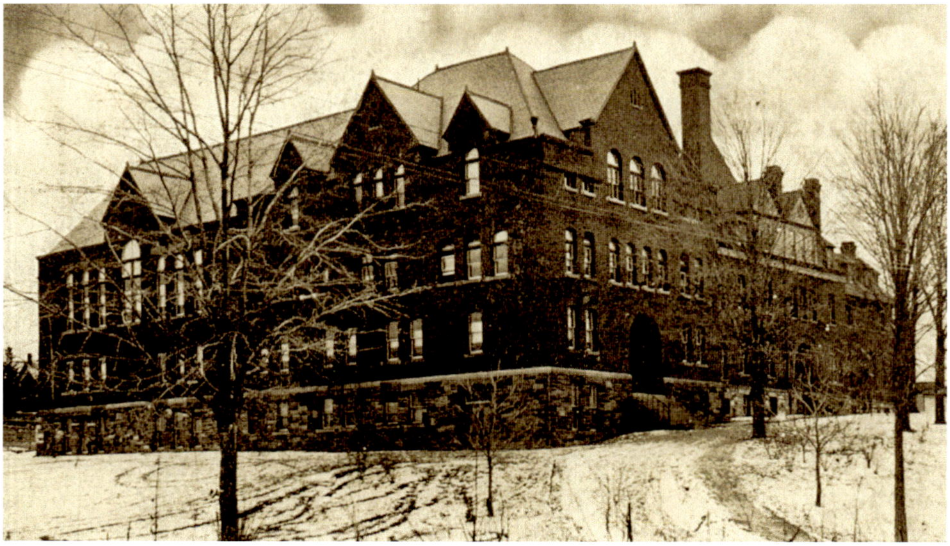

New Paltz Academy, New Paltz

SUNY New Paltz connects its history to the 1828 New Paltz Classical School that became an Academy five years later. Both were along the Wallkill River and north of the original Huguenot settlement. After a major fire in 1884 that burned the wooden Academy to the ground, rebuilding took place. Following contentious discussions, a decision was made to establish a state normal school at the site with a substantial new building that by 1889 became a "a massive four-story structure of brick and stone, steep-roofed and vaguely Romanesque" according to *In a Valley Fair*. Climbing expeditions to the Shawangunks were a regular activity for students and faculty.

At the end of Easter vacation in April 1906, an exploding oil lamp in the attic led to a furious fire that destroyed the building and its contents. A decision was made to rebuild on a spacious site called Harcourt Heights that provided room for future expansion less than a mile from the former location. This new, higher site offered clear views of the Shawangunk Ridge and was away from the noise and smoke of the trains along the Wallkill corridor. Today the site is occupied by the Town and Country Condominiums

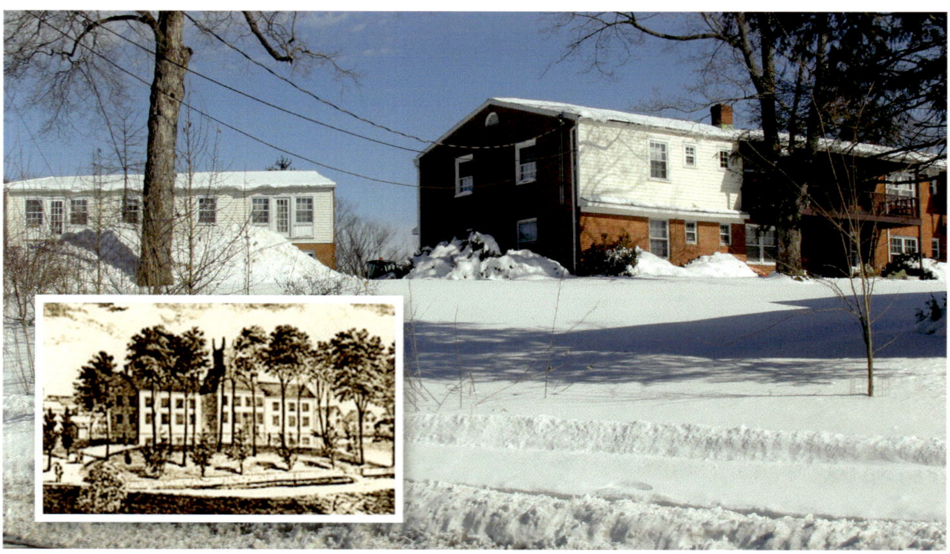

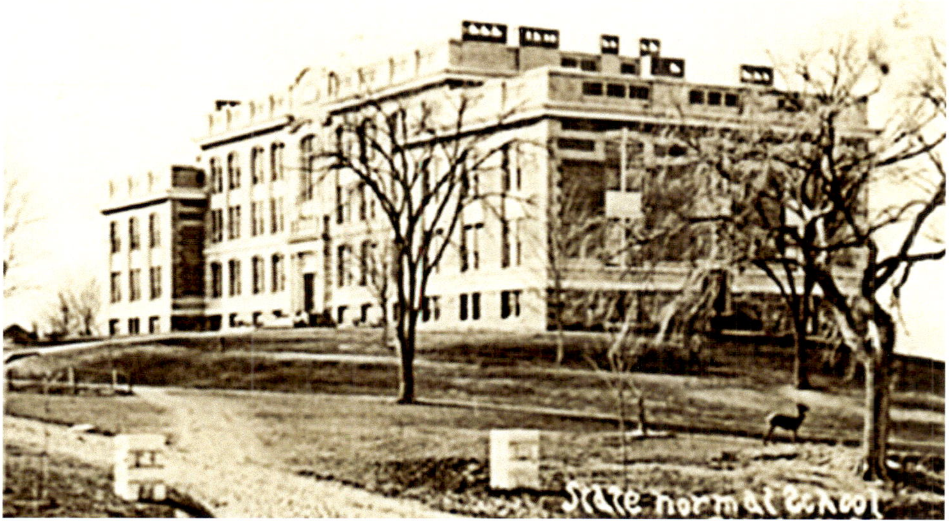

OLD MAIN, SUNY NEW PALTZ

Ground was broken in 1907 and dedicated in 1909 for the first building for the new Normal School building that—rechristened "Old Main"—now is the oldest building on the sprawling campus of the State University of New York at New Paltz.

Already 80 years of age, the venerable Albert K. Smiley of Mohonk and chairman of the local Normal School board, brought luminaries who had been attending one of the International Peace Conferences on the mountain to the dedication.

In 1919–20, the symmetry of the building was altered with a major expansion to the north that included a 1,200 seat auditorium. Over the years, the building has served many functions, including not only general offices but also that of the college president as well as classrooms. Upstairs on the south side was a gymnasium with a running track. For decades now, it appropriately has housed the School of Education.

After a major renovation in 1992, the auditorium was rechristened the Julien J. Studley Theatre. In 2011, the full building underwent modernization with sustainable building practices relating to water and energy consumption.

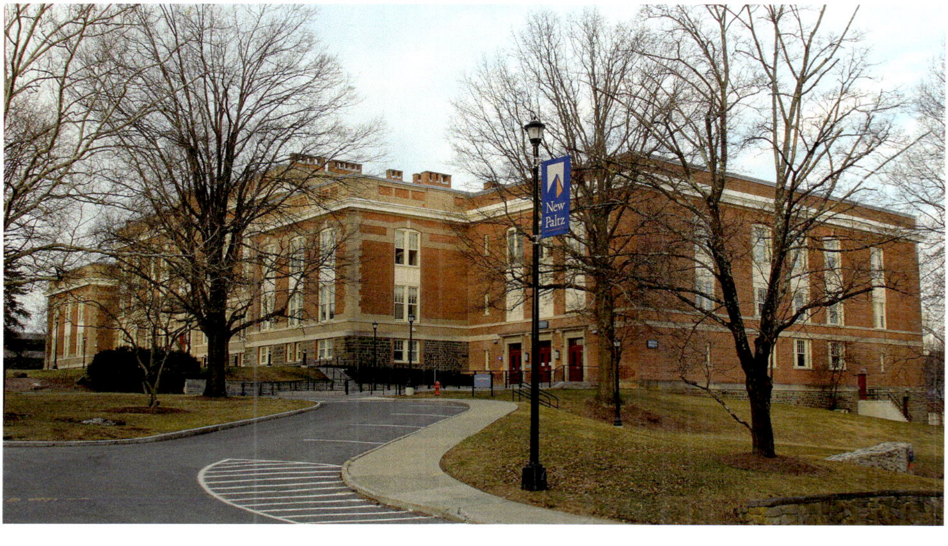

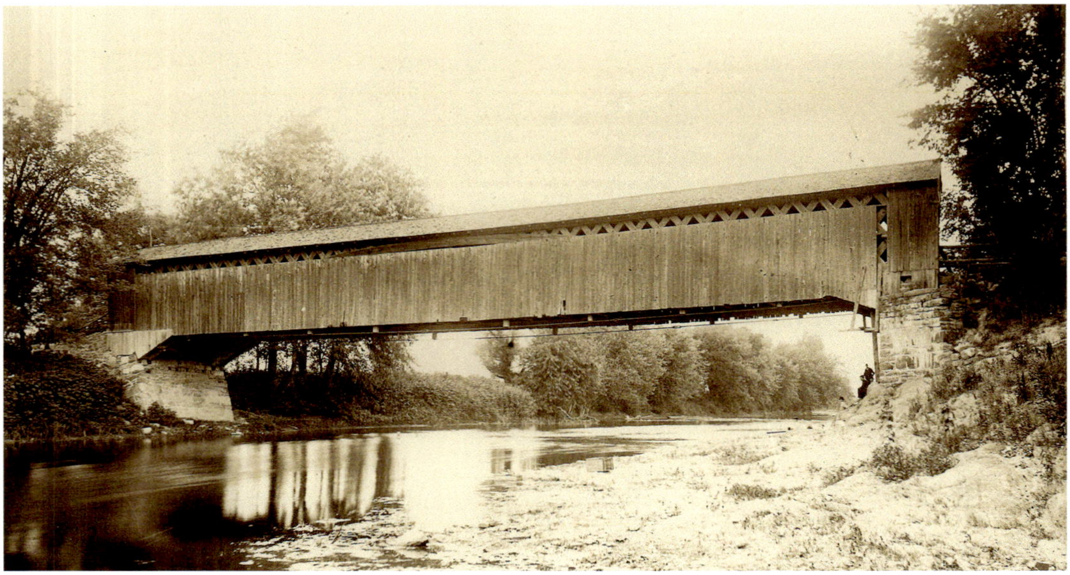

Wallkill River Bridges, New Paltz

Until the construction of a bridge across the Wallkill River, citizens of New Paltz depended on a rope-pulled scow as a ferry.

Only three bridges have spanned the river. The first, which was approved in 1845 and completed around 1850, was an imposing 153 foot long and 18 foot wide wooden covered bridge supported by a Town lattice truss and auxiliary arches.

The New Paltz covered bridge then was connected in 1856 with a dirt-surfaced turnpike as a toll wagon road between New Paltz in the Wallkill Valley and Wawarsing in the Rondout Valley via a route over the Shawangunk Mountains. Tolls were collected at the gap that is now spanned by the Trapps—Steel—Bridge. Within a few years, the toll road went bankrupt and the road from one valley to the next became a public road. Nonetheless, this route contributed significantly to the viability of the Trapps Mountain hamlet that had emerged on the ridge.

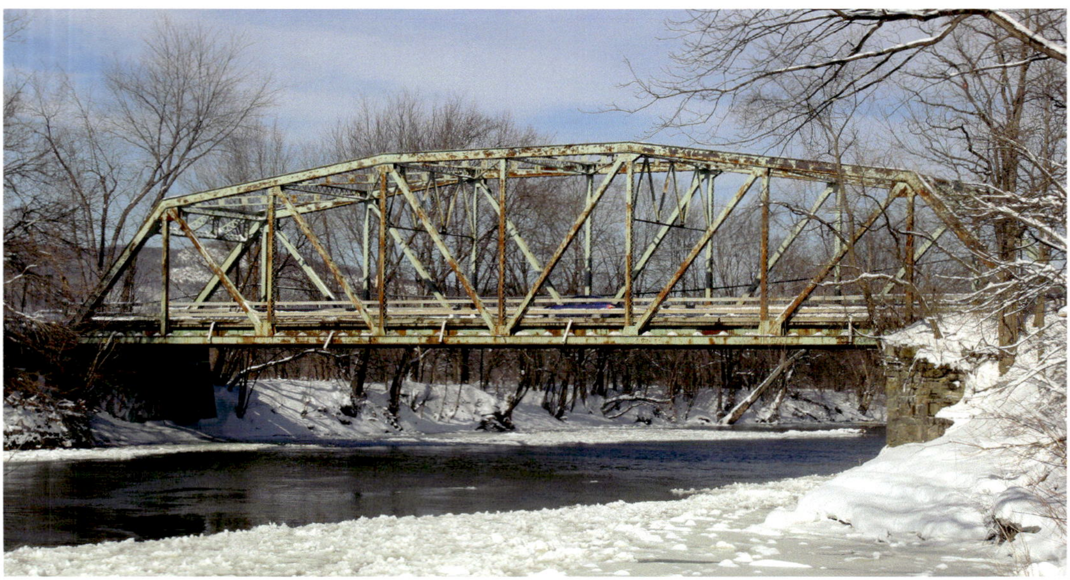

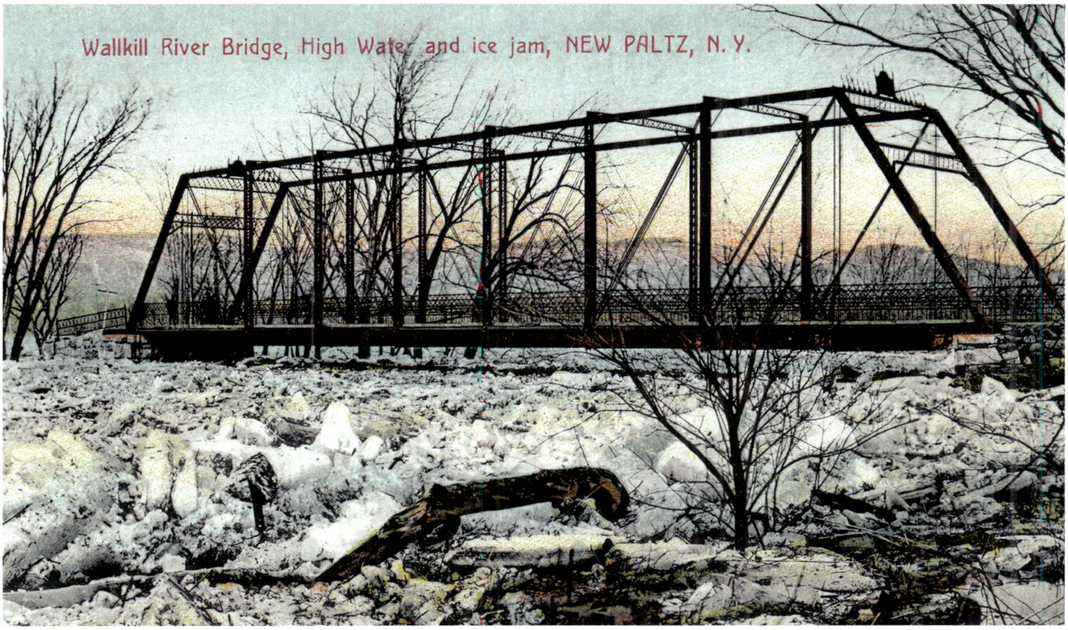

During repairs to the covered bridge in January 1869 folks crossed over on the frozen river ice to its north.

The covered bridge was replaced around 1891 by a "modern" iron bridge with a garden-variety Pratt truss that proudly showed the emblem of the Groton Bridge Building Company that was headquartered in the Finger Lakes region of upstate New York. Both the wooden and the iron bridge each lasted about 40 years. The old iron bridge was condemned in 1938 but not immediately dismantled. In 1941, when its successor was completed (as shown on the preceeding page), the iron components were sold for scrap that was melted to make weapons for the war effort.

In early 2014, it was announced that a new bridge would be completed across the Wallkill River by 2017.

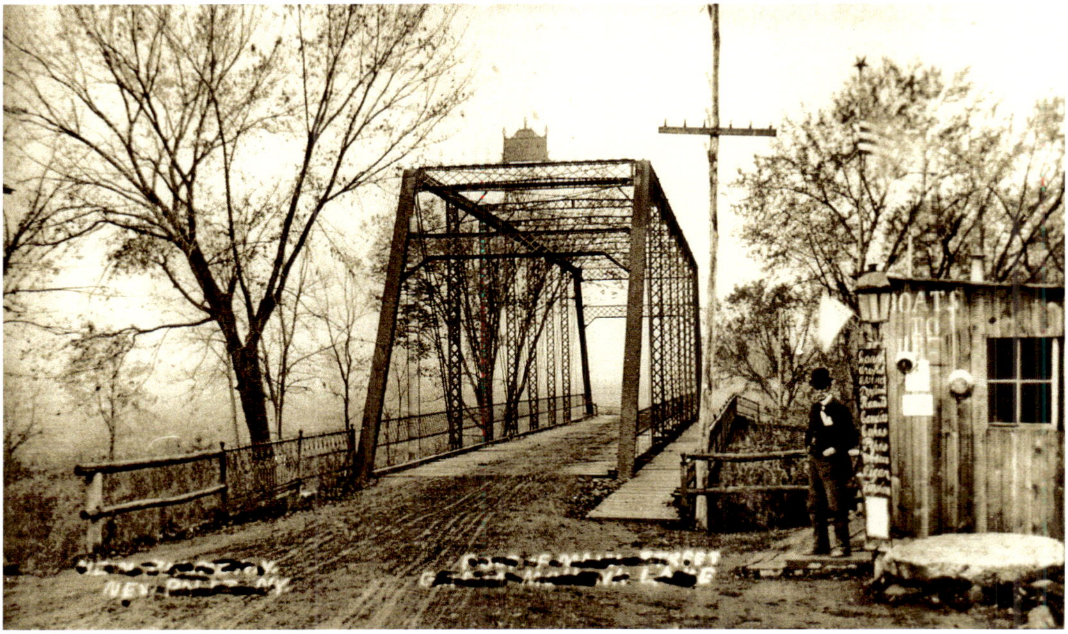

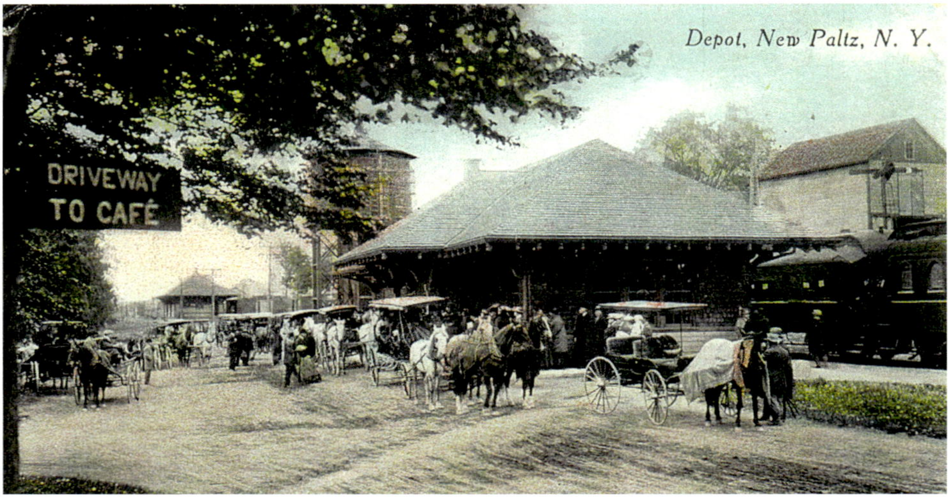

Wallkill Valley Railroad Depot, New Paltz

The Wallkill Valley Railroad reached New Paltz from the south in 1870 but it took two more years for it to service the county seat at Kingston fifteen miles to the north. For more than half a century, arriving guests of Lake Mohonk and Lake Minnewaska transferred to horse-drawn carriages for the journey to the Shawangunks. The railroad also served smaller summer inns in the area. It provided a means of transporting perishable fruits, vegetables, and milk from farms in the valley to urban markets beyond while also transporting hard goods to the stores and lumberyards that opened in New Paltz and environs. By 1933, passenger service had been reduced to one train a day and four years later halted. Freight continued on the line until 1977.

The New Paltz Train Depot burned down in 1907 but was immediately rebuilt with a hipped roof instead of the gabled roof on the original building. Once passenger service ended in 1937, the structure was essentially derelict until it was sold in 1959. By the 1980s, the structure had deteriorated badly leading to calls to demolish the no longer utilitarian building. Renovated again in 1988 after purchase by Robert Mark Realty, it was resurrected in 1999 and expanded in 2003 as La Stazione, an Italian restaurant. This was eight years after the Wallkill Valley Land Trust organization purchased the railway right of way adjacent to the depot as a rail trail for hikers, runners, bikers, and skiers.

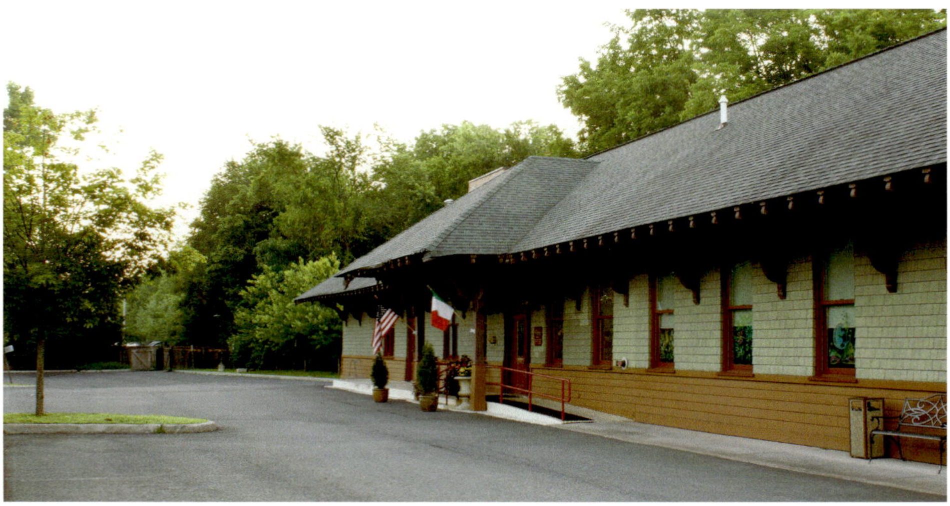

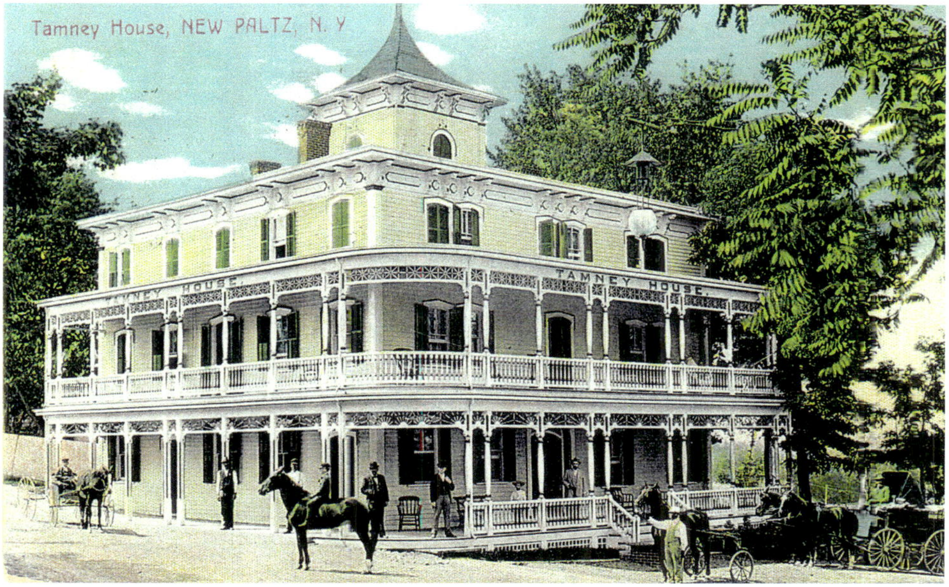

Main Street and Wurts Avenue, New Paltz

Located a short distance uphill from the train depot at the junction of Main Street and Wurts Avenue, Tamney House had several prior and later owners. Constructed in 1871 following an Italianate design, it had a regal appearance as a three-story wooden structure with a two-story wrap-around porch and a cupola. Initially the Shaefer House, which closed in 1874, it was taken charge of by Warren Chipp Tamney in 1888. In 1922, the hotel was renamed The Palmer House and retained that name until the late 1940s. Rooms were available by the day or week with boarding also provided for horses. Later it became the New Paltz Hotel, a use that continued into the 1970s. It is not clear when the balconies and utilitarian adornment were stripped away that left the structure barren and unremarkable in appearance. Today, it serves as a multi-family residence with only the surviving brackets under the eaves hinting at its former glory.

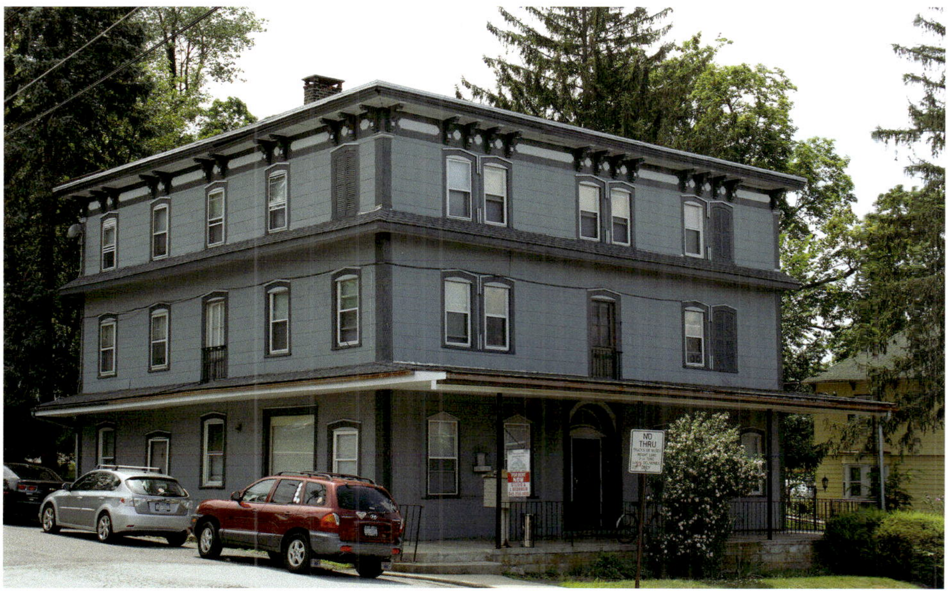

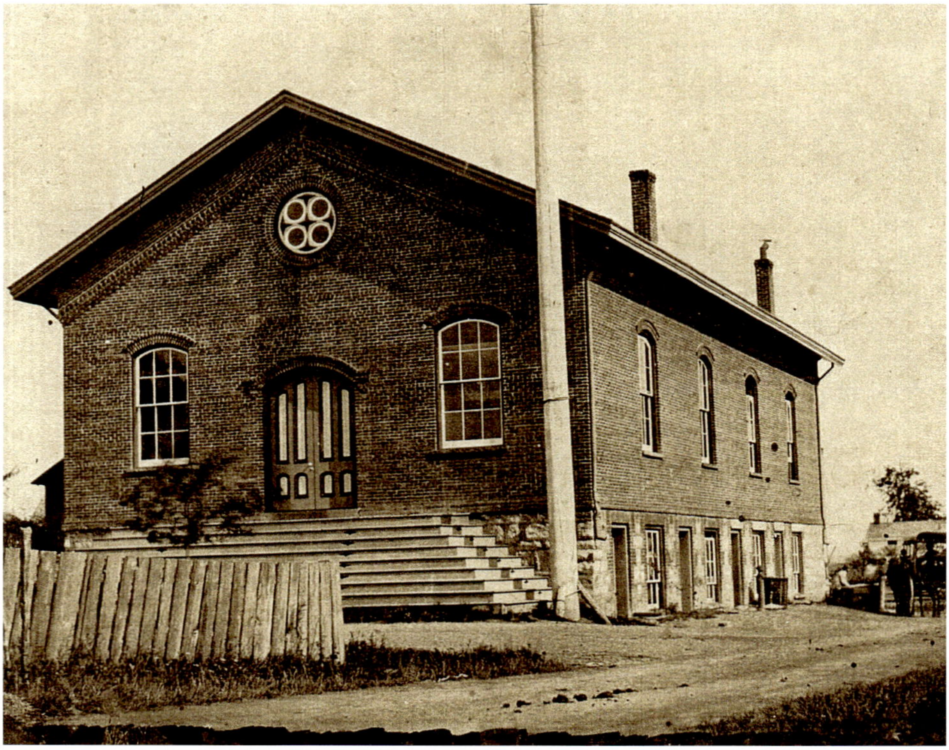

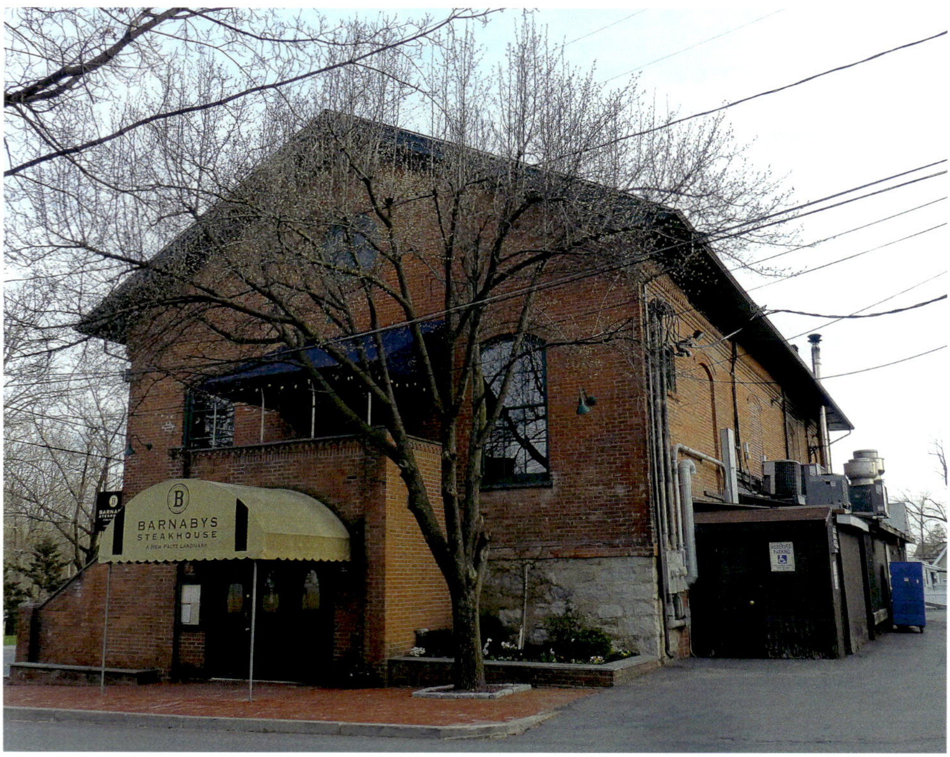
B
BARNABYS
STEAKHOUSE
A NEW PALTZ LANDMARK

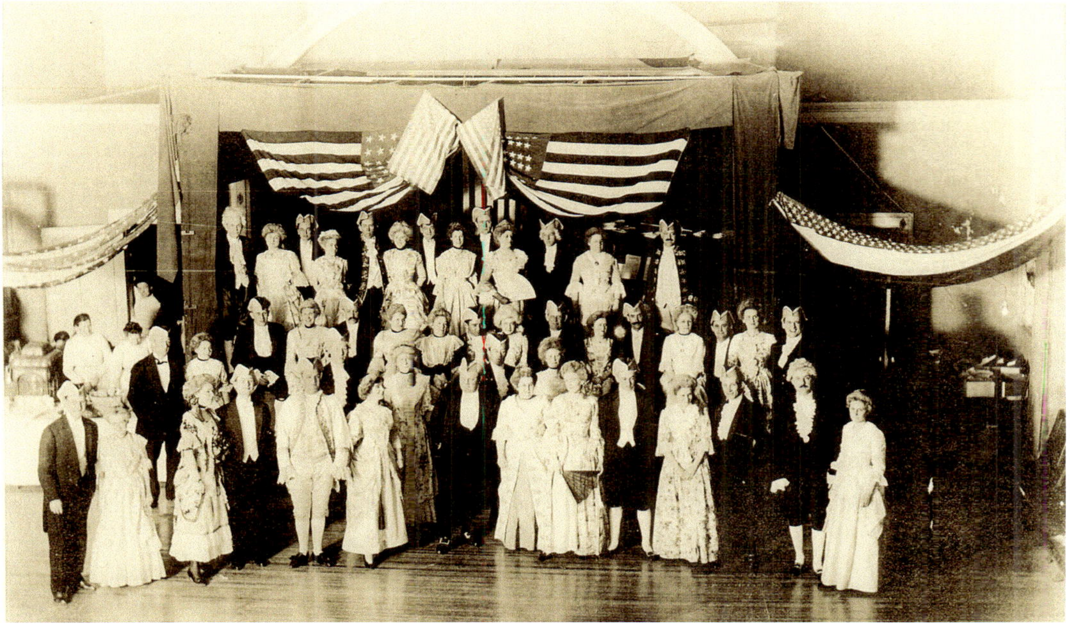

Village Hall, North Chestnut Street, New Paltz

Village Hall, constructed using locally produced red bricks on North Chestnut Street in 1863 by the New Paltz Literary Association, was not a seat of government but a community center with a generous space upstairs for performances and downstairs room for a restaurant and apartments. Over the years it served a range of cultural and social functions—a veritable community center—until 1929, hosting plays, music recitals, operettas, dances, lectures, vaudeville acts, and more, including as a venue for services for congregations without a church building and commencement for the State Normal School. As its mass suggests, the upstairs hall was commodious, capable of holding some 500 comfortably, indeed the total population of New Paltz at the time. The gathered crowd in the interior view were celebrating George Washington's Birthday early in the twentieth century.

For a while early in the twentieth century, St. Athanasius, now St. Andrew's Episcopal Church on Main Street, occupied the bottom floor. After the Ulster County Savings Institution foreclosed on the building in 1906, a new proprietor christened the multi-use building as the Opera House. In 1916, as motion pictures, first silent and then those with sound, began to be popular, a screen was added even as lectures and other events continued. However, in 1929, the Opera House closed down, and the next year St. Joseph's Catholic Church purchased the building as their parish center, holding it until the 1960s.

A developer subsequently acquired the building in 1966 in hopes of resuscitating it as not only a venue for the community but also the swelling number of students at the college. Because of a lack of necessary parking, his plans were frustrated by the Village Planning Board. In time, the spaces were renovated with a 300 seat movie house, the Academy Theatre, upstairs and a restaurant, Barnaby's Loaf & Tankard, beneath.

By the 1980s when a modern theater was opened in one the new shopping plazas on the east side of town, the Academy Theatre lost its audience even as Barnaby's Loaf & Tankard was able to prosper. In 1981, an all-black theater group, New Day Repertory Company, intended to bring live theater to New Paltz but their efforts faltered and the upstairs was vacated even as Barnaby's Loaf & Tankard continued to thrive, earning plaudits for their flame-broiled hamburgers. Under new ownership in 2001 and a change in name, business returned, but it was not until a year later when still new owners truly revived the old restaurant with a variant name and a new menu—Barnaby's Steakhouse—that went out of business in 2014. In early 2015, it was announced that the building would become the new home for the Goodwill Church, an Orange-county based Evangelical Presbyterian Church.

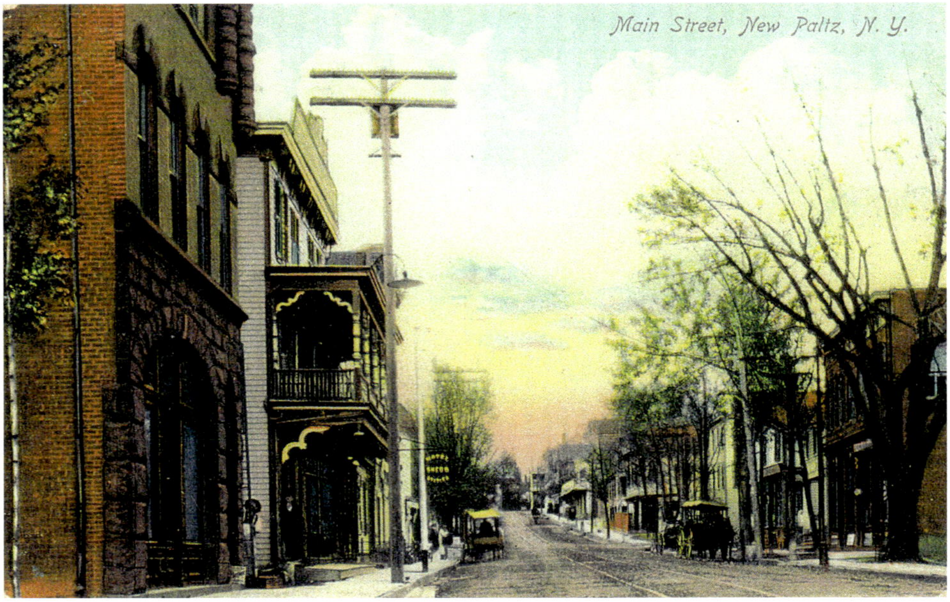

View Looking Up Lower Main Street, New Paltz

Looking up Main Street where it begins to level before rising again, there once were three prominent buildings on the north side, one being the town's leading bank, New Paltz Savings Bank that was chartered in 1871. The structure shown in the *Then* photo was completed in 1891. Considered the finest building in the village at the time, it was distinguished by its three stories that rose higher than any of the other frame or brick commercial buildings, a distinctive mansard roof, reddish brick and sandstone exterior, as well as a pair of banded cylinders with finials atop them. Adjacent to the bank was the Muller Hotel, a three-story building with a prominent balcony that was constructed in 1875 and razed in 1943. Due to expanded business, the old bank was demolished in 1970 and replaced by a sleek and more expansive one-story modern structure. The etched name New Paltz Savings Bank still is above the door, but over the years since it has had other names; today the illuminated sign declares the building is occupied by Wells Fargo.

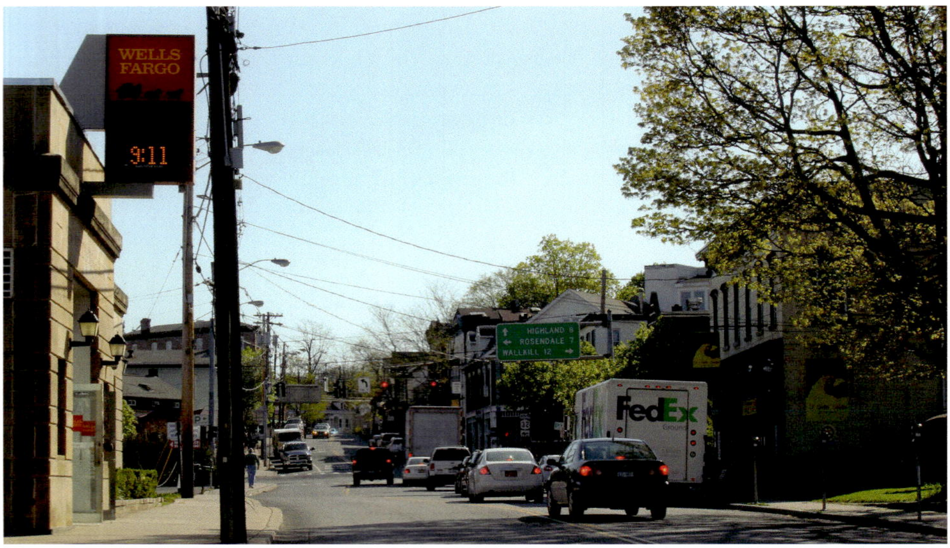

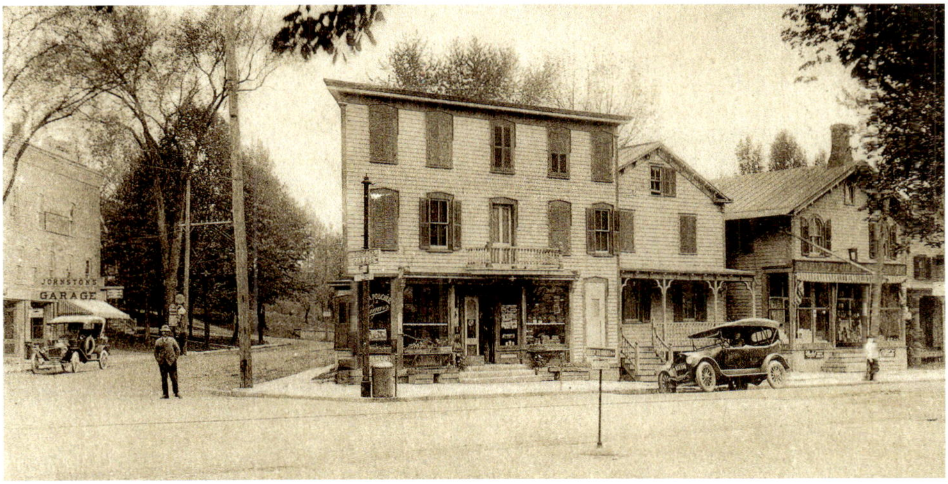

The Four Corners, New Paltz

Labeled lozenge-shaped in accounts at the turn of the twentieth century, the wood-frame structure is sited oddly at the acute-angled corner of Main and South Chestnut where roads from the four directions come together. This unique structure was constructed in 1891 and remains a village landmark. Its expansive entry was originally along Main Street, but sometime in the past was altered to be a recessed entrance accessible from both streets. As a prime location for sales, the building historically housed specialty shops. For fifty years from the 1930s, small eateries occupied the building, most notably one called The Triangle, until David's Cookies opened in the 1980s. Today, Mixture, an eclectic store that does signage as well as screen printing on all types of media, including t-shirts, caps, glassware, among many others, has set up shop.

The third storefront on the right has a long history as a retail establishment. Rock and Snow, which has become a near-legendary community institution purveying equipment and clothing for climbers, hikers, and skiers who enjoy recreation at the nearby Gunks, traces its roots to 1970 when it was opened by pioneer climber Dick Williams. In 1990, the old frame building erupted in fire destroying the store. A newly designed and larger building that complements well other old structures along the streetscape was opened in 1993. Rich Gottleib, once store manager, in 2000 purchased the business and continues to play a key role in servicing those who come to the Gunks for recreation.

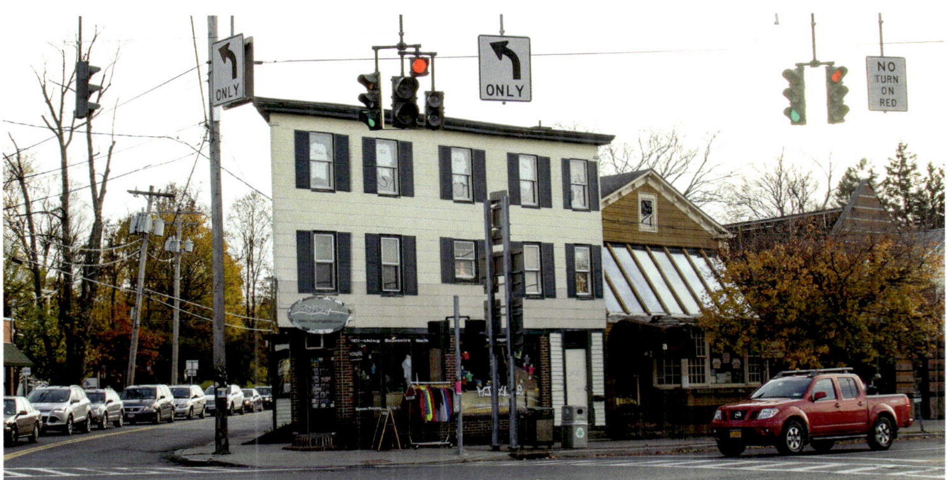

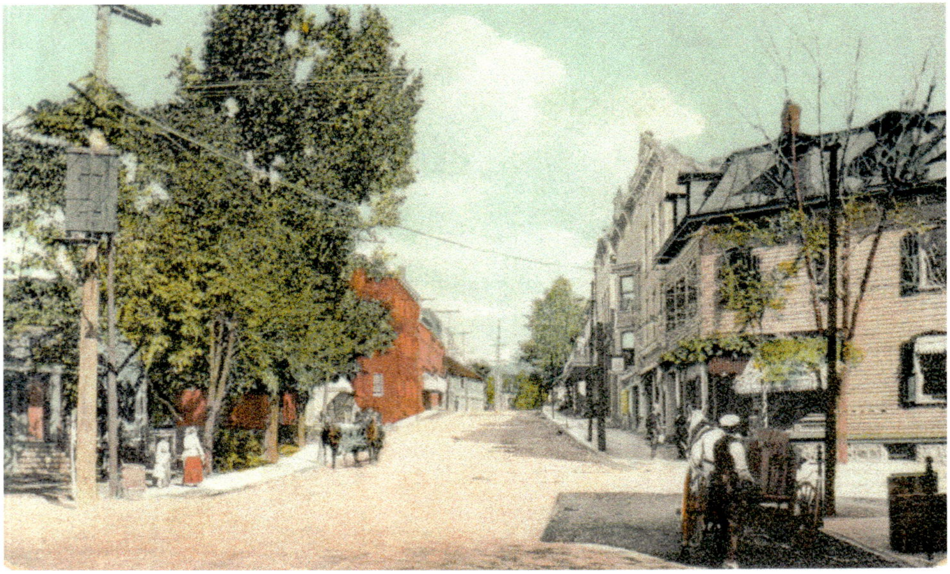

Main and Chestnut Intersection, New Paltz

The corner of Main Street and Chestnut Street is the principal four-way junction where three important highways converge. Behind the chestnut trees on the left was the residence of the Coe family, whose home with a front lawn was constructed in the 1860s. In the 1940s, it was converted into The Homestead restaurant. Because the trees and pole made turning difficult for trucks going north, they were removed in the 1980s. A patio was added in 1997 when the restaurant/bar was called Griffon, before then being transformed into Neko Sushi in 1998. Neko Sushi has a tori gate set off to an angle to improve the *fengshui* of the building. Across the street a three story structure was originally constructed with a gambrel roof in 1908 and leased to engineers who were supervising the building of the aqueduct along the Shawangunk Ridge. Fire consumed the building in 1987 and was replaced by a somewhat compatible brick building. Instead of trees, directional signs and lights populate the intersection today.

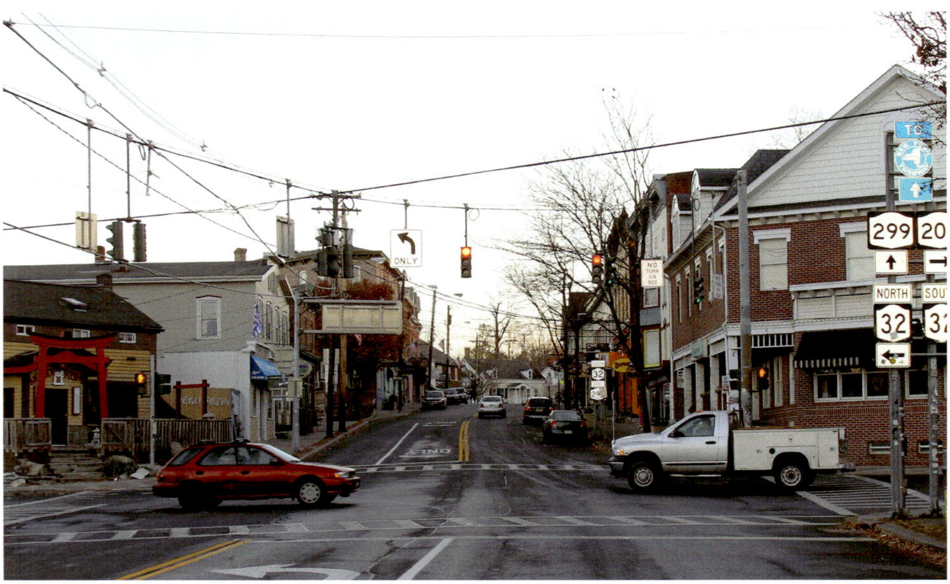

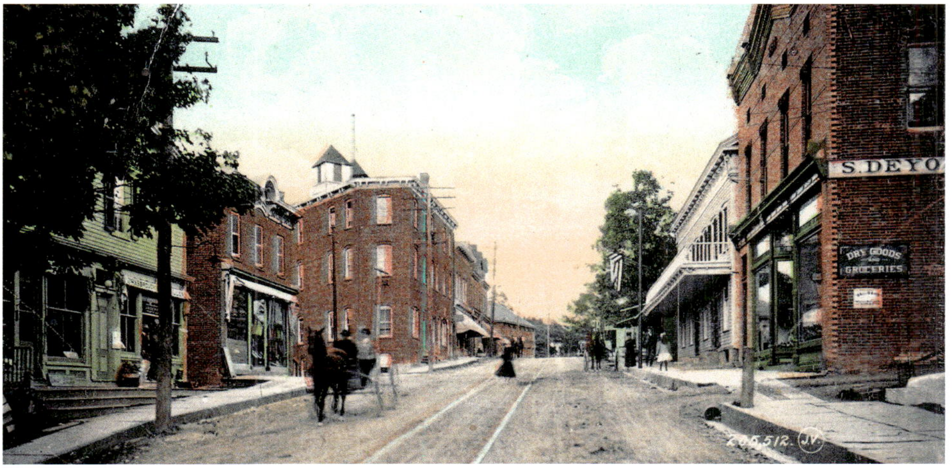

Looking Up Main Street, New Paltz

The commercial core of New Paltz retains today buildings that were there at the beginning of the twentieth century with a mixture of wood frame and brick structures. However, while once they met the shopping needs of average residents whose requirements are now met farther uptown, the spaces today are replete with restaurants, coffee shops, a meat market, a health food shop, antique shops, and contemporary clothing that caters to college students and visitors while still having a loyal base of residents who enjoy its eclectic mix.

Most of these buildings had large windows with those on the north side having as well roll-up awnings for use during the summer. Today, restaurants and specialty shops continue to occupy the spaces.

Near the center of the photo on the left is the distinctive 1893 Flatiron Building. With a three-story appearance and three storefronts along Main Street, the building also included an important basement level along Church Street. To its left is the Main Street Bistro, owned by Doug Thompson, which since 1993 continues to be packed with recreationists visiting the Gunks.

Over the decades, many small businesses, including barber shops, clothing stores, and a bookstore occupied the Main Street ground floor spaces while the basement housed the vehicles and equipment for the Ulster Hook and Ladder and Star Hose fire companies. Upstairs space was abundant for offices of many types. Today Krause's Chocolates, a branch of the well-known Saugerties shop, occupies the former fire house.

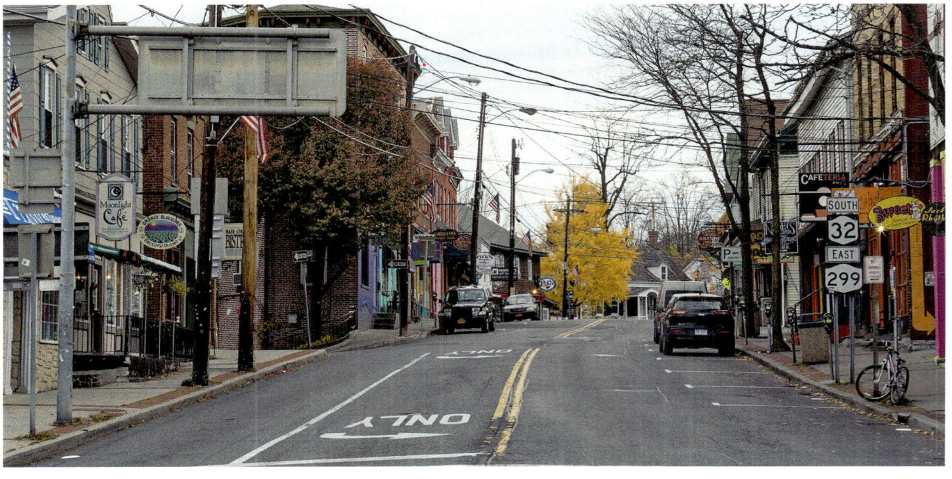

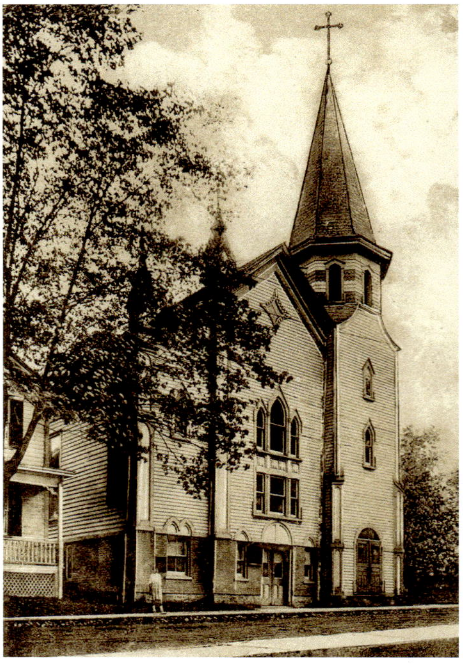 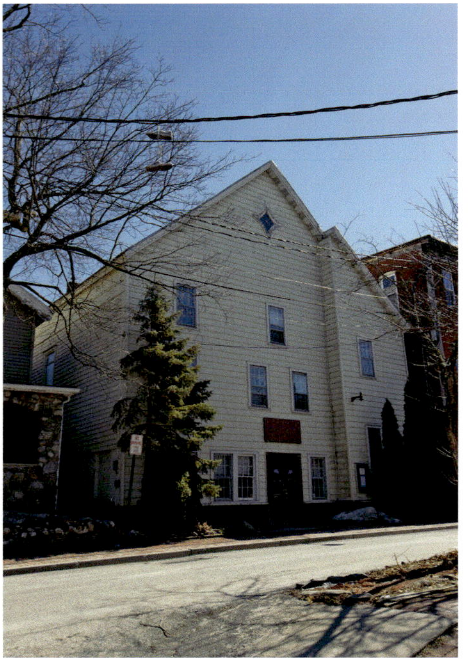

Methodist Episcopal Church/Jewish Congregation of New Paltz, New Paltz

This very old church, the only one on Church Street and "at the heart of the village" according to a news report of the time, has a history of adaptive reuse that reveals changes in the community at large.

From the late eighteenth into the early nineteenth century, the Methodist Episcopal community in New Paltz held services in private homes that were officiated by circuit riders who traveled by horse from town to town. With the support of fifty parishioners, a modest church was constructed facing Main Street at the junction with Church Street in 1840. In 1870, this structure was moved north and repositioned so that it faced Church Street. With the addition of a 70 foot tall steeple, a pair of pinnacles, and new windows, the facade was transformed into what art historian William Rhoads called "a vernacular version of Christian Gothic," a landmark church. A bell was placed in the steeple in 1892 that served as a village-wide fire alarm. Electric lights and stained glass windows followed a year later

As the congregation grew, discussions began about constructing a new church with plans developing from 1925 onward. In 1927, a spacious plot was secured at the junction of Main and Grove Streets with construction beginning in 1928 and dedication in June 1929 of what newspapers reported as "an adaptation of an English village church." The new church included a high half-timbered and stuccoed gable. The church weathered the Depression and burned its mortgage in 1945. Today it is known as the New Paltz United Methodist Church.

During the period of transition in 1928 as the Methodists were designing a new edifice, the old building on Church Street was purchased by the Sullivan-Shafer Post 176 of the American Legion, which replaced the stain glasses windows with "less ecclesiastical" ones according to the *New Paltz Independent*. In 1960, the Redeemer Lutheran Church acquired the building as its church until 1965.

Meanwhile, in 1963 some 35 people who met to discuss the possibility of establishing a Jewish center in New Paltz that would serve residents and students. Jewish worshippers held services in 1964 in the Lutheran Church, which had once been the Methodist Episcopal Church, and in January 1965 purchased 8 Church Street, dedicating it as the synagogue for Congregation Ahavath Achim. Lutherans continued worshipping as tenants until their new church was completed on Route 32 South. In 2001, having outgrown the Church Street site, the renamed Jewish Congregation of New Paltz purchased the former family restaurant called Dominick's as their social hall.

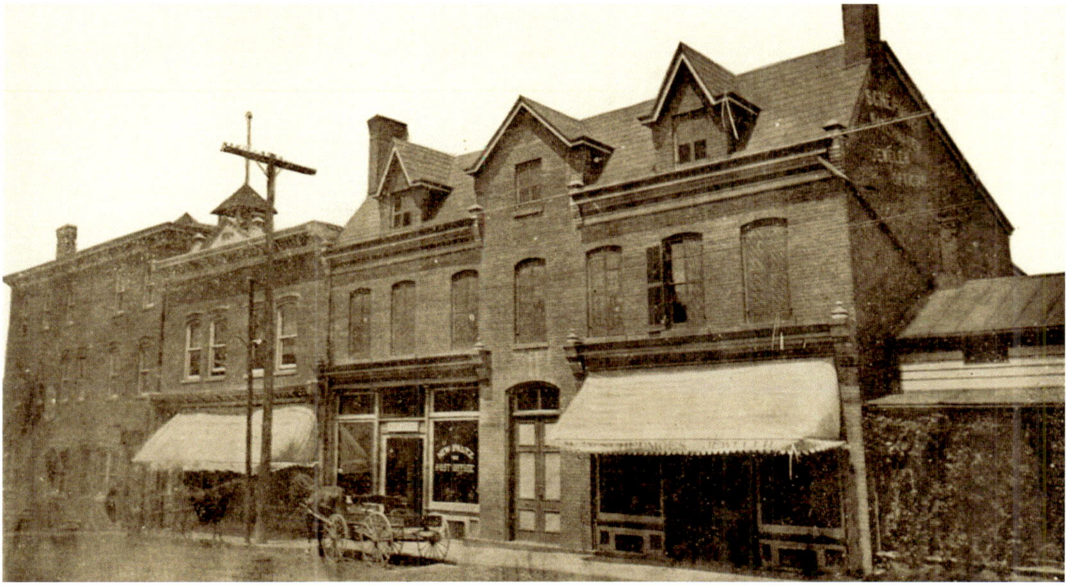

"Brick Row," North side of Main Street, New Paltz

Anchored by the Flatiron Building on the far left, the row of old brick buildings retains much of its past character. Each of the buildings is notable for its bracketed cornices and arched windows.

The imposing seven-bay brick building with three dormers and a gambrel roof was constructed in 1895 for M. Dewitt Schepmoes, a jeweler. Two storefronts with indented entrances and bright show windows, one for the jewelry shop and the other the post office and later a butcher shop, were separated by a stairway that led to the owner's apartment on the second floor. While the building once had a slate roof, today it is metal.

Today, the shop fronts lining Main Street are quite colorful and not changed much over the years except for the near elimination of awnings. Brightly lit throughout the day and year round the specialty shops appeal to tourists as well as locals.

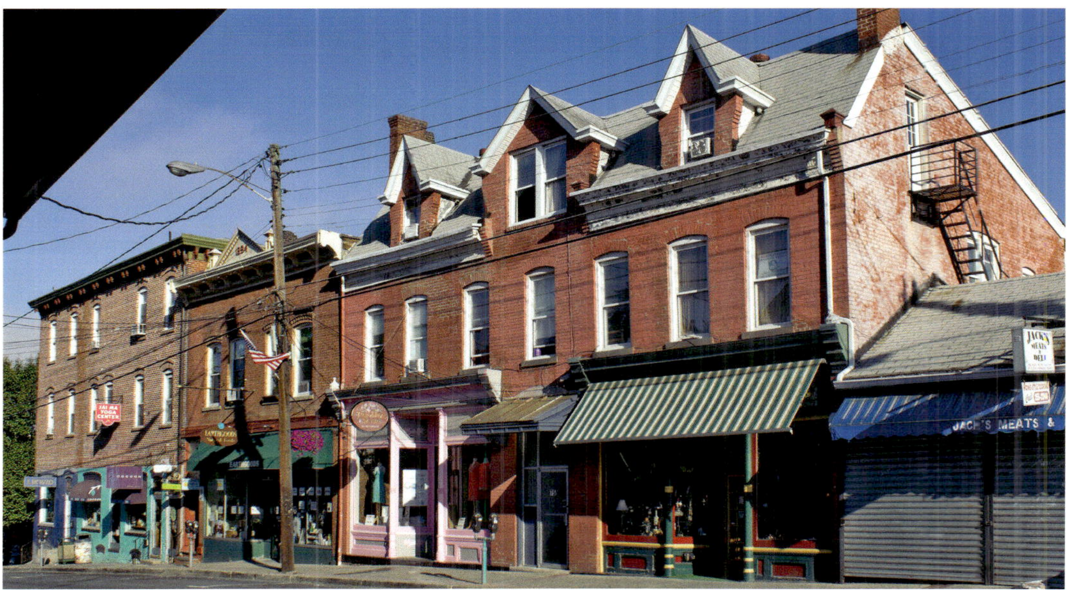

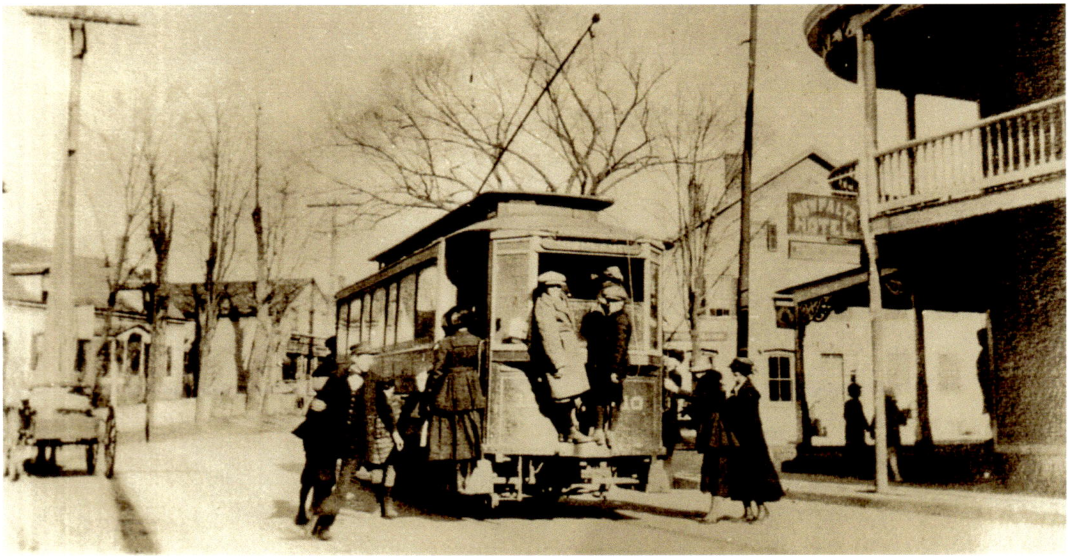

Main, Front, and Plattekill Junction, New Paltz

After leveling off, Main Street begins another climb at a corner that today mixes old and new buildings. The old are barely visible on the left, first the New Paltz Casino and beyond the Elting Library. On the right, the hotel with the veranda was replaced, first with a gasoline service station and bookstore, and more recently with a Starbucks. Across Plattekill Avenue, the commercial building was replaced with an elegant brick building for the Huguenot Bank, which is now occupied by Chase Bank.

Dominating the *Then* photograph about 1900 is a laden street car that linked New Paltz to Highland Landing where it was possible to take a boat to New York City and other locations along the Hudson River. At first, passengers had to take a ferry to reach Poughkeepsie before a rail connection carried cars across the high railway bridge. Playing a key role in wider visitation to New Paltz for both day and nighttime activities, the trolley ran from 1897 to 1925 when automobiles began to alter the patterns of individual travel. The *Now* photograph suggests that vehicular traffic is light in New Paltz, yet the truth is this is a very early morning shot.

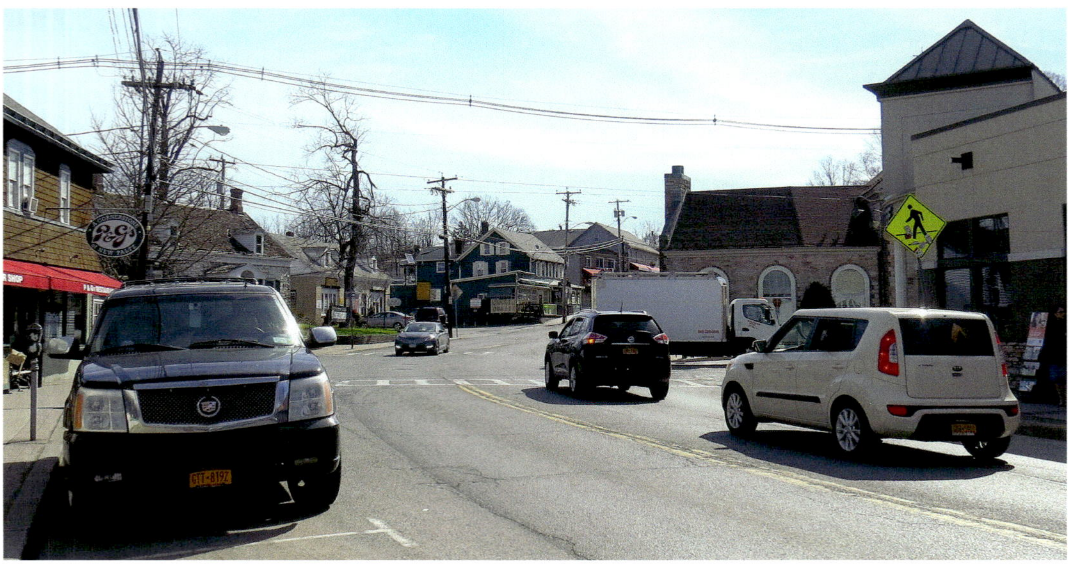

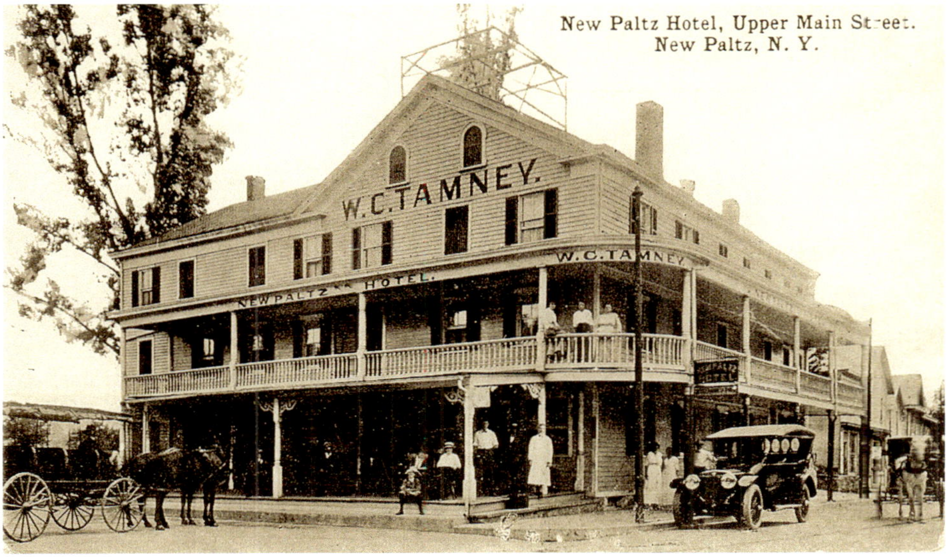

Main and Plattekill Intersection, New Paltz

Continuously from about 1774 until 1945, first a tavern and then hotels were located on the southwest corner of Main Street and Plattekill Avenue. When the surviving hotel was demolished is not clear.

The Upper Main Street W.C. Tamney New Paltz Hotel pictured in the *Then* image took that name in 1914 after it had been purchased from William Steen who had transformed a plain hotel by adding a second-story veranda and calling it first the Steen Hotel and subsequently the New Paltz Hotel.

In 1976, an Amoco gas station was constructed on the site, which in 1978 was transformed into the Ariel Bookstore that underwent needed expansion twice as it became a highly regarded institution in the college town.

More recently, the corner is noted for Starbucks, the only one in Ulster County outside the city of Kingston. Attached bookstore spaces became first a Mexican restaurant, called Blockheads, and now Ariel Dentistry.

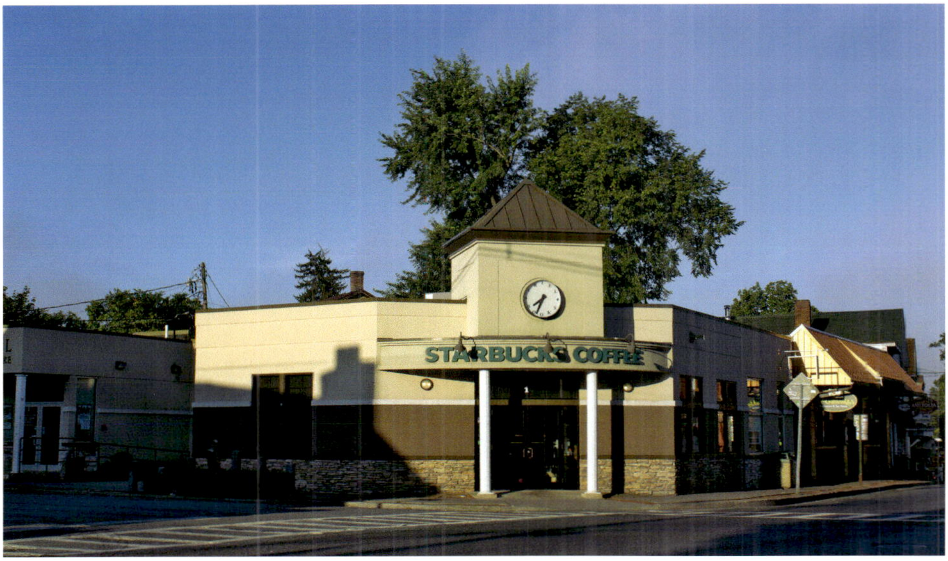

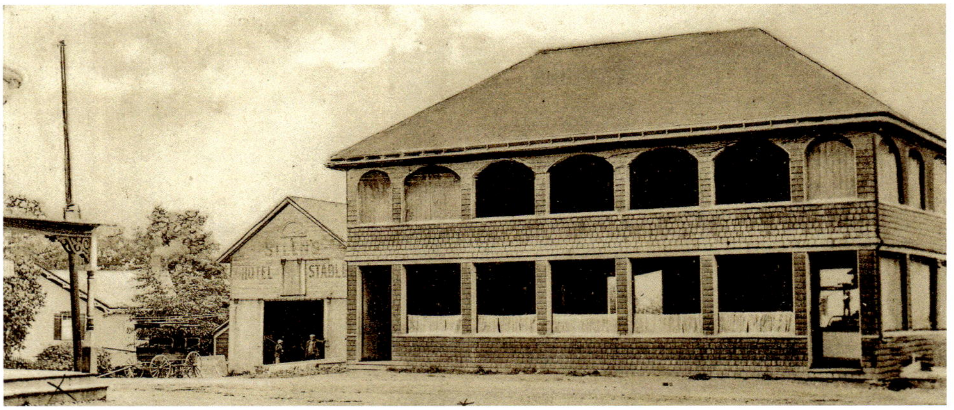

THE CASINO AND P&GS, NEW PALTZ

The lot directly across the street from Steen's New Paltz Hotel was a common stable and barn with livery service for guests. In 1900, just to the east of the barn, The Casino, a two-story, pavilion-type open structure with a hipped roof, was constructed.

This was not a place to gamble, but was a venue for summertime patrons to come sit, enjoy ice cream, read, and relax during the day. In the evening, regulars from throughout the area, summer boarders, and casual visitors from afar arrived to enjoy band music and dancing. A fountain and potted palms on the first floor gave the room a welcoming space. The Casino continued as a cornerstone of New Paltz even when it was enclosed as an inn before being converted to other uses such as a clothing store, drug store, and real estate office.

The Casino changed hands in 1921 and was renamed the Blue Crane Inn, continuing the tradition of providing dancing and music. Its prominence decreased with the demise of the Highland to New Paltz trolley and the increasing popularity of private automobiles that provided access to greater entertainment opportunities beyond the village of New Paltz. For more than a decade after, the building served a variety of retail purposes including being a drug store, clothing store, real estate office and in the 1940s Dick's Bar and Grill.

In 1947, the bar and grill was purchased by Pat Cafferty and George Jayne, two Lake Mohonk employees, giving it the name Pat and George's that was shortened by regulars as simply P&G's, a name that has been carried forward by Edwin Beck who bought the business in 1969. Over the past 45 years, first Ed, then his civic-minded son Mike, and his children continue to run a restaurant and bar loved by area residents of all ages, tourists, and countless SUNY New Paltz students who recognize its heritage and value among the proliferating competing restaurants and bars in New Paltz.

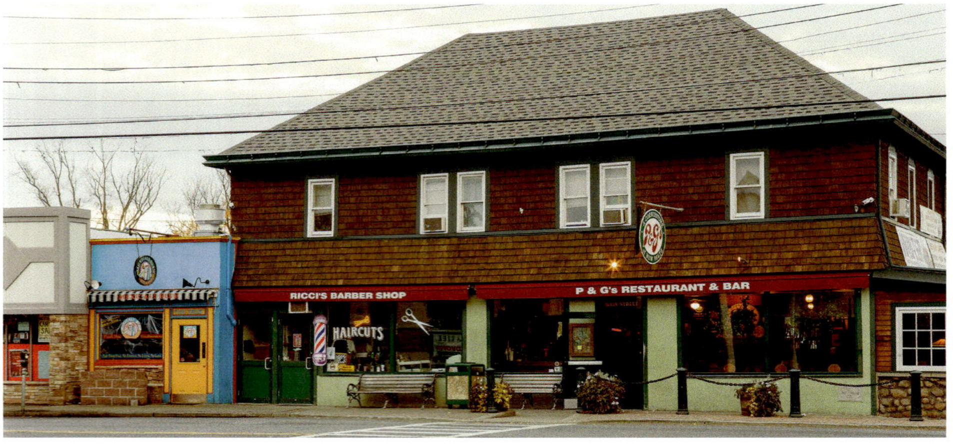

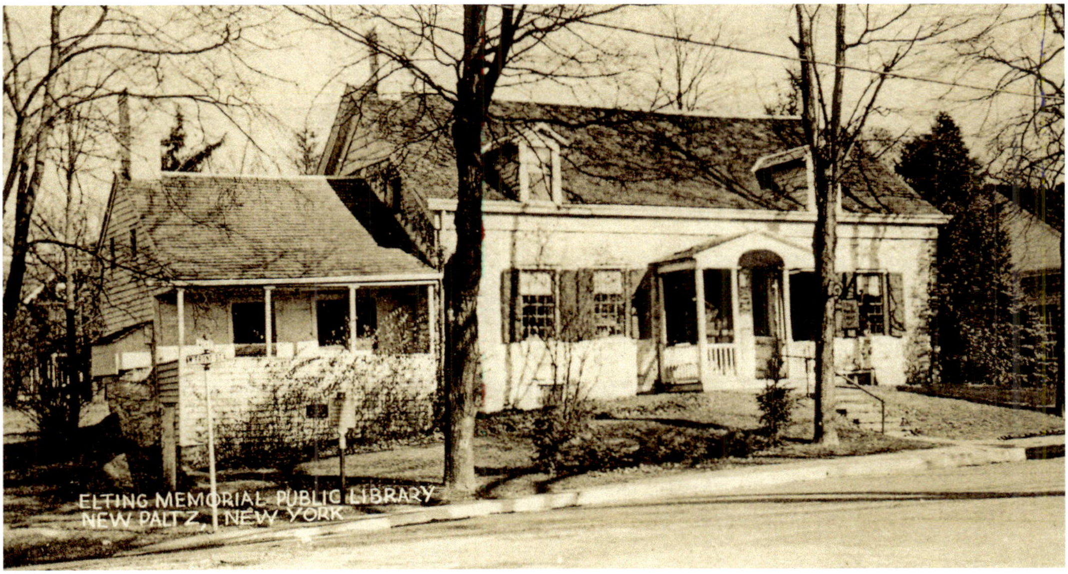

Elting Memorial Library, New Paltz

Diagonally across from the early W.C. Tamney Hotel and opposite The Casino was the only stone house on Main Street, a structure dating from either the late eighteenth or early nineteenth century. Records reveal that the one-story-and-a-half residence with its symmetrical facade was purchased in 1817 by Solomon Elting, who also acquired the undated attached frame structure.

For a decade after it was provisionally chartered in 1909 as a free library association, the New Paltz Library occupied various spaces along Main Street. With an increasing collection and patron demand, the association was fortunate to benefit from the gift of the old Elting residence by Philip Elting, a New Paltz son who had become a wealthy paint manufacturer in Chicago all the while retaining close roots with New Paltz, in 1920.

Known since then as the Elting Memorial Library, the historical building is much loved by the community especially as it remains intact after an expansion of the library in 2006 that tripled its size.

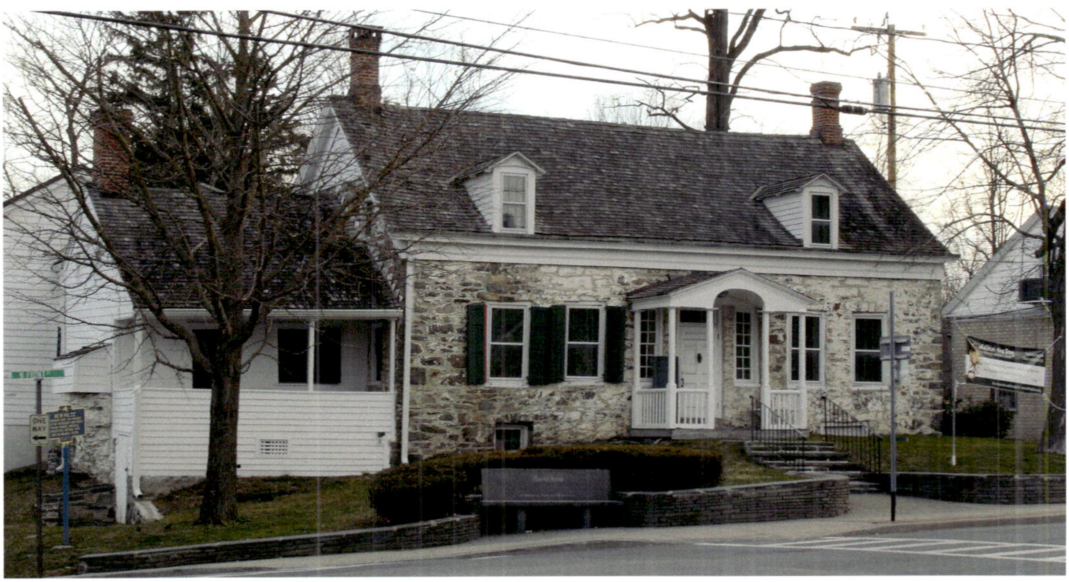

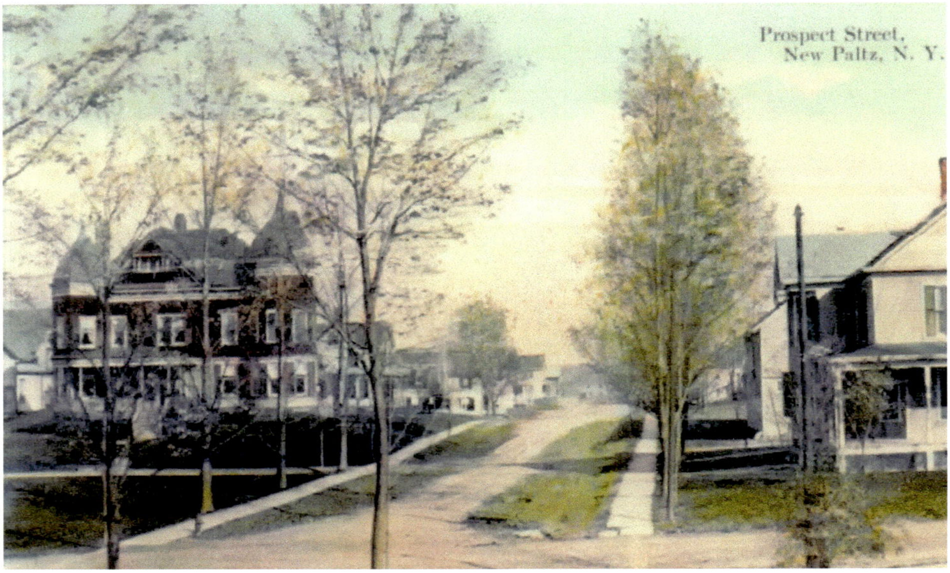

Main and Prospect Looking North, New Paltz

Continuing up along the north side of Main Street at the junction of Prospect Street was a grand turreted home that had been constructed in 1893 before being purchased in 1899 by the State of New York as a residence for principals of the New Paltz Normal School. Later, the residence became merely a collection of apartments before it was consumed by fire in 1991. Its demise as a stately residence with a broad lawn reaching to Main Street was accelerated once a Gulf service station (now Citgo) was constructed in front of it along Main Street.

Across the unpaved Prospect Street, an extensive livery stable and barns belonging to Louis DuBois were constructed behind his home in the late nineteenth century. Some of the stables and barns were consumed in a fire in 1923. Although it is not clear when the home on the corner was torn down, some of the livery buildings were transformed into the passenger waiting room for the new New Paltz Trailways Bus Station in 1962.

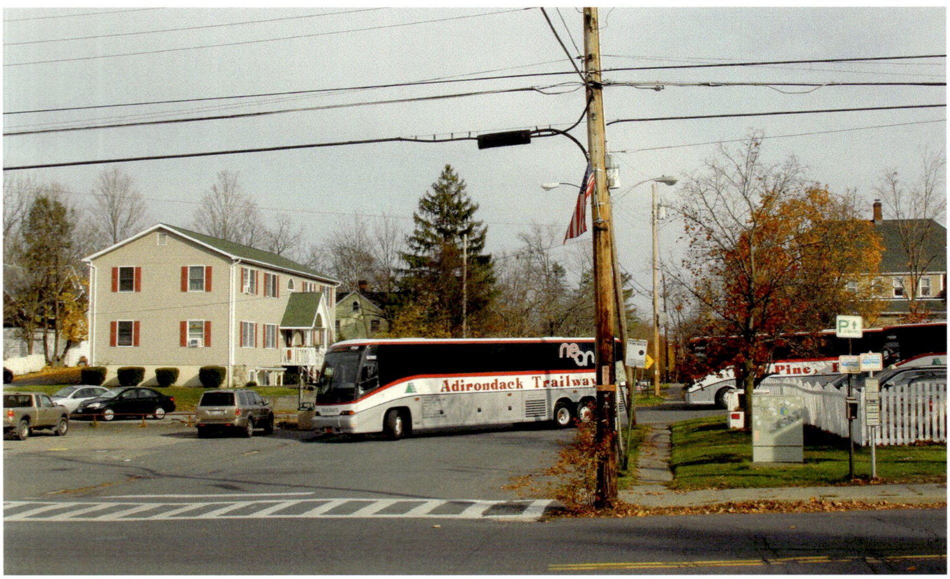

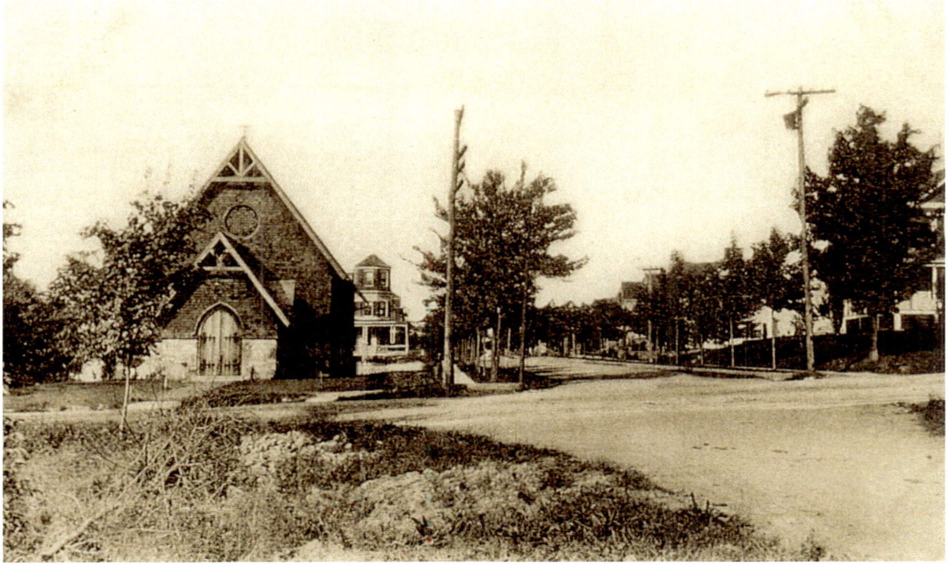

ST. ANDREW'S EPISCOPAL CHURCH, MAIN STREET AND NORTH OAKWOOD TERRACE, NEW PALTZ

As early as 1844, an Archdeaconry Mission group with the name St. Athanasius was established in New Paltz, a young congregation that met at various venues throughout the village for more than 60 years. It was only in 1906 when the congregation had grown sufficiently large that thoughts turned to acquiring land and constructing a church. This was accomplished on the northwest corner of North Oakwood Terrace when David Storr, a wealthy merchant and recent New Paltz resident began to develop new streets and interesting houses on the east side of the old village.

When the church was completed in 1909, it was named St. Andrew's Episcopal Church. An adjacent vicarage in similar style was completed in 1928.

The young trees and the vacant lot across the street in the *Then* image suggest the freshness of the area, quite a contrast with the heavily wooded scene and the service station opposite it today.

Today, instead of a grassy area, the church faces an auto repair shop and a Gulf station.

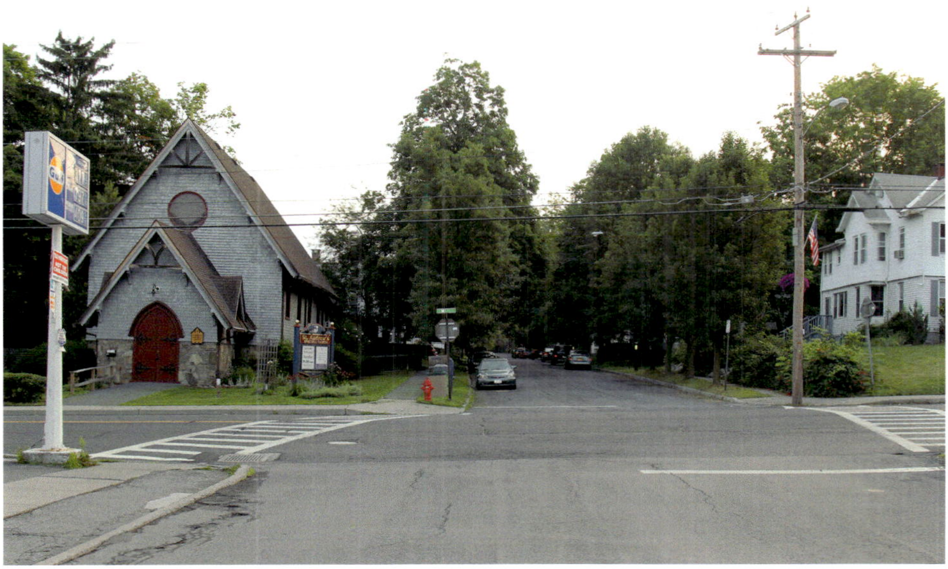

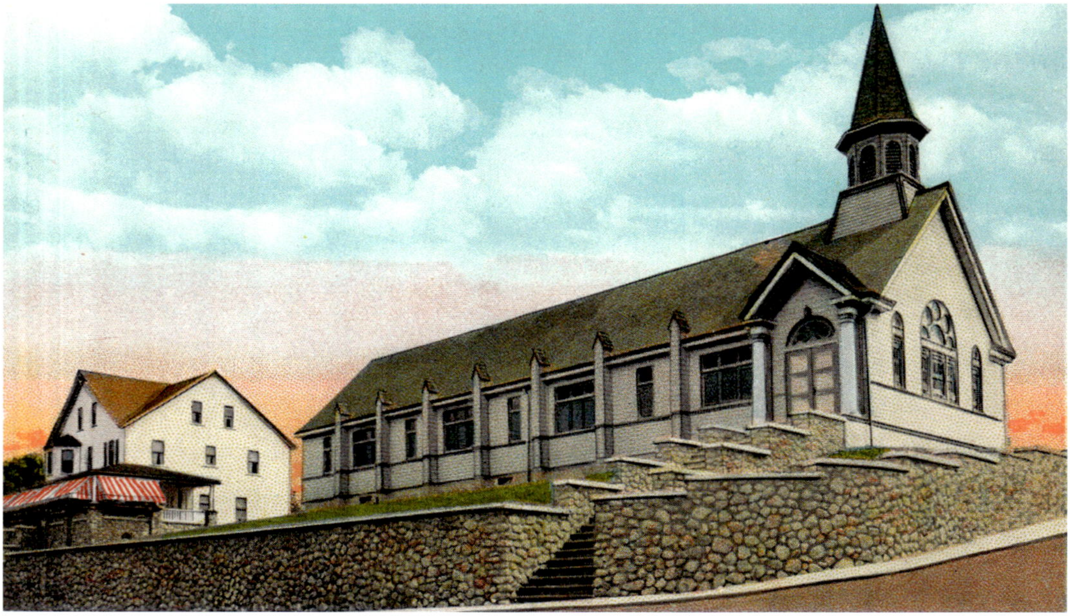

St. Joseph's Catholic Church and Parsonage, New Paltz/ Charles Borromeo Catholic Church, Gardiner

While St Joseph's Catholic Church in New Paltz dates from the period 1891–1893 and was dedicated in 1894, it had its beginnings decades earlier to the south in Tuthilltown and Gardiner. In Tuthilltown, the small community of Catholics were serviced by a circuit riding priest, but after the Wallkill Valley Railroad came north and spurred developments at the new hamlet of Gardiner Station after 1850, a need arose for a Catholic Church and regular services, which at first were held in a barn owned by James Clinton. In 1882, the wood from that barn was used to construct St. Charles Borromeo Catholic Church at Ireland Corners in Gardiner shown in the image at the top of the next page.

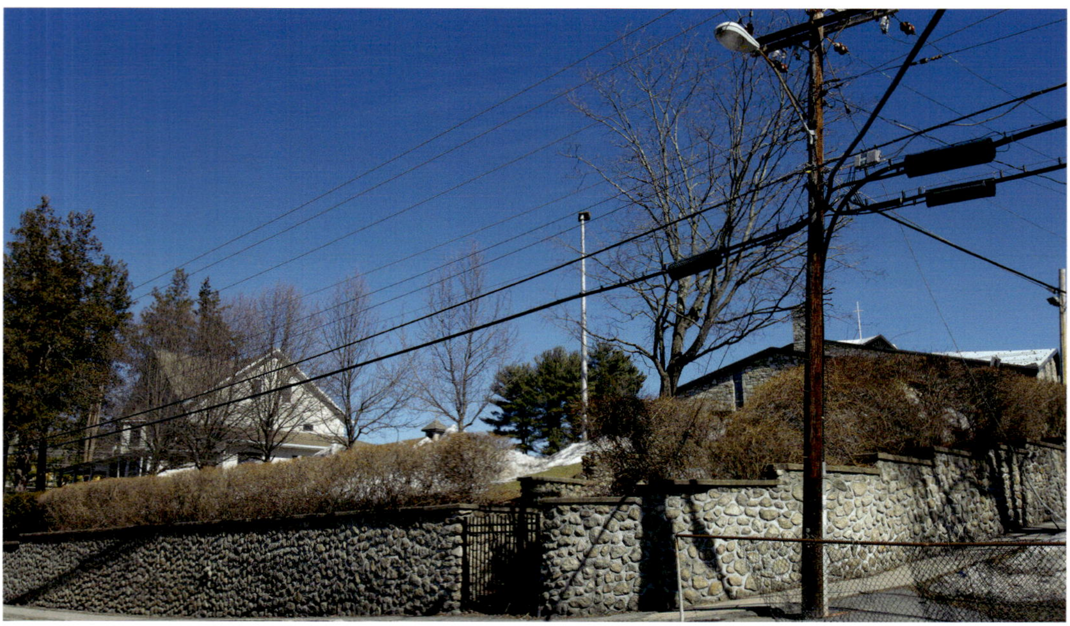

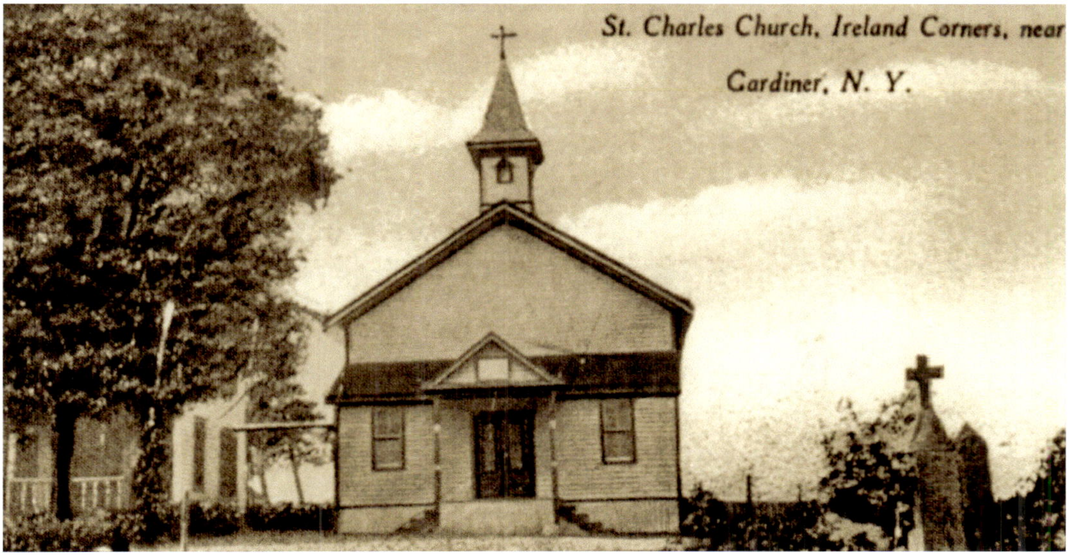

As both the Catholic population in the village of New Paltz and at the nearby State Normal School increased, a decision was made at St. Charles to begin the construction of a new church in New Paltz. The first site chosen was on Church Street in the Village and a cornerstone was laid in 1885, but these plans were laid aside. Subsequently, it was decided to purchase an acre of land on South Chestnut Street between Hasbrouck and Mohonk Avenues. The cornerstone at the former site was then moved to the new site—midway between 'downtown' New Paltz and the college—in 1891. Construction took place in 1893 and the church was dedicated in 1894. After Cuban students began attending the Normal School in 1901, services were offered also in Spanish

The adjacent parish house was completed in 1928 as work continued on building retaining walls of stone, which were collected on the ridge, to frame the South Chestnut and Mohonk Avenue flanks of the property as seen in the *Then* photograph. During this period of vigorous growth, St. Joseph's in 1930 purchased Village Hall on North Chestnut Street after the Opera House closed, to serve as the St. Joseph Center.

As the Catholic community continued to expand in succeeding decades, an addition was added that led ultimately to groundbreaking for a new church on February 7, 1965. It is this grand, modern church that today is St. Joseph's Catholic Church The large parish house on the left in the *Then* photo is still standing.

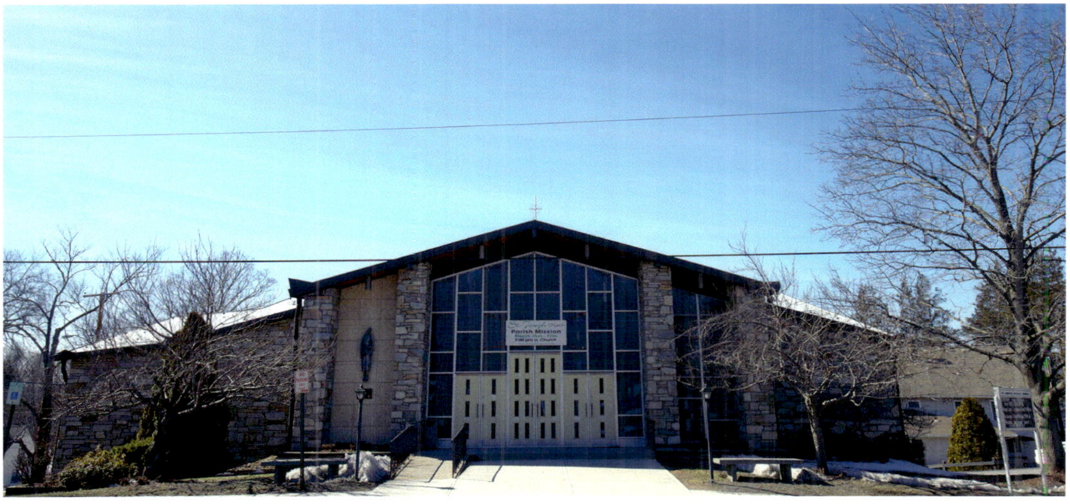

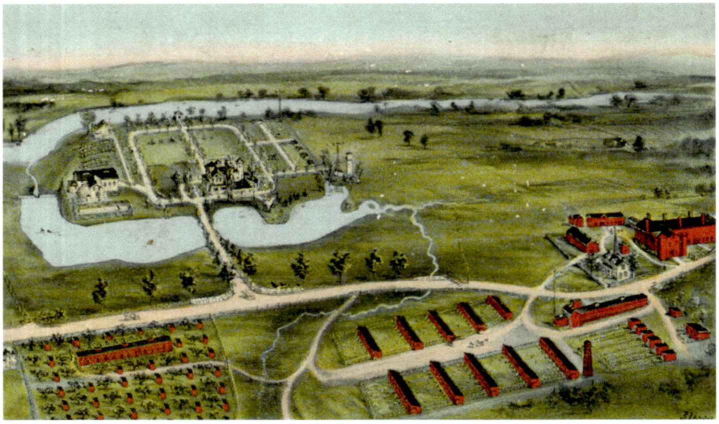

Oscar Tschirky Estate/The Culinarians' Home, New Paltz

The towns surrounding the Shawangunks have had many well-known residents—Sojourner Truth, Floyd Patterson, and Robert DeNiro, to name just a few—but none had the renown of Oscar Tschirky, who today is all but forgotten.

Born in Switzerland in 1866 and arriving in New York in 1883, he rose in stature in the hospitality industry from the lowly position of busboy at the Hoffman House. He joined the original Waldorf-Astoria Hotel just two months before it opened in 1893 serving there in many capacities for a half century. For decades he was maître d'hôtel and host extraordinaire until retiring in 1943. Popularly known as "Oscar of the Waldorf," his fame derived from his association with presidents, royalty, and the elite of the world who resided at the Waldorf-Astoria when they were in New York City. His birthdays, anniversaries, dinners, and even the marriages of his children were all chronicled in the *New York Times* often with the location as New Paltz. Many considered Oscar the arbiter of culinary taste and fine dining.

Although not a chef, he published a cookbook and is acknowledged as the creator of the Waldorf Salad, Veal Oscar, and Thousand Island Dressing.

In 1889, he purchased farmland four miles north of the village of New Paltz along the Wallkill River with the Shawangunks as backdrop. There he established what became known as "Oscar's Farm" as new and old farms were added to his property over the next decade in what was called the Bonticoe area of New Paltz. The property was bisected by the road north to Kingston, which today is the less traveled Old Kingston Road. Early travelers witnessed a veritable estate as they passed through the property. Here he built a main house in the Queen Anne style as his farmstead facing East over a double pond that was created by channeling water from the Wallkill River. Local carpenters, masons, farmhands, gardeners, and laborers with many skills were hired to bring his ideas to reality. Behind, as shown in the 1920s *Then* postcard view, he landscaped the area to the river as a park. Numerous farm buildings were constructed as well, mainly to the east and across the road to Kingston, including some that were used to raise young pigeons that found their way to the Waldorf-Astoria kitchens as squab, a hotel delicacy at the time. Leghorn fowl, ducks, and Berkshire hogs also were part of his farm-to-table operation.

At the beginning of 1942, Oscar deeded his 320 acre country estate to The Société Culinaire Philanthropique, the oldest association of chefs, cooks, and pastry chefs in the United States. According to the *New York Times*, he did so "for the welfare and well-being of the aged members of The Société, which named his estate The Culinarians' Home fashioning it as a retreat, a retirement home for chefs who then generally didn't have pensions. He built a Swiss chalet for himself, where he lived until he died in 1950.

For decades, this worked well, but by the 1980s the home was opened to the general public as a residence for ambulatory senior citizens. Today, some 15 residents occupy the main Victorian structure, which sits on but 40 acres of the once large estate.

Although today the main house, ponds, and outbuildings behind the house survive amidst the landscape acreage that slopes back towards the Wallkill River, much of the surrounding acreage has returned to woodland or remains as meadow. The extent of the once vibrant farming operation is no longer evident.

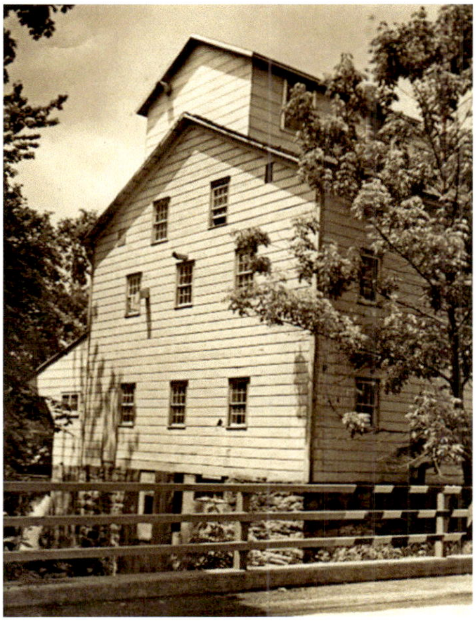
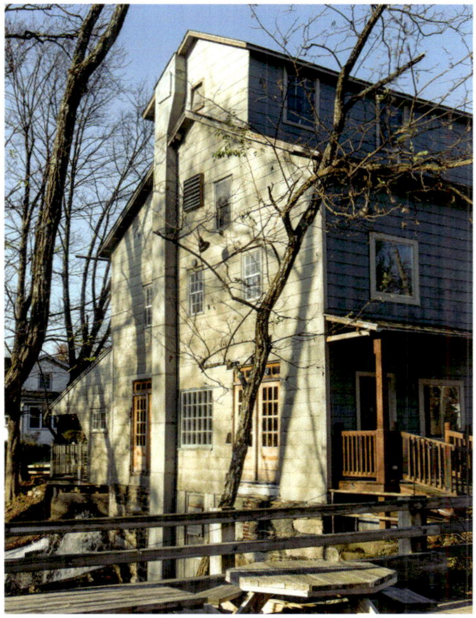
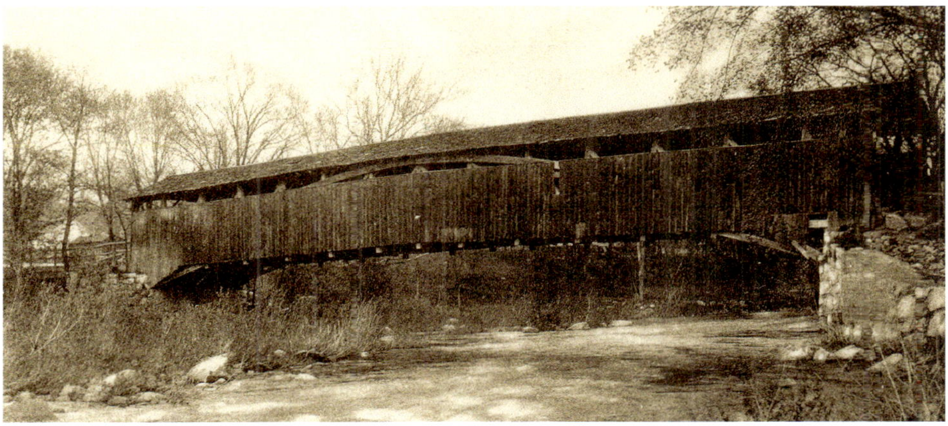

Ganahgote, Tuthilltown, Gardiner

The south-to-north flowing Wallkill River is joined by the Shawangunk Kill at Ganahgote, a nineteenth century hamlet adjacent to Tuthill about a mile west of the center of today's Gardiner hamlet. It was the need to cross this stream, which rises on the Shawangunk Ridge and flows to the valley, that a wooden covered bridge with a Burr arch truss was constructed around 1845. This was a critical link in along Farmers Turnpike well before the railroad reached the area farther east.

In 1872, the Ganahgote area included two hotels, a school house, shops, a wagon shop, a harness shop as well as a variety of mills—grist mill, saw mill, and a carding and fulling mill—that depended on the rushing waters of the Shawangunk Kill. However, with the arrival of the railroad line farther east and the subsequent development of the Gardiner hamlet, Ganahgote fell into decline. When an iron bridge across the Wallkill River was constructed in 1902, the covered bridge became redundant and was removed in the 1930s. Today one can still see the abutments.

One surviving exception is the three-story Tuttletown Grist Mill, which dates to the late eighteenth century and operated into the twenty-first century. Today, the building has been converted into a restaurant as part of the Tuthilltown Spirits complex, which is New York's first whiskey distillery since prohibition.

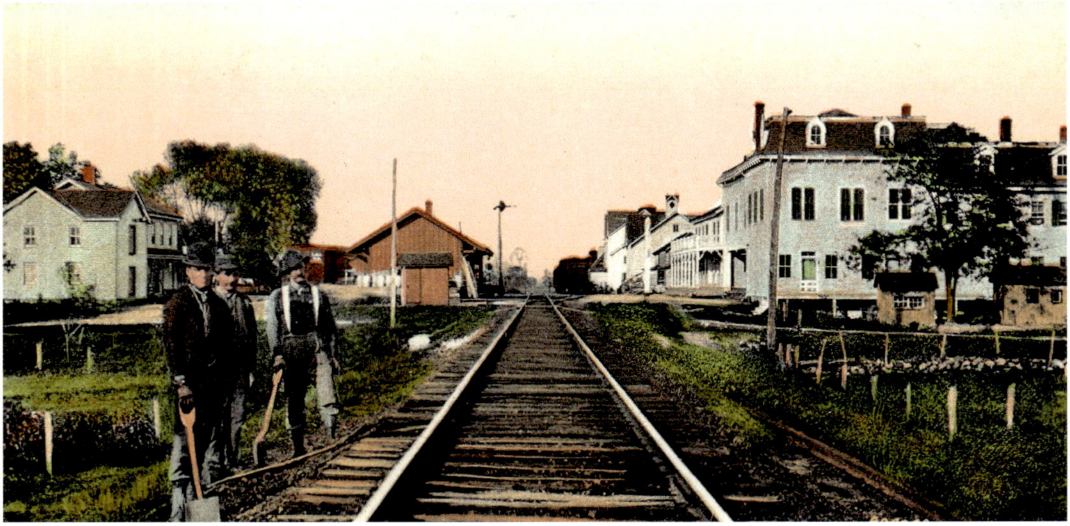

Gardiner Hamlet

Although the *Then* photo is looking south, the "iron bands" of the single track Wallkill Valley Railroad continued north to New Paltz in 1870. While passenger service was reduced to one train a day in 1933 and then halted four years later, freight continued on the line until 1977 before that too stopped.

Once railroad ties and iron rails were removed, most of the old line reverted to untidy brush as Conrail tried to find municipalities and others to purchase the linear route. A decade later through the foresight of municipal authorities in New Paltz and the not-for-profit Wallkill Valley Land Trust, a way was sought to acquire each of the three sections, including four miles in the Town of New Paltz, three miles in the Village of New Paltz, and five miles in the Town of Gardiner. With assistance from the Trust for Public Land, the linear parcel was purchased even in the face of many doubters and opponents, and shortly thereafter the Wallkill Valley Rail Trail Association was formed to clear and maintain the rail trail. As the late historian Carleton Mabee summarizes, "where engines used to huff and hiss, walkers stride. Where freight trains used to rattle by, birdwatchers peer through their binoculars. Where children once rode the train to school, they bicycle. Still a few householders, as they quiet down for sleep, miss the comfort of train whistles blowing in the night."

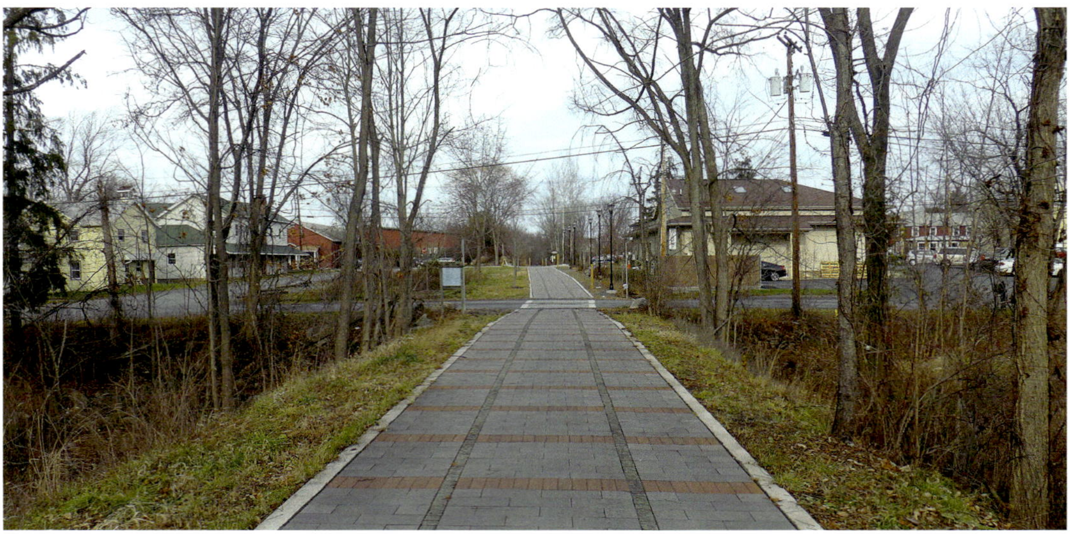

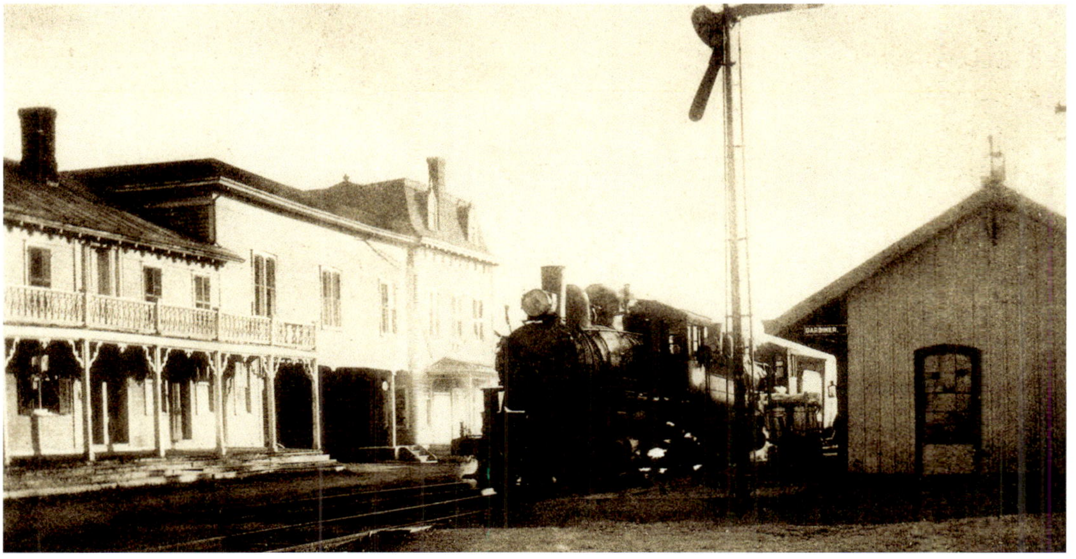

Gardiner Train Depot and Callahan Hotel

Although the Town of Gardiner was formed in 1853, it was not until the tracks for the Wallkill Valley Railroad from Goshen in the south reached the area in 1869 that the farm fields around the train depot began to be transformed into a checkerboard pattern of streets.

The once thriving hamlets at Ganahgote and Tuthill a mile west were eclipsed. The late historian Carleton Mabee calls Gardiner "a classic railroad village" in that the depot at Gardiner Station in a short time morphed into Gardiner hamlet. Adjacent to the tracks and across from the depot, the McKinstry House, "a first class hotel," was opened in 1869 (or 1888) and by 1929 was known as the Callahan Hotel. Locals and visitors simply referred to it as the Gardiner Hotel. The hotel was demolished in 1974, leaving vacant land that has assumed other commercial uses including Pasquales Pizza & Restaurant.

More than a half century later, the old rail line was transformed into a rail trail via a convoluted process of citizen engagement. The Wallkill Valley Rail Trail that once ran only from Gardiner to New Paltz now stretches over the Rosendale Trestle to Kingston, as the rail line itself once ran.

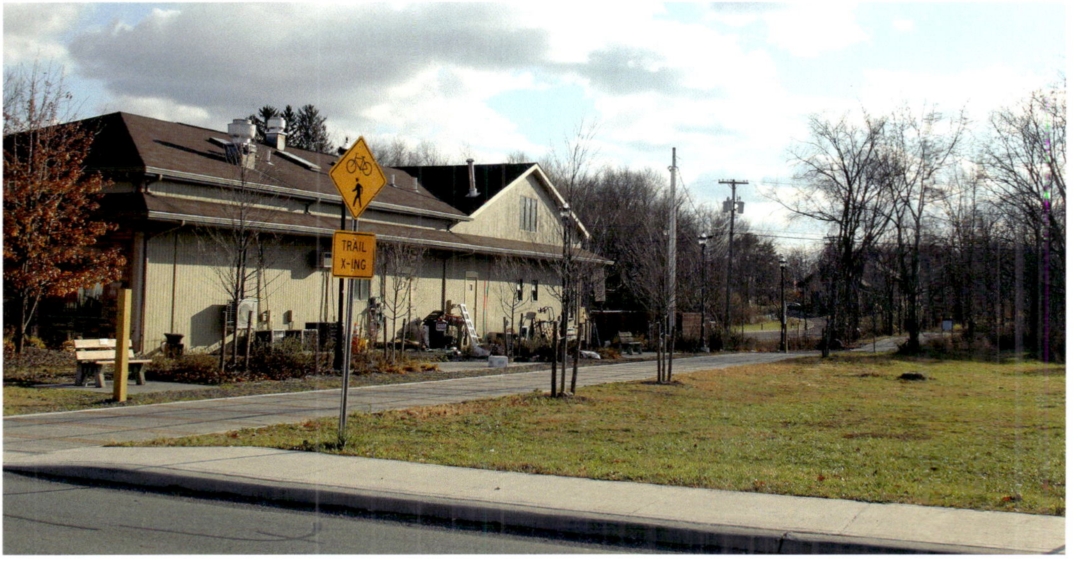

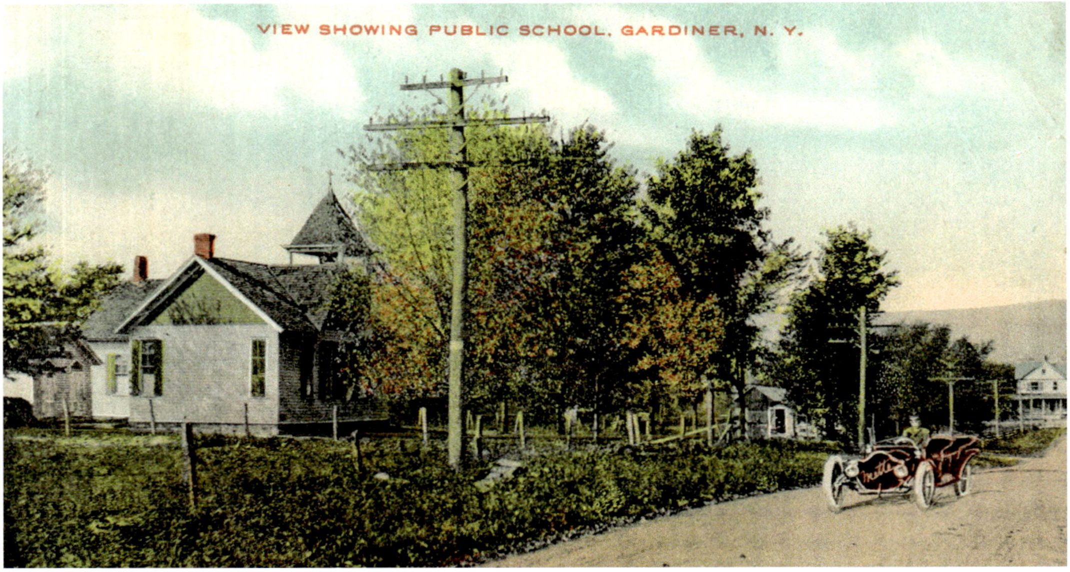

Gardiner Schoolhouse/Town Hall

On the left is the Gardiner Schoolhouse, a one-room structure that was erected in 1880, one of approximately fifteen one-room school houses in the town at the time. The building was expanded in 1895 with a second room and a prominent bell tower. It was located a short walk from the rail depot and the developing residential Gardiner hamlet. The schoolhouse was one of the few buildings to survive Gardiner's 1825 fire that ravaged other buildings farther west in the hamlet

From the 1920s onward, one-room school houses slowly closed one after the other as school districts centralized instruction. The Gardiner School was a holdout, not closing until 1981.

Subsequently, after much community discussion and votes, this historic building became Gardiner Town Hall and has undergone significant renovation even as its outward appearance has not changed significantly.

US Routes 44/55 run west through the hamlet of Gardiner and then over the Shawangunk Mountains.

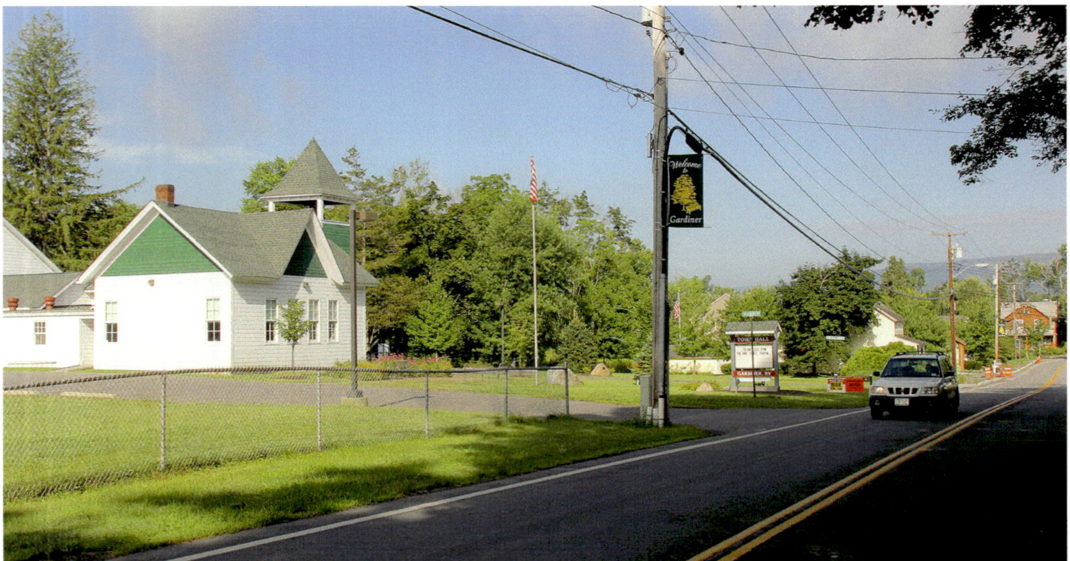

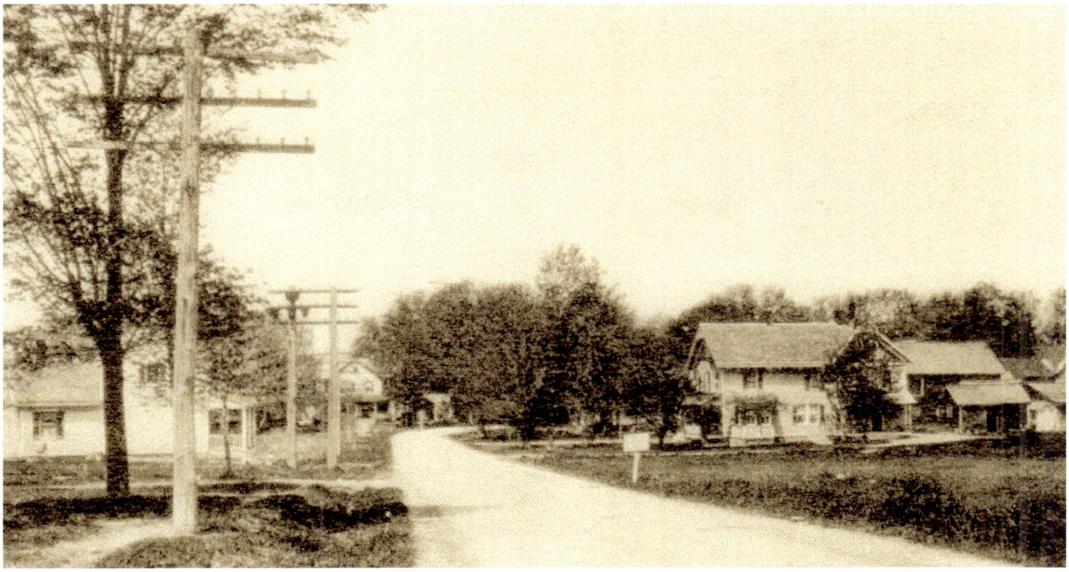

Gardiner at the Turn

Heading west in Gardiner past the historic Gardiner Schoolhouse, which is just off to the left, the road jogs a bit before returning to its westward path and proceeding past the site of the old train depot and heading towards the Shawangunk Ridge along what locals refer to as the Minnewaska Trail.

Much of this road, even as a US highway, still retains its open rural feeling.

The grassy area on the right in the *Then* photo is now occupied by the Station #2 of Gardiner Fire Department, which has been serving the hamlet since 1953. An all-volunteer fire company protected Gardiner beginning in 1912 from Station #1 at a location where the Gardiner Library today is located. Since 1977, an emergency rescue and first aid squad not only has served the hamlet but also assisted injured recreationists on the nearby ridge.

The early hand pumper was used up through Gardiner's 1925 fire, after which a new Sanford Fire Engine was purchased to meet the needs of an expanded fire district.

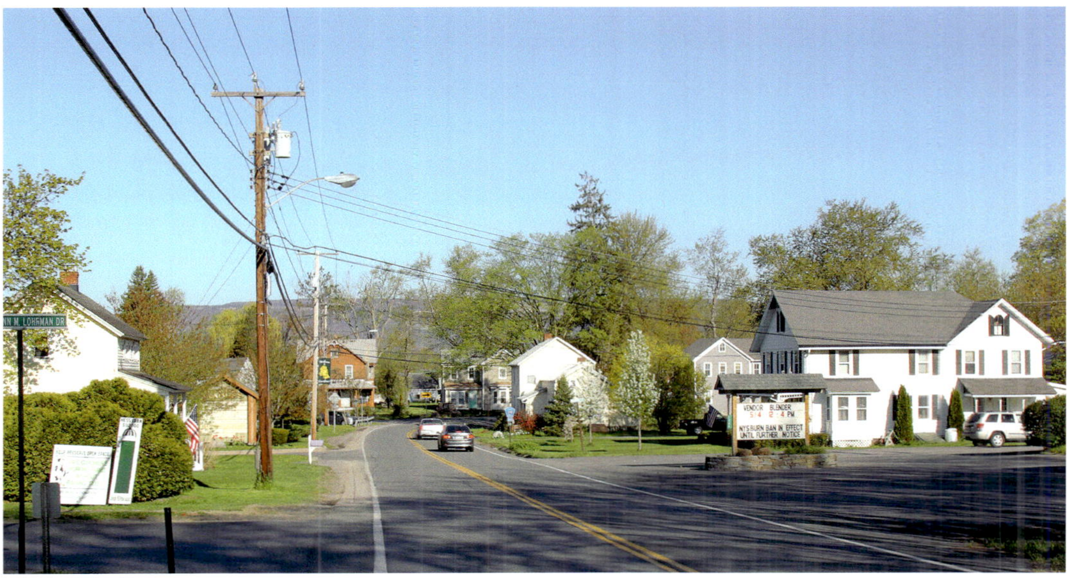

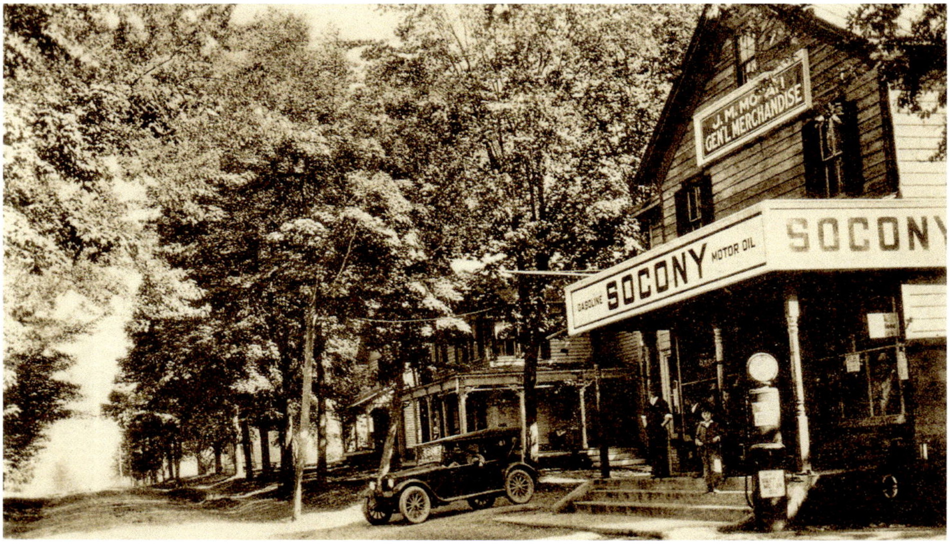

MORAN GEN'L MERCHANDISE/MAJESTIC'S HARDWARE, GARDINER

Constructed around 1900 on Dusinberre Road near Gardiner's Main Street, this gable-fronted store has a storied history. John M. Moran, as a 15 year old worked as a clerk in the store and subsequently became its proprietor. Literally a cornerstone of the hamlet, it boasted 'Gen'l Merchandise'—groceries to hardware—as well as being a Socony (Standard Oil Company of New York) gas and motor oil station. A Gardiner stalwart who served as Town Clerk from 1941–1946, John M. Moran died in 1956. His service to the community was honored with the designation of the field adjacent to Town Hall as the John M. Moran Field.

With wide windows, dramatic signage, and a porch on which to tarry, this store provided general merchandise required by hamlet residents for decades. Socony was a major American oil company that began in the second decade of the 20th century. It was a precursor of Mobil Oil that merged with Exxon in 1999 to form ExxonMobil.

Since 1963, Majestic's Hardware, a mainstay of the hamlet, has operated in the historic building. The residences beyond preserve the historic streetscape of the hamlet.

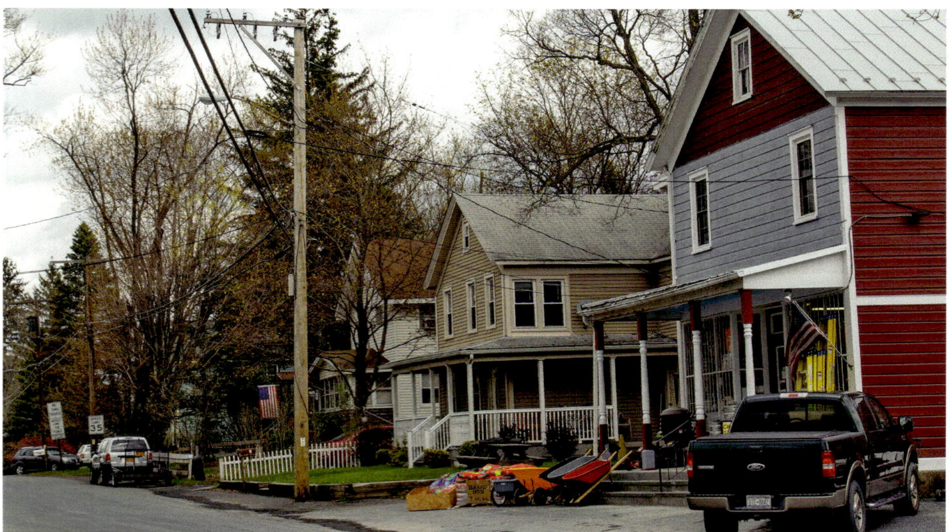

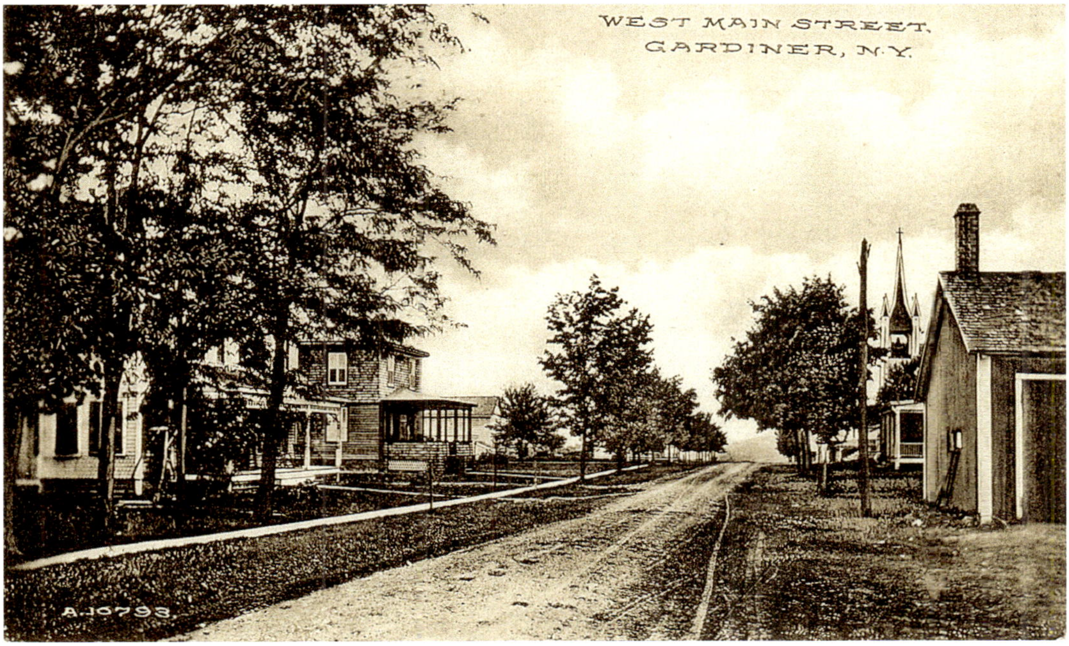

West Main Street, Gardiner

Looking west along Main Street towards the Shawangunk Ridge, the changes along the hamlet road principally focus on the paving of Route 44/55 (Main Street), the addition of sidewalks and curbing, as well as a heavier overlay of electric poles with electric, telephone, and cable lines. Some trees have died or been removed while others are thriving.

A 35 mile per hour speed limit encourages those living in the hamlet and those passing through to slow down to enjoy the pace of Gardiner life.

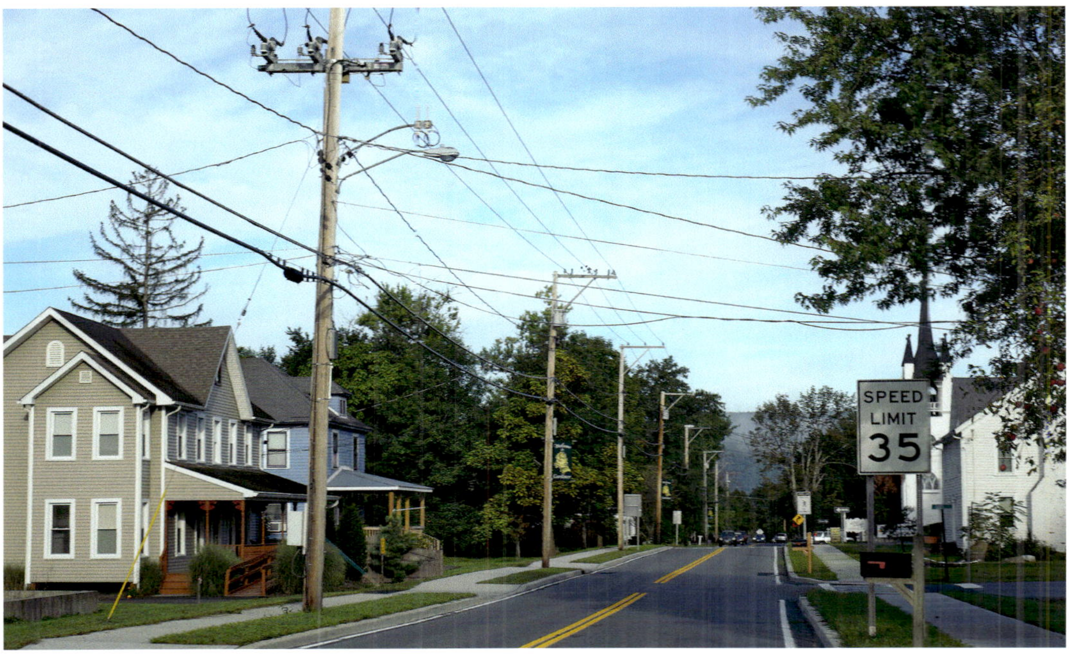

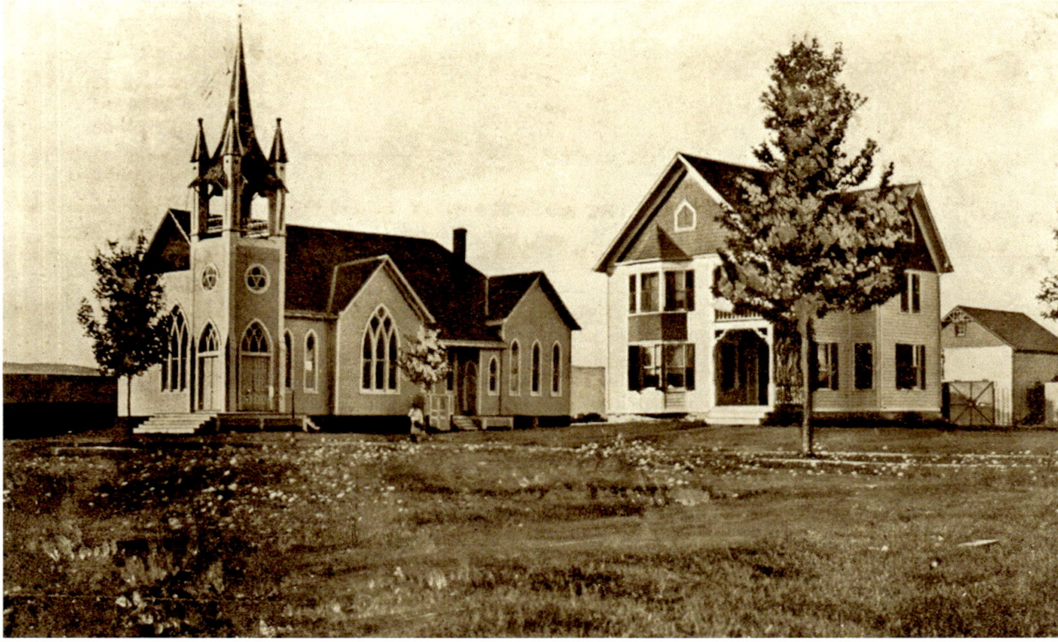

Reformed Church and Parsonage, Gardiner

Just to the west of the old Gardiner Train Depot is the Gardiner Reformed Church, a congregation that was organized at the end of December 1890. The striking church with its belfry, spire, and finials as well as the parsonage were originally built in 1892, dedicated in 1893, and then expanded and remodeled to its present extent in 1926. A manse for the minister was completed in 1896. The *Then* photo clearly reveals the starkness of the farmland site that was being transformed into the hamlet even several decades after the arrival of the first Wallkill Valley Railroad trains.

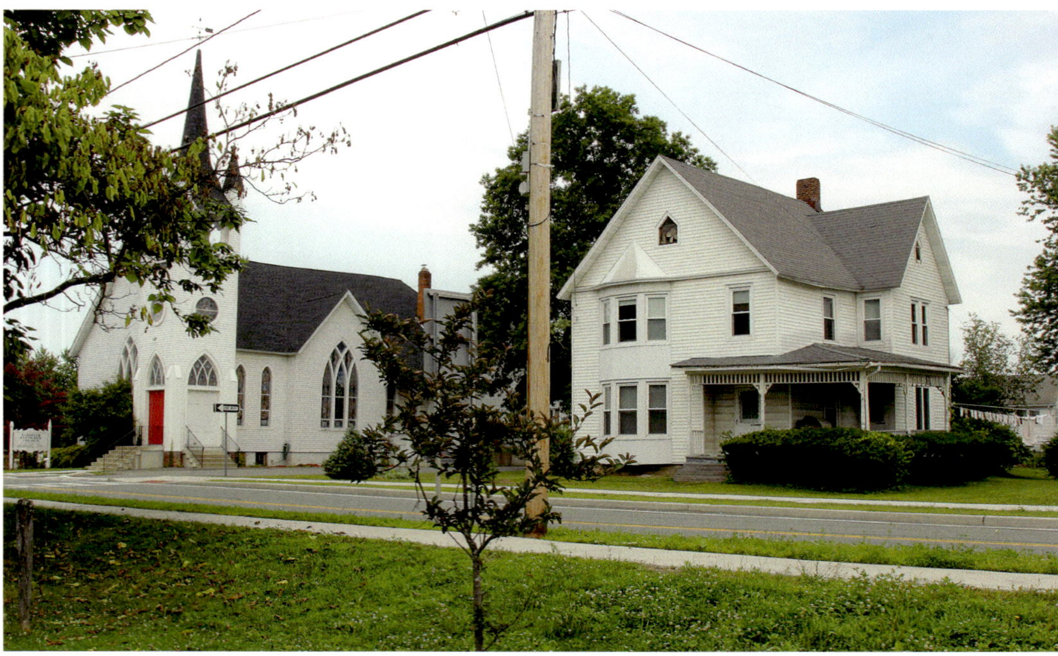

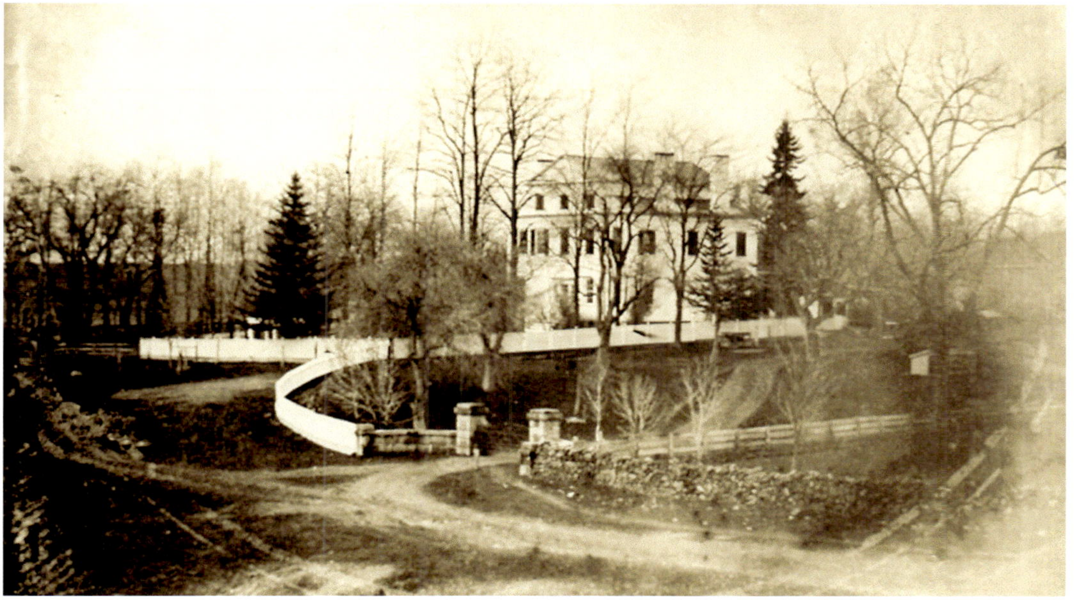

Josiah Hasbrouck Home, Gardiner

One of the outstanding old homes in Gardiner is the Josiah Hasbrouck House, which is popularly known as Locust Lawn, a Federal-style residence that dates to about 1814. It is adjacent to the 1738 Evert Terwilliger homestead on the bank of Plattekill Creek.

With a stone entrance and wall on the right and surrounded by a white fence on a large piece of land, Locust Lawn looked in the 1860 albumen silver print image more like an estate than a local residence. A successful local politician and congressman, Hasbrouck and his descendants resided in the home until 1959 when it was gifted to the Huguenot Historical Society. However, in 2010, HHS feeling that this Hasbrouck home was beyond their mission transferred ownership to Locust Grove, a Poughkeepsie-based historic preservation institution that owns and manages the Morse-Young home.

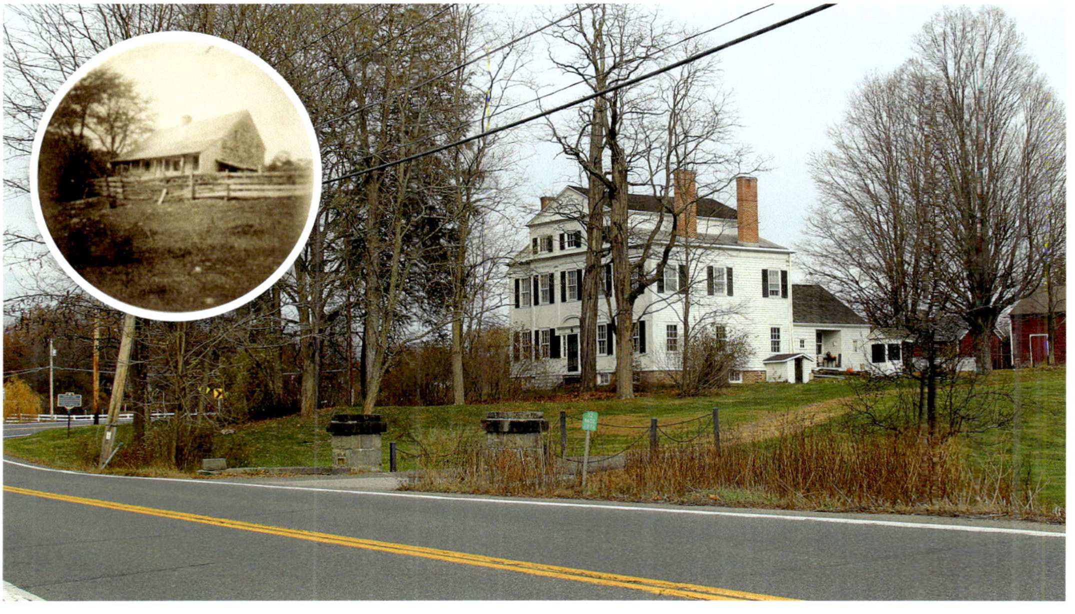

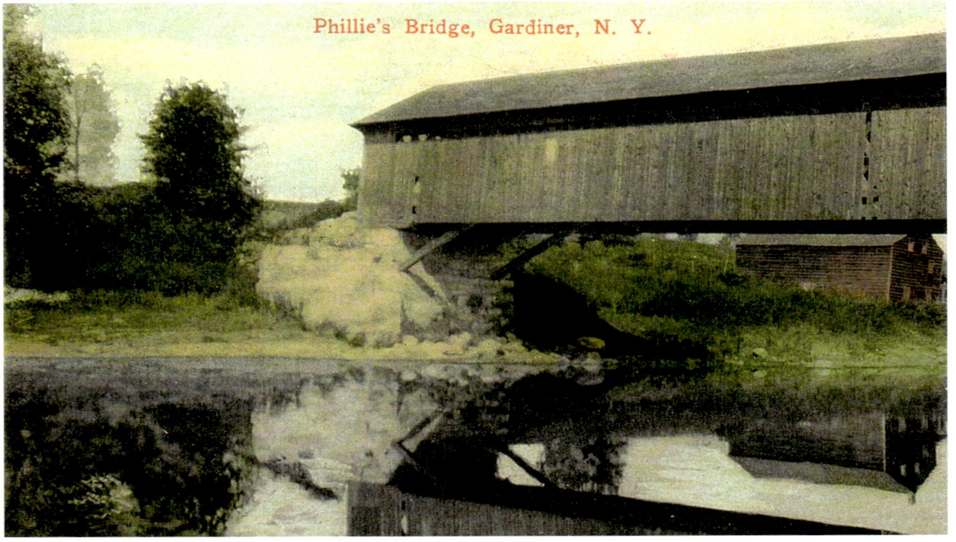

Phillie's Covered Bridge, Gardiner

The successor of an earlier bridge (whether covered is uncertain), this covered bridge was constructed soon after 1843 when other covered bridges were being contemplated or constructed in Ulster County, including in New Paltz and in Rifton. In 1843, an act to raise money to pay for rebuilding a bridge across the Wallkill was passed.

Early in the twentieth century, the bridge began to deteriorate because of the lack of repair due to the fact that traffic patterns had shifted to other areas with bridges crossing the Wallkill, such as in Gardiner and in New Paltz. Repairs were made in 1906, but the covered bridge was condemned again in 1948 after a hundred years' service. On August 16, 1952, according to the *Kingston Freeman*, sections of the bridge collapsed into the river. While high school students and others rallied to save the bridge, the authorities in the Town of Gardiner decided the prudent thing to do was to set it on fire in order to reduce liability.

Today only the stone abutments remain. Looking from Gibbons Lane on the west side of the Wallkill, the estate property behind trees and an embankment belongs to the actor, Robert De Niro.

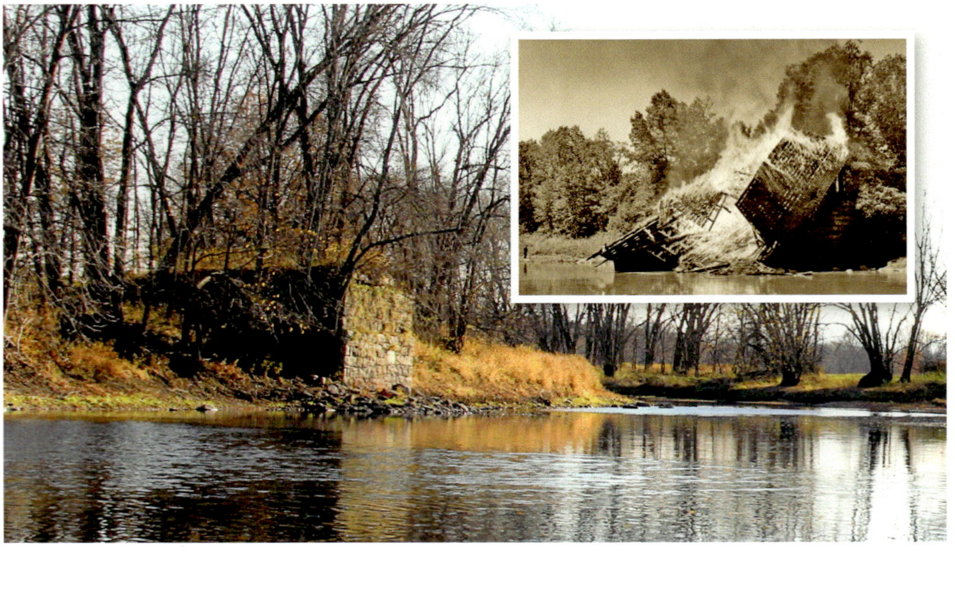

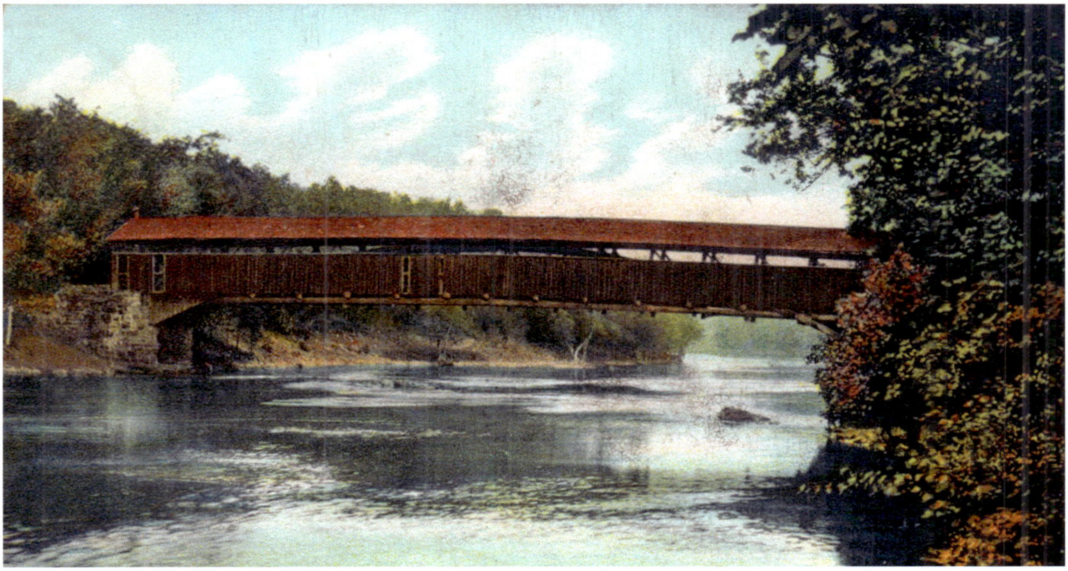

Perrine's Bridge, Towns of Esopus & Rosendale

Although the identifying label on the 1907 postcard indicates that the Perrine's Bridge was in New Paltz, N.Y., the covered bridge actually spans the Wallkill River at Rifton between the towns of Esopus and Rosendale. Perrine's Bridge was originally built *c.* 1844–1850 by Benjamin Wood using a Burr truss made of chestnut for the 154 foot span that was wide enough for a wagon full of hay to pass. It is the second oldest covered bridge in New York State after the Hyde Hall covered bridge near Cooperstown but has a longer Burr arch than the Hyde Hall covered bridge.

After being closed in 1930, the bridge deteriorated. In the 1950s, many called for removing the bridge since it was believed its protruding abutments accentuated flooding in New Paltz. Restoration work was carried out in 1969 and then again in 1993.

The *Now* photograph was shot from beneath the high bridge that carries the New York Thruway I-87 towards Albany. Many Thruway travelers catch a fleeting glimpse of the covered bridge as they travel north.

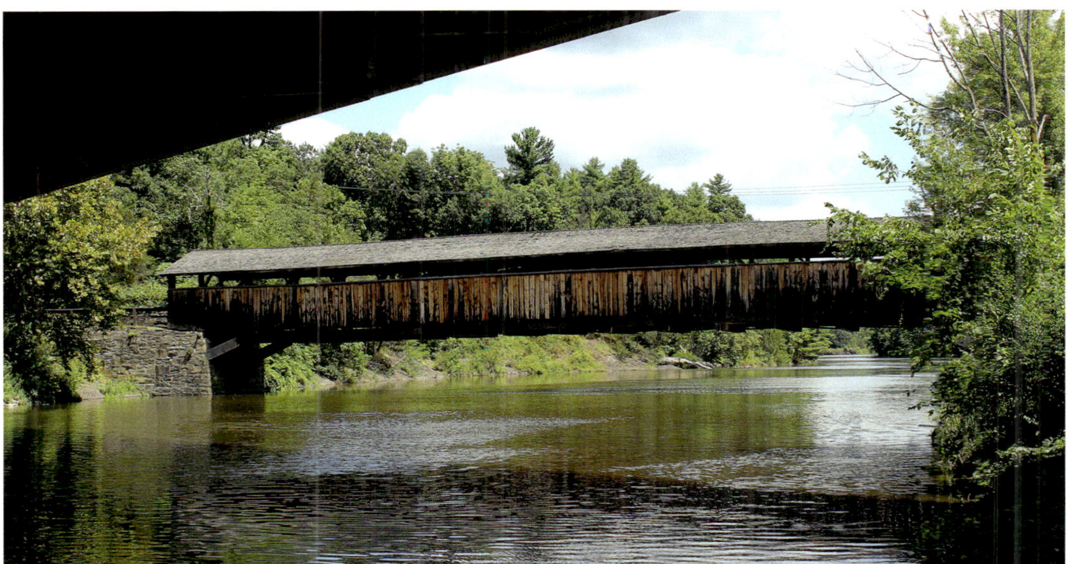

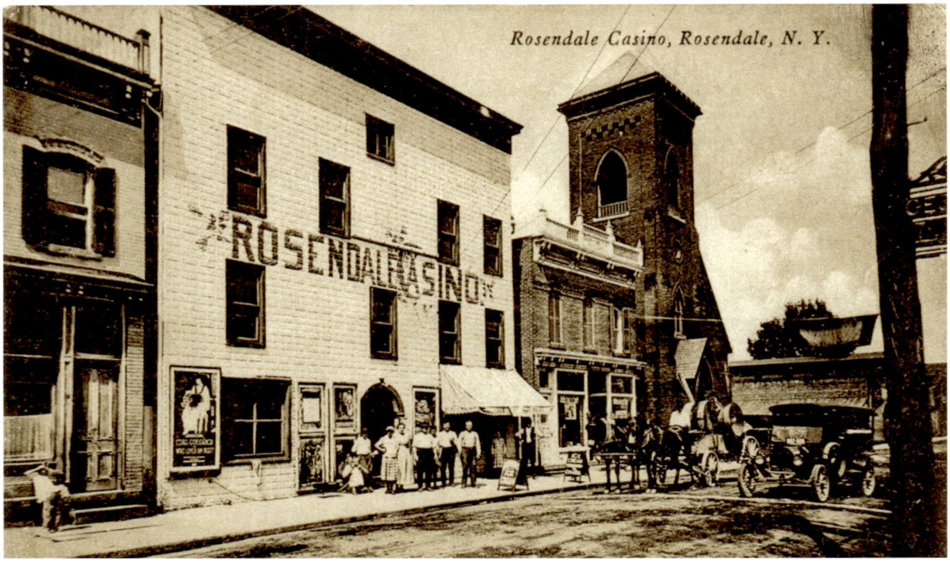

MAIN STREET, ROSENDALE

The village of Rosendale is located at the northernmost extent of the Shawangunk Mountains where their heights diminish as they reach the Rondout Creek, which flows northeast through the town. While there was settlement here in the seventeenth century, the broader town began to thrive after 1825 with the development of a high quality natural cement industry and the digging of the Delaware and Hudson Canal, which had brought anthracite coal from Pennsylvania to the Hudson River.

As both a link and a node in the evolution of nineteenth century transportation, Rosendale further prospered with the arrival of the Wallkill Valley Railway in 1871.

The decline of the canal system in the latter half of the nineteenth century and the weakening of the cement industry greatly impacted Rosendale. A further challenge emerged as a result of an extensive fire in 1895 that wiped out nearly half of the shops and homes lining Main Street.

Though Rosendale is not booming today as it once did, it is a lively and cosmopolitan community with many historic buildings that have benefited from adaptive reuse.

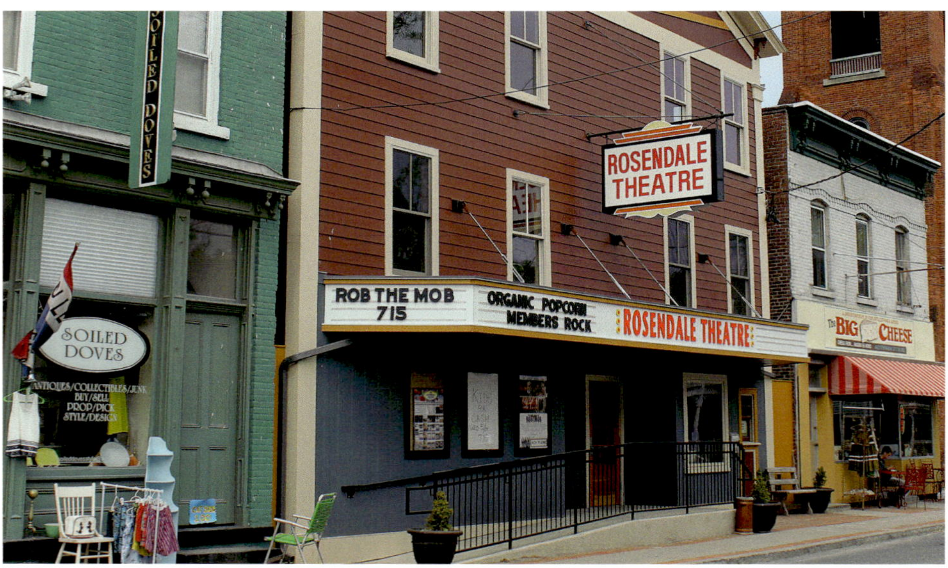

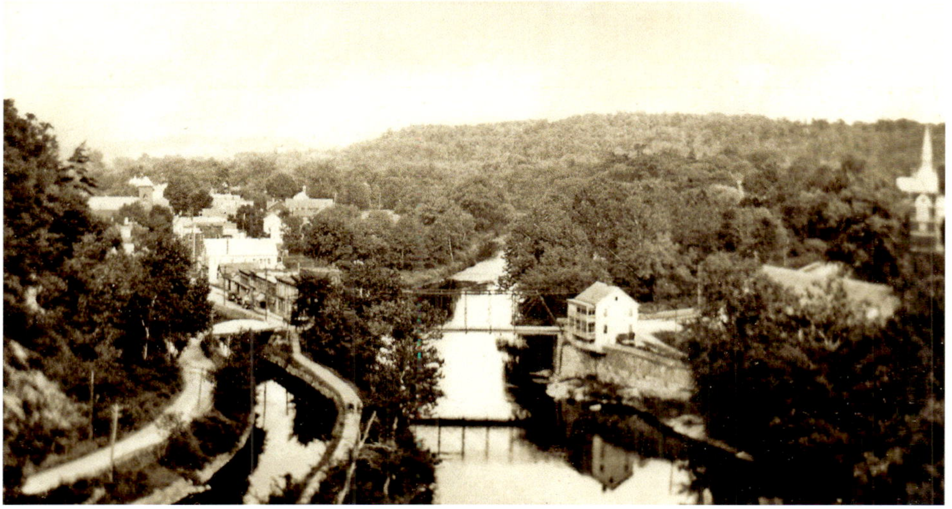

D&H CANAL AND RONDOUT CREEK, ROSENDALE

Looking east in the *Then* photograph from the Wallkill Valley Railroad trestle, the village of Rosendale is on the left on a low-lying flood plain at the foot of Joppenbergh Mountain with the steeple of St. Peter's Church rising above the trees on the right at a higher location.

Until the early twentieth century, the highway leading into Rosendale from the west was adjacent to the Delaware and Hudson Canal with the towpath on an embankment above the Rondout Creek. The inset image shows the canal boats beneath the trestle.

The canal ran behind the stores and residences on the north side of Rosendale's Main Street with cement mines and mills along its northern bank, which facilitated the transport of cement to the Rondout wharves at the Hudson River. Once the canal company ceased operating in 1898, many saw the canal as merely a 'ditch' that needed to be filled in.

Floods impacted both the D&H Canal and the Rondout Creek over the years. After serious floods in 1928 and 1936 as well as two in succession in 1955, the US Army Corps of Engineers reconfigured the creek, dredging sections, constructing a flood wall to the south of the village, as well as raising portions of Main Street. The *Now* photograph reveals clearly not only the realignments but also the obliteration of any trace of the nineteenth century D&H Canal.

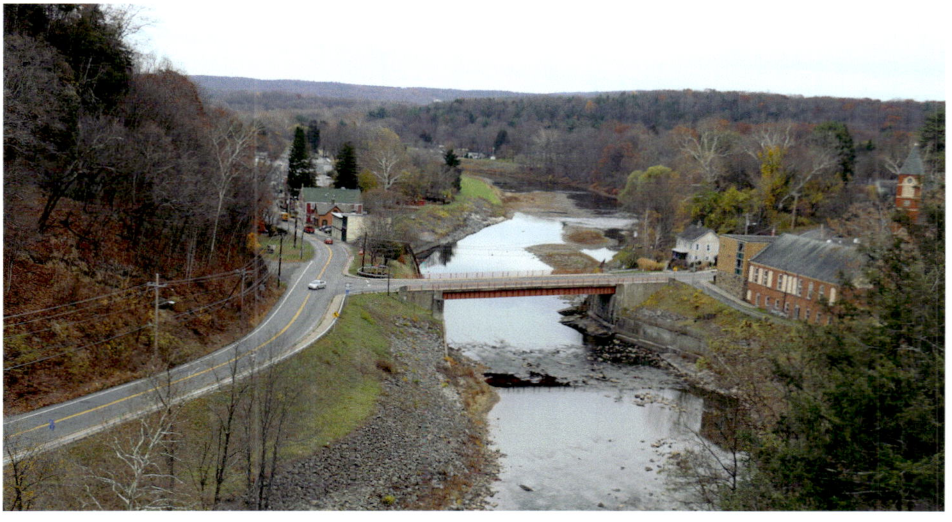

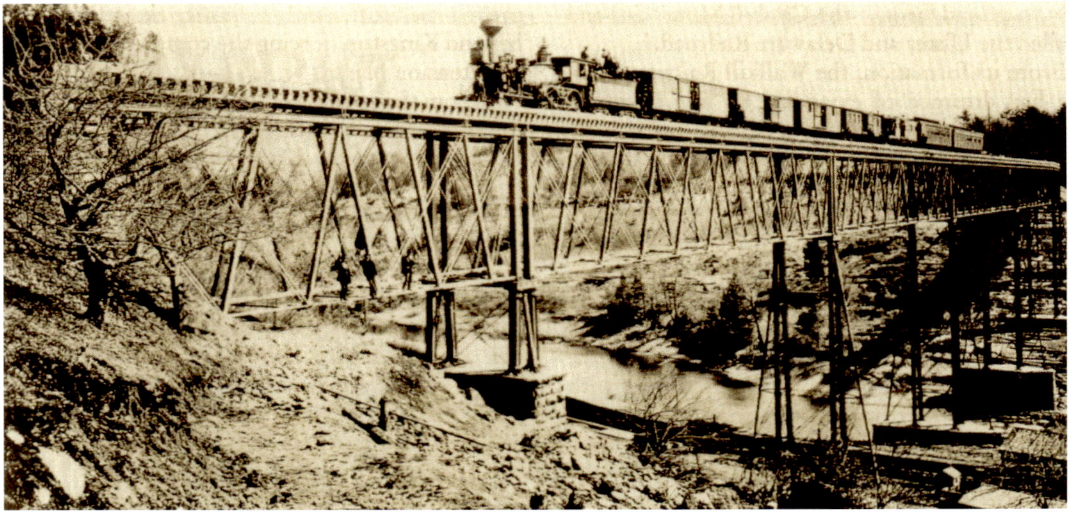

Rosendale Trestle, Rosendale

Much of the line followed by the Wallkill Valley Railway crossed level land. A major obstacle faced those constructing the line in Rosendale where a 150 foot deep chasm over the flood-prone Rondout Creek and the Delaware and Hudson Canal presented a formidable barrier. According to the *New York Times*, abutments were in place by Fall 1870, but the placement of falsework beneath to support the structure was delayed a year because of quicksand that had to be overcome before the superstructure of two short wooden spans and three iron ones could be set in place.

When the 940 foot trestle was completed in 1872 with an overall span of 988 feet, the *New York Times* declared it as "the highest span bridge in the United States" and "deserves to be placed among the wonders of railroad construction." The first train crossed it in April 1872. The trestle was rebuilt in 1895–96 of steel because of concerns about its stability. The bridge remained in service until 1977.

In the decades since, various plans emerged to give it a new use, including a tourist rail line to Kingston and as a site for bungee jumping in the 1990s and early 2000s.

In 2009, the Wallkill Valley Land Trust and Open Space Conservancy purchased the derelict trestle when the property was foreclosed. After an engineering survey and substantial fundraising, new decking and railings were added. On June 29, 2013, a celebration was held opening the high bridge to the public.

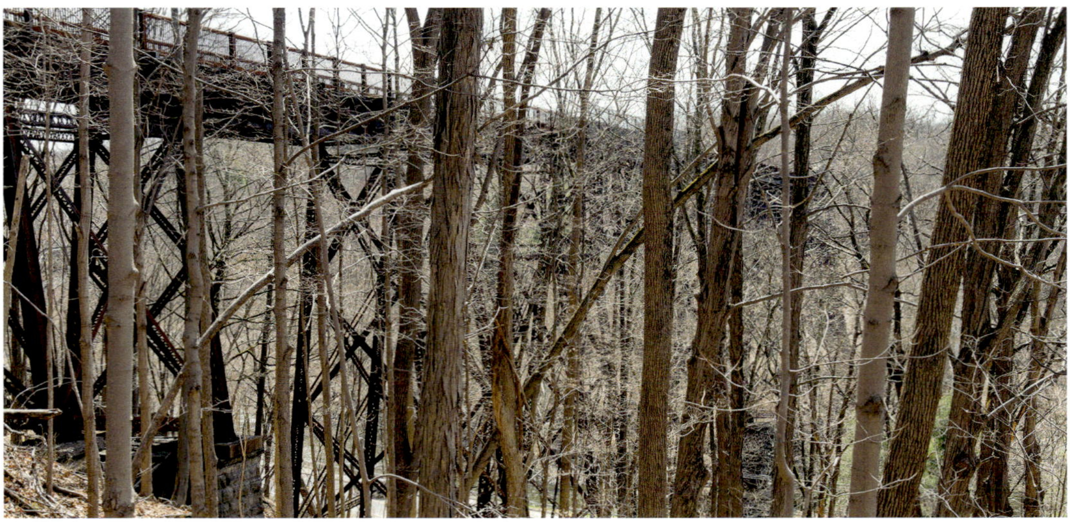

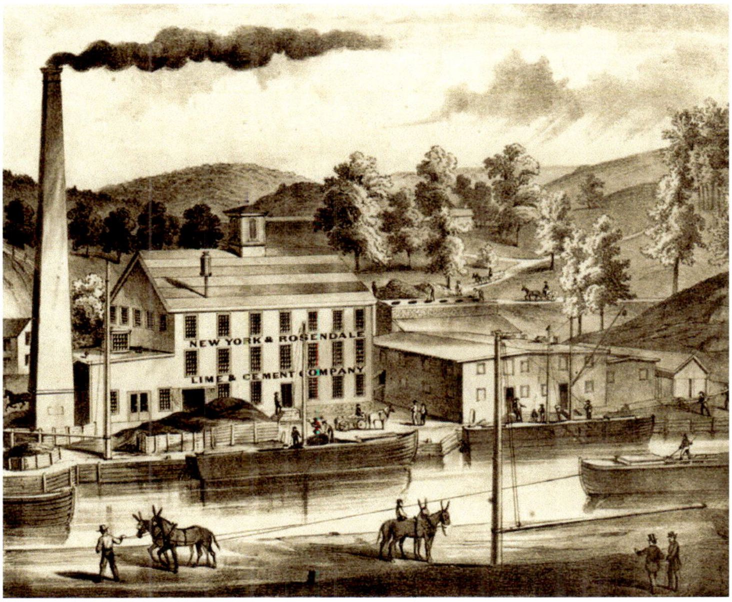

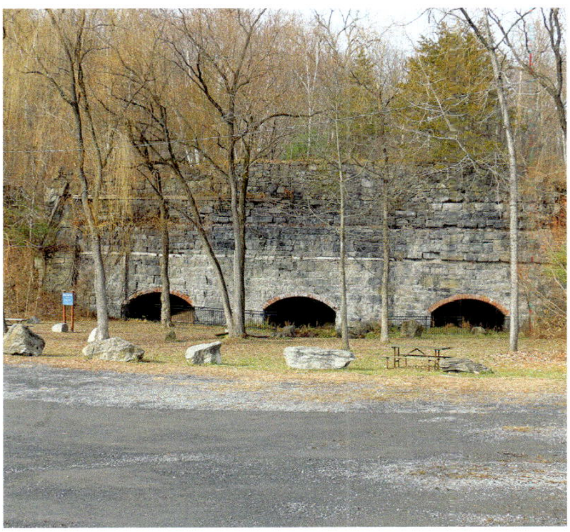

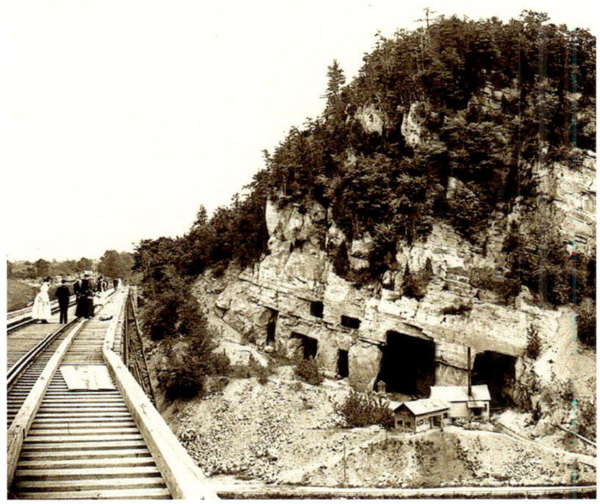

Rosendale's Cement Industry

As depicted in 1875 *Then* engraving, the New York & Rosendale Lime & Cement Company and other local firms provided approximately half of the country's cement production at the time. With the hillside behind providing easy access to the raw resource and space for constructing the high draw kilns needed to burn the stone, the cement companies added grinding mills and storage facilities. Frontage on the D&H Canal eased access to markets via cheap barge movement. As shown in the inset, the trestle for the railroad passed above some open mines below Joppenbergh Mountain.

What is not revealed in this view of an industrialized landscape is that adjacent to the foreground was the rear of buildings on Main Street, the fronts of which are shown on page 88.

Today when one drives behind the Main Street theater and restaurants, virtually all evidence of the cement industry is gone except for the apertures of old mines and kilns tunneled into the hillside that stand as forlorn relics of Rosendale's industrialized past. The canal has been filled in and is today a paved area while the site of the mills is now a grassy park. Without interpretation, they offer few clues of what once dominated the canal-side site that brought prosperity to Rosendale.

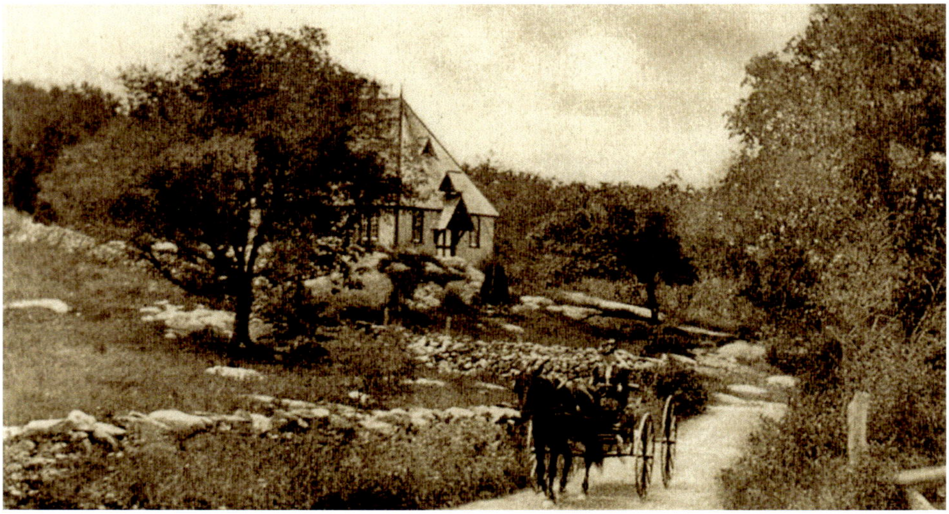

Clove Chapel, Marbletown

The picturesque Clove Chapel is on the western slopes of the Shawangunks below the Mohonk Mountain House in what was once called Yeapletown, a tiny community. Nearby are cellar holes of long gone dwellings as well as small family cemeteries, some of which are overgrown and untended. Today the chapel is within a triangular salient of the town of Marbletown that includes the Mohonk Mountain House and Sky Top.

This simple one-room board-and-batten structure with a hipped roof was constructed between 1875 and 1876. Assistance was provided by nearby congregations in Alligerville and the Clove as well as guests at the Mohonk Mountain House who also supplied Bibles and hymnals. Pastors included the chapel in their regular circuit and were supplemented by some ministers who officiated at the Mountain House.

While church services are no longer offered, the Clove Chapel is regularly used for weddings and commitment ceremonies as well as an annual Christmas Eve service.

The Stokes Family, who are descendants of Adam Yaple (sic) whose late eighteenth century log cabin is on Mohonk Mountain House property, today maintain the Clove Chapel and the nearby Stokes Burying Ground through a family association.

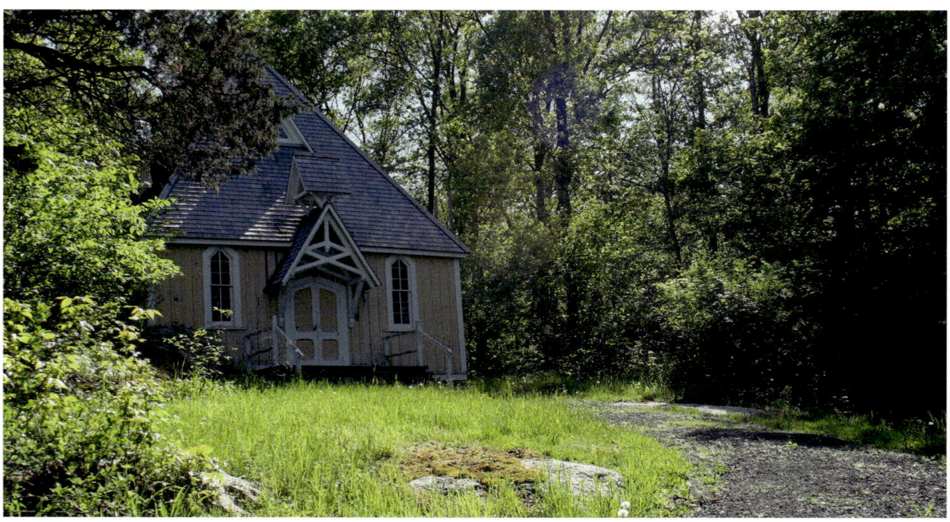

Acknowledgments

Then Images (i = inset)

Todd Clark Collection: 87
Matt Colardo: 6
Cragsmoor Library: 8, 48
D&H Canal Historical Society and Museum: 89
Elting Memorial Library, Haviland-Heidgerd Historical Collection: 23, 26, 54, 57, 60, 61, 63, 70, 71, 86i
Historic Huguenot Street: 50, 51, 52
Paul Huth: 21
Library of Congress: 9, 10, 16, 43, 44, 46
Locust Lawn Collection: 85
Carleton Mabee: 90
Mohonk Mountain House Archives 17i, 18, 19, 19i, 20, 25, 27, 28, 29, 30, 32i, 33, 34, 35, 36, 37, 40–1, 92
Mohonk Preserve, Daniel Smiley Research Center: 31, 32, 42, 47
Dennis O'Keefe Collection: 22, 24, 55, 57, 63, 64, 68, 69, 81, 72, 77, 81, 83, 86
Ronald G. Knapp Collection: 3
Rosendale Library: 15
Alfred Smiley Collection: 45
Theodore Burr Covered Bridge Resource Center: 56
Vivian Yess Wadlin Collection: 14, 17, 53, 54, 57, 59, 62, 65, 66, 67, 70, 73, 74, 75, 76, 78, 79, 80, 82, 84, 86, 88
Wikipedia Commons: 7, 91

Now Photography

Fred Gerty: 25, 46i
John Hayes: 11
Maxine Kamin: 50, 87, 88
Glenn Koehler: 20, 22, 26, 34, 35, 37, 38, 45, 46, 70, 77, 90
Susan Koehler: 17, 29, 39, 44, 47, 48, 52, 58, 59, 63, 65, 67, 69, 82
Susan Lehrer: 89, 91, 92
Michael Neil O'Donnell: 4, 5, 9, 10, 12, 49, 51, 53, 53i, 66, 74, 75, 83, 96
Carol Rietsma: 18, 19, 21, 23, 24, 27 30, 31, 32, 33, 36, 42, 43, 54, 55, 56, 60, 62, 64, 68, 71, 72, 73, 78, 79, 80, 81, 84, 85, 86
Pril Smiley: 28

With Gratitude for Their Assistance

Carrie Allmendinger, Historic Huguenot Street
Nell Boucher, Mohonk Mountain House Archives
Harvey Flad, Vassar College
Paul Huth, Mohonk Preserve, Daniel Smiley Research Center
Carol A. Johnson, Elting Memorial Library, Haviland-Heidgerd Historical Collection
G. Steve Jordan
May T. Knapp
Joan LaChance, Mohonk Mountain House Archives
Rebecca Mackey, Historic Huguenot Street
Bill Merchant, D&H Canal Historical Society and Museum
Gretchen Reed, Mohonk Preserve
Eric Roth, Mohonk Preserve
Marion W. Ryan, Elting Memorial Library, Haviland-Heidgerd Historical Collection
Pril Smiley, Mohonk Mountain House Archives
Kenneth Snodgrass, Locust Grove Estate & Locust Lawn Farm
Linda Tantillo, Rosendale Public Library
Jane Taylor
John Thompson, Mohonk Preserve, Daniel Smiley Research Center
Hattie Grifo, Cragsmoor Library

BIBLIOGRAPHY

"A Bit of Extraordinary Railroad History–The Great Rosendale Bridge of the Wallkill Valley Railroad–Other Railroad Items." *The New York Times* March 19, 1872.

Benjamin, Vernon. *The History of the Hudson River Valley*. New York: The Overlook Press, 2014.

Burgess, Larry E. *Mohonk, Its People and Spirit, A History of One Hundred Years of Growth and Service*. New Paltz, NY: Smiley Brothers, Inc., 1980.

Flad, Harvey. "The Parlor in the Wilderness: Domesticating an Iconic American Landscape," *Geographical Review* 99.3 (July 2009): 356-376.

Fried, Marc B. *Shawangunk Place-Names*. Gardiner: Published by the Author, 2005.

Jordan, G. Steve. *Strength Beauty Spirit: Images of the Mohonk Preserve and Shawangunk Ridge*. Stone Ridge: Clove Editions: 2003.

Josephson, Robi and Bob Larsen. *An Unforgiving Land: Hardscrabble Life in the Trapps, a Vanished Shawangunk Mountain Hamlet*. Delmar, NY: Black Dome Press, 2013.

Josephson, Robi. *Mohonk Mountain House and Preserve*. Charleston: Arcadia Publishing, 2002.

Johnson, Carol A. *New Paltz Revisited*. Charleston: Arcadia Publishing, 2010.

Johnson, Carol A. and Marion W. Ryan. *New Paltz*. Charleston: Arcadia Publishing, 2001.

LaBudde, Keith. "The New Paltz-Wawarsing Turnpike," *Shawangunk Watch* 15.1 (Fall 2010): 2.

Larsen, Robert A. and Jack Fagan. *Trapps Mountain Hamlet: An Interpretive Walk Through a Vanished Shawangunk Community*. New Paltz, NY: Mohonk Preserve, Inc., 1999.

"Life Among The Rocks At Lake Mohonk, *New York Times* August 14, 1882: 5.

Lowenthal, Larry. *From the Coalfields to the Hudson: A History of the Delaware and Hudson Canal*. Fleischmanns, NY: Purple Mountain Press: 1997.

Mabee, Carlton. *Gardiner and Lake Minnewaska*. Charleston: Arcadia Publishing, 2003.

Mabee, Carleton. *Listen to the Whistle: An Anecdotal History of the Wallkill Valley Railroad in Ulster and Orange Counties, New York*. Fleischmanns, NY: Purple Mountain Press, 1995.

Matteson, Benjamin H. and Joan A. LaChance. *Story of Sky Top and Its Four Towers* . New Paltz: Mohonk Mountain, House, 1998.

Moffett, Glendon L. *Down to the River by Trolley: the History of the New Paltz-Highland Trolley Line*. Fleischmanns: Purple Mountain Press, 1993.

Partington, Frederick E. *The Story of Mohonk*. Fulton: Morrill Press: 1911.

Roth, Eric J. "'where ye walloens dwell': Rethinking the Ethnic Identity of the Huguenots of New Paltz and Ulster County, New York," *New York History* 89.4 (Fall 2008): 346-373.

Snyder, Bradley and Karl Beard. *The Shawangunk Mountains: A History of Nature and Man*. New Paltz, NY: Mohonk Preserve, 1981.

Sylvester, Nathaniel Bartlett. *History of Ulster County, New York with Illustrations and Biographical Sketches of its Prominent Men and Pioneers*. Philadelphia: Everts and Peck, 1880.

Terwilliger, Katharine T. *Wawarsing, Where the Streams Wind: Historical Glimpses of the Town*. Ellenville, NY: The Rondout Valley Publishing Company, Inc., 1977.

"The Shawangunks," *Open Space* 2 (Summer) 2004: 4-11.

Townshend, Mike. "Tavern Lore: Barnaby's Building Played Huge Role in New Paltz's Past," *New Paltz Times* (February 10, 2014)
Trueblood, Benjamin F. "Mohonk and Its Conferences," *New England Magazine* 16 (1897): 447-464.

Websites

About Town: The Mid-Hudson Valley Community Guides *abouttown.us*
Century House Historical Society—Cementing History and Art *www.centuryhouse.org*
D&H Canal Historical Society and Museum *www.canalmuseum.org*
Elting Memorial Library, Haviland-Heidgerd Historical Collection *www.eltinglibrary.org/hhhc*
Friends of the Shawangunks *shawangunks.org*
Harris, Wendy E. *The Story of the Shawangunk Mountains Region*
Prepared for the Shawangunk Mountains Scenic Byway Steering Committee
cragsmoorconsultants.com/scenic%20byways/Scenic_Byway_Paper.html
Historic Huguenot Street *www.huguenotstreet.org*
Hudson River Valley Heritage *www.hrvh.org*
Hudson River Valley Institute *www.hudsonrivervalley.org*
Hudson River School Art Trail *www.hudsonriverschool.org*
Hudson River Valley National Heritage Area *www.hudsonrivervalley.com/Home.aspx*
Hudson River Valley Review *www.hudsonrivervalley.org/review*
Lake Minnewaska *www.lakeminnewaska.org*
Mohonk Preserve *www.mohonkpreserve.org*
Mohonk Mountain House *www.mohonk.com*
Minnewaska State Park Preserve *nysparks.com/parks/127/details.aspx*
New Paltz Historic Preservation Commissions' Historic Property Map *hpc.townofnewpaltz.org*
New Paltz Historic Preservation Commissions' New Paltz Then & Now Morphing Photos
hpc.townofnewpaltz.org/index.php?option=com_content&view=article&id=1876&Itemid=91
New York State Historic Preservation Office *nysparks.state.ny.us/shpo*
New York State Historic Preservation SPHINX system on Landmarks
nysparks.state.ny.us/shpo/online-tools/disclaimer.aspx?pgm=spx
Panoramic View from Sky Top
www.360cities.net/image/albert-k-smiley-memorial-panorama#-116.62,-28.77,70.0
Shawangunk Mountains Scenic Byway *mtnscenicbyway.org*
Stone Ridge Public Library *www.stoneridgelibrary.org/collections.html*

www.gunksthroughtime.com

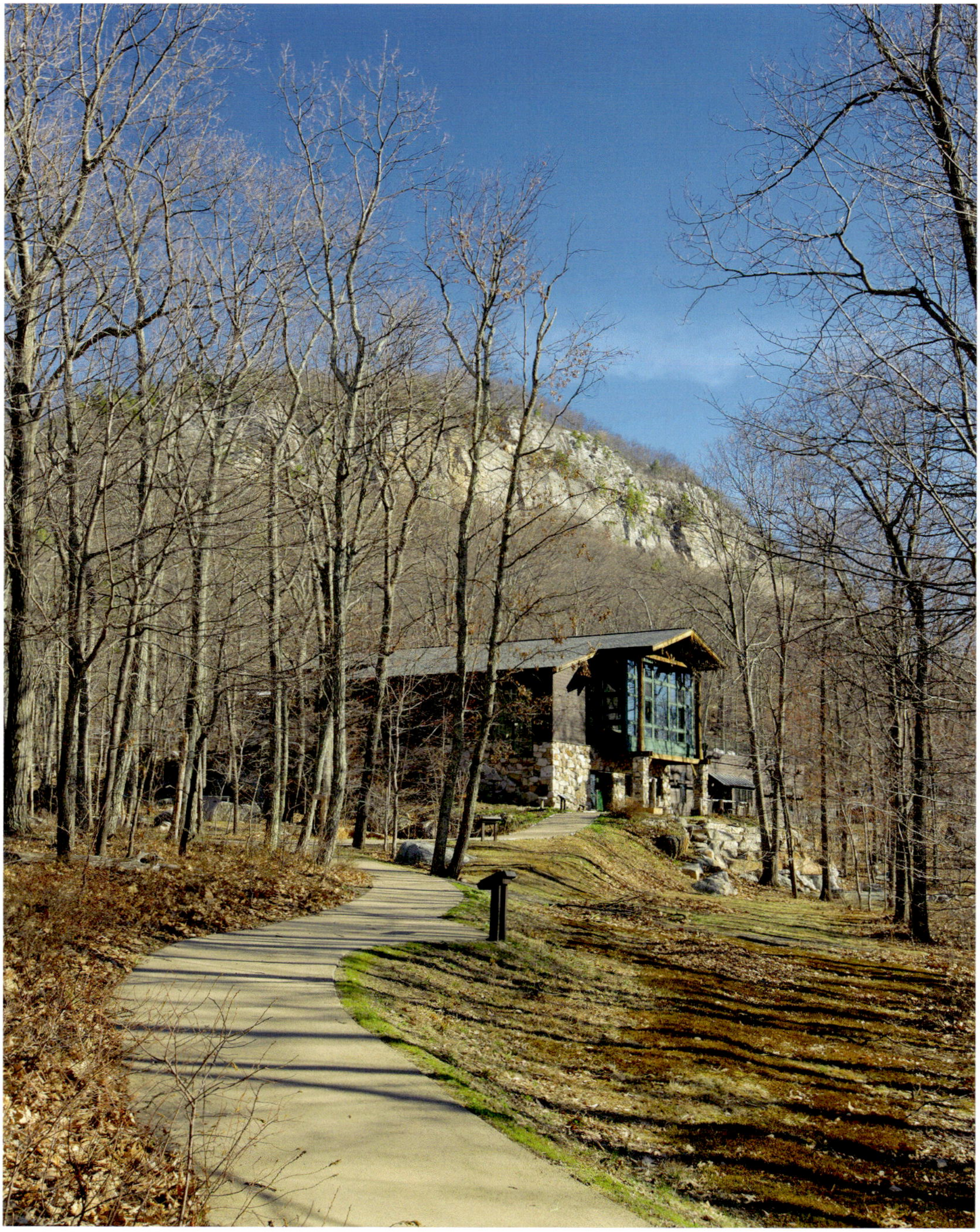

View from the rear of the Mohonk Preserve Visitor Center looking up towards the spectacular cliffs known as The Trapps, the most popular venue for rock climbing in the Northeast USA. Just below the cliffs is Undercliff Carriage Road, a historic route that once linked the Mohonk Mountain House along Lake Mohonk with the The Cliff House and Wildmere above Lake Minnewaska. Today the route is suitable for the enjoyment of those who hike, bike, snowshoe, cross-country ski, bird, or come simply for a stroll or to contemplate nature.